Branded Lives

T0313734

Branded Lives

The Production and Consumption of Meaning at Work

Edited by

Matthew J. Brannan

Lecturer in Management, Keele University, UK

Elizabeth Parsons

Senior Lecturer in Marketing, Keele University, UK

Vincenza Priola

Lecturer in Organisation Studies, Aston University, UK

Edward Elgar

Cheltenham, UK • Northampton, MA, USA

Published by
Edward Elgar Publishing Limited
The Lypiatts
15 Lansdown Road
Cheltenham
Glos GL50 2JA
UK

Edward Elgar Publishing, Inc.
William Pratt House
9 Dewey Court
Northampton
Massachusetts 01060
USA

A catalogue record for this book
is available from the British Library

Library of Congress Control Number: 2011927317

ISBN 978 1 84980 092 1 (cased)

Printed and bound by MPG Books Group, UK

Contents

Contributors

Matthew J. Brannan is Director of International Partnerships and a lecturer in Management at Keele Management School. His research focuses upon the contemporary experience of work, especially service work, and employs predominately ethnographic techniques of investigation.

Margo Buchanan-Oliver is Professor of Marketing and the Co-Director of the Centre for Digital Enterprise (CODE) at the University of Auckland Business School. Her research concerns interdisciplinary consumption discourse and practice, cultural identity projects and social semiotics.

Jean Cushen is a lecturer within the Management School, Queen's University Belfast. Jean teaches Human Resource Management and Research Methods and her research explores Human Resource Management, Knowledge Work, Labour Process Theory and Critical Realism.

Martin R. Edwards is a senior lecturer in Human Resource Management and Organisational Behaviour at the Department of Management, King's College London. His research has involved investigating organizational identification in parent-subsidiary contexts with a particular emphasis on multi-foci organizational identity issues, as well as longitudinal research examining the impact of mergers and acquisition on employee identities and employee well-being.

Scott A. Hurrell is a lecturer in Work and Employment Studies in the Institute for Socio-Management at Stirling University. His research interests include skills, work organization and recruitment and selection with a particular focus on front-line service workers and the non-profit sector. Scott has worked with policy bodies such as Futureskills Scotland, the former Equal Opportunities Commission (Scotland), the Scottish Council for Voluntary Organisations and Scottish Government Departments.

Elisabeth K. Kelan is a lecturer in Work and Organisation in the Department of Management at King's College London. Prior to this appointment she was a senior research fellow at London Business School. She received her PhD from the London School of Economics and Political Science. Her research interests lie in the area of gender in organizations, diversity, identities and organizational cultures.

Christopher Land is a senior lecturer in Management at the University of Essex and visiting fellow at the University of St Gallen. His research covers a range of topics including representations of work and organization in literature, the relationship between the arts and political economy, community as an organizational discourse, and ethical branding.

Elizabeth Parsons is a senior lecturer in Marketing at Keele Management School. Her current research interests lie in two key areas: the cultures of second-hand markets and the construction of gender and identity in organizational life. She draws from social theory, material cultural studies and post-structural feminism for inspiration. She is Assistant Editor of the journal *Marketing Theory*.

Vincenza Priola is lecturer in Organisation Studies at Aston University in the UK. Her research interests centre on the general field of management processes and practices with a particular focus on gendered processes in organizations. She is interested in managerial and gender identities and how these are constructed within organizations.

Stephanie Russell is a PhD student in Keele Management School, Keele University. Her research focuses upon the impact and experience of deregulation, with particular emphasis on institutional theory and critical theory. Attention is also given to Foucault's work on power and the enterprise discourse. She has particular interest in ethnographic and qualitative research methodologies.

Dora Scholarios is Professor of Work Psychology in the Department of Human Resource Management, University of Strathclyde. Her research interests span the areas of recruitment, assessment and selection, skills and employability, well-being, and work/life boundaries, with special focus on call centres, service work, software/IT and the voluntary sector.

Melanie Simms is Associate Professor of Industrial Relations in the IROB group at the University of Warwick. She researches trade union renewal, organizing campaigns, and comparative employment relations with a particular interest in the ways in which trade unions try to recruit and engage new groups of workers.

Sandra Smith is currently a lecturer in the Department of Marketing at the University of Auckland Business School, New Zealand. She has completed her doctoral thesis on employee constructions of a service brand and has a special interest in the use of narrative analysis to unveil the complexity of organizational worlds and, moreover, the branded identity within organizations.

Veronika V. Tarnovskaya is Associate Professor at the School of Economics and Management, Lund University. She is a researcher in strategic marketing and branding with a special focus on emerging markets. She has published several articles in journals such as the *Academy of Management Executive* and *International Marketing Review* and is the author of *The Mechanism of Market Driving with a Corporate Brand* (VDM Verlag, 2009). She lectures in international marketing and brand management.

Scott Taylor currently works as a senior lecturer at the Centre for Leadership Studies, University of Exeter Business School. He has worked at Manchester Metropolitan, Open, Birmingham, and Essex universities. His research centres on the religious or spiritual beliefs and values people bring to workplaces.

Hugh Willmott is Research Professor in Organization Studies, Cardiff Business School. He co-founded the International Labour Process Conference and the Critical Management Studies Conference. He has a strong interest in the application of social theory to the field of management and business. He currently serves on the board of Academy of Management Review, Organization Studies, Journal of Management Studies and is an Associate Editor of *Organization*.

Preface

Cad-dill-lac... Cad-dill-lac... the Lac... I saw you drive up... De-ville se-dan,
'79!... Last of the great ones... Did you see Goodfellas?... Cad-dill-lac... hmm.

The syllables rolled around his mouth and off his tongue as if he were tasting
them or feeling them for size like bits of broken-up gobstopper in his mouth.
Humbert Humbert did not have more fun rolling 'Lo-lee-ta' around his mouth,
neither was he more obsessed with syllables of a name, nor with its fetishized
object. I had just bought a 79 Cadillac Deville from a car drive in Princeton,
New Jersey. It was part of the estate of a woman who had died at the age of
99 and had been in her garage from new. It had 70,000 miles on the clock and
there was a wheelchair in the trunk, honest! I had driven it down to a clas-
sics motor centre in Philly to get an idea of its place in the pantheon of the
US golden age. The 72-year-old owner, Steve, owned and ran the place, 500
American antiques from the 1940s to the 1970s piled in line on a shabby lot,
most of them in reasonable condition, some very well preserved in a big old
shed, some mint-condition gleaming in a small showroom. It was not just the
Cadillac name that rolled off his tongue, he seemed to like saying Olds-mob-ile
too; there were many models he recited, a bit like a poem, or Chuck Berry or
Johnny Cash rattling off place names in classic American pop. Chev-rolet, Bel
Air, Pont-tiac Bonne-ville, Bu-ick Wild-cat. The 56 Ford Thun-der-bird started
at the first flick of the ignition; as he slipped into the bench seat it roared into
life a bit like he launched the syllables from between his lips. Steve lived and
breathed these cars, said he was born with them and had grown up with them:
their story was his story. Knew the history of every car, some had passed down
three generations before getting to him. He was gonna work till he dropped
unless he could get his son to take over, to see that the shabby lot was a field
of dreams. Of course he'd like to sell me a car but thought I was just fine with
mine. If he sold ten a month he could get by. Steve seemed a happy man,
branded to his core and loving it.

Of course the experience of the workers embedded in the specific factory
conditions and social relations of production which produced these cars in
the 1950s, 1960s and 1970s were far from the experiences outside the factory
gate then and now. The glossy brand was a project for the marketers to work
on unconnected with the grime of the factory regime. Now the brand name
is coming back inside the factory, inside its social relations and inside the

workers' heads. Walmart has replaced General Motors as the world's biggest corporation and on the back of every employee's blue uniform it says, 'Can I help you?' Customers are everywhere. In or out of the factory, the corporation would like you to intersperse the syllables of its brand name into every interaction in or out of work. The history of marketing repeats itself, first as dream, then as farce now as nightmare in the factory.

When my Cadillac was made there was still a sign above the factory gate, 'Entry Forbidden'. It was a 'hidden abode' of production. Remember the famous quote from Marx? Freedom, equality and Bentham rule on the labour market. But it is a different story after the labourer has made a contract to sell their labour-power:

> we can perceive a change in the physiognomy of our dramatis personae. He, who before was the money owner, now strides in front as capitalist; the possessor of labour-power follows as his labourer. The one with an air of importance, smirking, intent on business, the other, timid and holding back, like one who is bringing his own hide to market and has nothing to expect but – a hiding. (*Capital*, p.155, George Allen & Unwin, 1957)

More recently Bruce Springsteen sings of seeing 'death in the eyes' of the workers ('The Factory') as they make their way through the factory gate for the morning shift. The 'behind closed doors' nature of the employment relationship profoundly affected the nature of work experience and of factory cultures. Spatially and symbolically, the factory was removed from everyday experience, also from its norms and conventions. Having nothing to lose but their hides, workers could abandon polite convention and shape their own cultures of survival and bonhomie, with sexism and racism and homophobia rife, with no other social actors (or even of intruding bosses in labour controlled lines) to challenge the basis of their cultures, its transgressions and inversions of external status orders and norms. Steve never went into the factory to check out how his cars were made. Now it is routine. At many car plants, right up to Bentley Motors, the forces and social relations of Production are specifically put on show to visitors, for triple use. As always there is material production; they are further used as marketing strategies to draw customers in to see how 'their car' is made; but now their very visibility is used to keep 'the line' in line, every one as ambassadors of the marque. As they force the workers to take down their pin-ups and tidy up their clothes and benches, how the managers must long for them to roll 'Bent-te-ley' around their mouths lovingly as they work.

There is an urgent need for a revival and reconfiguration of industrial sociology, albeit a more careful one extending beyond the factory gate and without Marxist guarantees but which looks very carefully at the nature of how materiality and culture are intertwined now. Re-inscriptions of the social relationships of the employment contract bring new forms of domination, declaring themselves as new forms of freedom: the freedom to dance to work and to take a hiding as privilege so long as there is a brand name on the hide. This volume contributes to the tasks of renewal by providing a precise and carefully located discussion of the specific forms and development of new working practices and some examples of the latest and most visible of the ways in which the dominance of the market, of market institutions and marketing drive ever further back not only into the making of commodities and delivery of services but into the very social relations of production and now, putatively, into the very subjectivities and emotions of workers. The face-to-face relation and 'customer rules' have long been part of the service economy unprotected by any 'hidden abode'. Their inequalities may be even greater than in manufacturing and its contradictions must be brought out by ethnographic inspection. One of the interesting things this book brings out about employee branding is that it further plunges whole sectors of the working class, formerly interacting only with themselves, into wider and visible social relations of expressive and communicative exchange and behaviour. This brings its own tensions and contradictions of re-shaping to conformist moulds, but further now, adding irony to contradiction, some sectors try to trade on leisure pursuits and styles which may continue important proletarian or oppositional themes.

So far the discussion of the branded employee has been an above-ground, user, 'operations' thing conducted in the mainstream literature. This book releases another current suggesting that employee branding will not always work in the favour of capital. There are submerged mines of potential and real subversion and radicalism, unnoticed or not yet fully deployed, within these new employment relationships and the new mystifications of demands placed on subordinated labour, and as the case studies of this volume show so well, on the body. The elasticity demanded of the body, its emotions and expressions, is multidimensional and allows creative, autonomous and organic elements of cultural practices. Cultures which magically think they are free and are encouraged to see in paid work a seamless extension might turn to real resistance, though, when they meet the grit of underlying compulsion. Cultural production of meaning may be deployed against, not always in line with, employer expectations. Mediated via the body, these meanings can open up different ways of being, thinking and sensing in a multitude of ways in social groups from below in a period of epochal change.

The accounts in this volume are broadly qualitative, being either explicitly ethnographic or case study based, and help to maintain a rich ethnographic tradition based on respect for, and careful recording of, situated conduct and experience. Further, the materials presented here are exemplary in combining ethnographic recording and respect with an analytic strategy that attempts to dig through layers of meaning to show how particular sites of autonomy and cultural experience are always historically and structurally located and owe something of their internal form to their surrounding economic structures and forms, also in complicated, often unintended ways, helping to reproduce and maintain these structures. The chapters explore the ways in which those who are subject to employee branding practices actively produce and re-produce their effects and affects, even while viewing them with cynicism or even in real and meaningful critique. In doing so, this book encompasses but moves beyond descriptive qualitative accounts to show a particular and new element in the circuit of capital in its cultural and subjective moment.

Steve, read this book! Think again before you ask your son to join you among the oversized tail fins and fish tail running lights. Let him keep his day job and his soul.

Paul Willis, Princeton University, December 2010

Acknowledgments

The editors would like to thank Mihelea Keleman, Pauline Maclaren and Paul Willis for their guidance support and friendship. We would also like to thank Francine O'Sullivan as commissioning editor and all those at Edward Elgar for their professionalism and confidence in the project. A note of thanks also to Terry McNulty and the European Academy of Management conference 2009, for allowing us space to initially develop many of the ideas contained within this book.

1. Introduction

Matthew J. Brannan, Elizabeth Parsons and Vincenza Priola

The growth of emotional, aesthetic and identity work within organizational contexts has led to epochal changes in the way that people are managed at work and, as a consequence, the way that work is experienced by employees. This volume explores the experience of employee branding, a very concrete and specific employment practice, that has become increasingly popular in recent times. This focused approach provides an aperture through which we can gain insight and provide analysis into a much wider and more complex picture of dynamic social relations mediated through the changing contours of the employment relationship. With, for example, many employees being increasingly encouraged to bring 'more of themselves' into the workplace (Fleming, 2009), the question of what constitutes appropriate selves, and how this is formulated, remains open to question and a vital topic for critical debate and engagement.

Working in the tradition of industrial sociology, this volume presents a range of theoretically informed empirical accounts that document the pleasures and pains of living the brand as a mode of both production and being in the world. The chapters also chart the ways in which employees may potentially become constituted as 'portraits' of organizational brands, and the prospects for securing competitive advantage that this may confer on organizations goes some way to explain the extraordinary lengths that some have gone to in order to embed these processes within institutional architectures. As the following quote proselytizes:

> If genuine commitment is to be achieved amongst front-line people, the brand ideology must touch the core of why people work in the organisation... If they are to ensure continued success in a competitive market, organisations must engage in team training that encourages individuals to connect and become the Living Brand® for both their internal people and external customers. The Living Brand® experience looks inside the mind and behaviour patterns of front-line people and answers the questions of how to turn even the most cynical of team members into a true Living Brand® Champion. (Smith, Bridge Training and Events, 2009)

Taken from commercial consultancy promotional material, the quote above might be read with a degree of cynicism but nonetheless highlights the two key mechanisms through which employee branding operates in the contemporary organization: control and consent. The promise to 'turn even the most cynical into true… brand champions' is redolent of an impetus toward compulsion, colonizing employees' hearts and minds in the strict service of accumulation. In terms of consent, the brand simultaneously works to mollify, touching 'the core of why people work in the organisation', offering employees a set of ideals to buy into, an ideology to strive for and ultimately a sense of meaning in a meaningless world. In becoming a 'brand champion', employees are invoked to embody, and thus animate, the brand, both for fellow employees and for customers in a complex series of relations that serve to produce and reproduce brand equity. As our point of departure, this example illustrates the central theme of the volume; an attempt to understand the power of brand rhetoric in contemporary organizations through an exploration of the production and consumption of meaning at work and the attendant politics of this process.

HISTORICAL CONTEXT

In studies of work and employment it is commonplace to draw attention to the changing face of organizations as they adapt to increased competition, rapidly changing product markets and global forces that work to restructure the way in which organizations must compete. While in recent decades the content of work and employment has undoubtedly changed significantly, there have also been profound changes in the form that work takes, meaning that it is not just *what* we do at work that has changed, but also *how* the work is done that has undergone radical transformation. Very broadly speaking, the growth of employment in the tertiary industries in most advanced industrial economies has meant that employment in services has become dominant. Working in the service industry is often characterized by workers engaged in emotional, aesthetic and identity work and, some argue, this has necessitated profound changes in the ways that people are managed at work.

Key to understanding the distinctiveness of work and employment in the global service economy is the spatial and temporal collapse of production and consumption; meaning the act or work can no longer be separated or abstracted from the consumption of its product. While on the one hand services are seen as playing a fundamental role in most economies, their evolution is also having a significant effect on society and the ways in which work is organized in all other sectors (including manufacturing). Sectors are becoming interrelated with the bundling between services and products, and the outsourcing of service-based functions to specialized firms, becoming key factors in this development. Information and communication technologies (ICT) are also fundamental in contributing to the interconnections between sectors and in narrowing the differences between various economic activities as well as the business development opportunities offered to large enterprises and to small organizations (OECD, 2000). The consequences that flow from this are both complex and contested and are still yet to be fully understood. However, we do know that working people are increasingly being encouraged to embrace the 'corporate lifestyle' and model themselves to organizational images while, paradoxically bringing more of themselves into their work and workplace.

One possible response aimed at achieving the fuller involvement of employees has been the development of employee branding strategies where workers are encouraged to buy into symbolic representations of organizational values by, for example, consuming the companies' products or 'living the brand' away from the workplace (Miles and Mangold, 2004). In this way employees, through both display and performance, are increasingly being induced to reinforce and represent the brand image both within the workplace and without. The image presented to an organization's customers and stakeholders through its employees becomes more crucial in the current era where ICT allows employees to share their work experiences and views of their organizations and products with the rest of the world via blogs, websites and social network sites. Therefore the employee brand, it seems, has never been more important for organizations and employees have the potential to create positive and negative brand images by influencing stakeholders and customers alike (Mangold and Miles, 2007).

In this volume we seek to explore the idea of 'employee branding' from a number of different perspectives. Our interest in the area is mirrored by a general increase in the awareness of employee branding from a corporate and practitioner point of view and this is, in part, due to a number of large organizations enthusiastically adopting the cause of employee branding as a key aspect of their human resource management (HRM) strategy (see Barrow and Mosley, 2005). The notion has also come to prominence in the functional and prescriptive management literature and there have been a number of studies that have sought to explore and promote the idea more widely (e.g. Gotsi and Wilson, 2001; Martin and Hetrick, 2006). Yet despite the enthusiasm with which the idea has been met with in some quarters, the practice has also encountered a degree of suspicion and hostility. Some authors have, for instance, suggested that the concept is hollow, or merely a reinvention of an older style 'employee engagement' strategy, or part of an attempt for HR managers to align their own role more closely with the strategic initiatives of the organization (Collins, 2003; Martin et al., 2005). Given that the contours of successive strategies to manage the employment relationship are littered with attempts to gain the control and consent of employees, we think it important to engage critically with the notion of employee branding and seek to offer an evaluation that is both historically and theoretically informed.

Our contribution to the employee branding debate seeks to explore the practice of employer and employee branding by focusing upon the lived experience of working under what might be termed branded conditions. More specifically, we seek to present a series of organizational case studies of employee branding 'in action' in an attempt to delineate the practice from both an employer and employee point of view. In this respect the chapters cover a diverse range of sectors and organizational contexts to include: clothing and furniture manufacture; retail; heavy industrial manufacture; hotels and the leisure industry (casinos); financial services providers, high technology providers and charitable service providers (Scope and Typetalk).

From the outset we wish to make clear that for us strategies and practices of employee branding are necessarily contested activities; always partial and always in process. Their effects are neither inviolate nor intransitive, and are always open to negotiation and contestation. Yet it is precisely this malleability that offers employers potential in terms of shaping notions of idealized workers and this makes the concept very appealing and worthy of serious empirical engagement and interrogation. Moreover, our case study approach is based on the knowledge that, to use Karen Legge's (1995) phrase, the rhetorics and realities of the employee relationship frequently and powerfully diverge and our commitment is to explore processes of branding from an in-depth, 'as it happens', perspective. While such an approach will be unable to comment on the wider significance of branding, it may open up an initial empirically informed theoretical understanding of the dynamics of branding in action and its impact for employers, managers, subordinates, consumers and society more widely. We include case studies from a number of employment sectors that are geographically dispersed, albeit heavily euro-centric. This, we believe, follows the pattern of adoption of employee branding practices but we are keen to note that further studies of employee branding in the regions that we do not cover will clearly enhance our understanding. As too will survey level work, which will add breadth to, and thus complement, the work presented here.

The volume approaches the topic of employee branding from a number of different disciplinary backgrounds, which we consider germane to the topic at hand. Branding is largely seen as a marketing phenomenon and this is therefore our starting point. However, the task of engaging with employees speaks directly to our shared interests in organization studies, and its prescriptive cousin, HRM. Our multi-disciplinary approach draws attention to the economic, social and often political context, which fashion and continue to shape practices of employee branding. Yet despite this, what unites us with each other as editors, but also with the other contributors to this volume, is a deeply held view of the importance of fine-grained qualitative research and for the attendant possibility of sociological analysis that this presents. Scepticism surrounding the idea of employee branding is, we think, well placed; as noted previously, we can point to many attempts to gain the control and consent of workers. A useful starting place is, therefore, to ask ourselves what exactly is employee branding and how is the term being used?

WHAT IS EMPLOYEE BRANDING?

We perceive employee branding to be an exercise in organizational communication that extends beyond the strict confines of the employment relationship. The specifics of the brand, often partially formed and lacking in full codification, work to promote ideas of idealized types of workers (Pettinger, 2004), that is to say: 'the sort of workers who work here'. Stakeholders, much wider and broader than simply management and employees, receive and process this communication as part of everyday life. Indeed, it is this wider audience and the wider perception of the employee brand that, in our view, makes the concept so worthy of study. Just as potential employees are part of the audience for the performance of the employee brand, so too is the potential customer (Merz et al., 2009). This is significant from an organizational perspective because it means that much of the work that once was restricted to the materiality of the product, such as the embodiment of capital, quality, ethos etc., can now be communicated by other means.

Some argue that this shift results from moves towards a knowledge economy. Arvidsson (2006, preface), for example, views the brand as symptomatic of a shift from industrial to informational capital, seeing it as 'an institutional embodiment of the logic of a new form of informational capital – much like the factory embodied the logic of industrial capital'. As such the brand is not only entirely implicated in the management and motivation of workers but also, as Arvidsson observes, puts to work the capacity of consumers and other actors to 'produce a common social world through autonomous processes of communication and interaction' (2006, preface). Thus while the brand is often made visible through its effects on employee recruitment practices (Brannan and Hawkins, 2007) (i.e. employees must embody the look and feel of the brand), these same employees are also 'put to work' in developing and maintaining a shared terrain for its subsequent communication. Here an individual's attitude or personality often take precedence over specific, more traditionally defined, skill sets. Arguably workers' ability to engage in, and reproduce, specific forms of communication has become central to both their continued employment in an organization and their ability to 'get on' in increasingly dynamic employment markets. Moreover, from an HR perspective, the task of communicating 'what it means to work here' can have already begun long before an employee clocks on for work for the first time. Put succinctly, employee branding extends the frontier of control, albeit tentatively, beyond the physical boundaries of the organization. This is illustrated by the so-called 'war for talent'[1], which saw the development of competitive recruitment strategies used by large corporations from the early 2000s to attract and retain key talented workers. Martin Kornberger (2010, 124) gives a good example of how such a recruitment strategy has been put into practice in his discussion of IAG's 'recruitment revolution'. In fitting with this perspective another appropriate example can be seen in the burgeoning range of self-help books where the practice of 'branding yourself' is advocated as central to career success (Peters, 1999; Andrusia and Haskins, 2000; McNally and Speak, 2003), demonstrating the extent to which the working lives of professionals are currently exposed to the discourse of employee branding. The mantra 'you are your own brand' has become particularly relevant to professionals' occupations, including academic careers. Noble et al. (2010), for example, relate one's academic career to a 'personal brand-building project' aimed at achieving eminence or career success mainly by publishing in 'A'-rated journals. As such the brand acts to structure modes of self-governance in the institution or organization: as employees are entreated to reproduce the brand they also simultaneously reproduce themselves as organizational members.

WHY EMPLOYEE BRANDING? WHY NOW?

While it is almost certainly true that attempts to 'brand employees' have a long history, systematic attempts to design the look and feel of idealized workers in such a robust and explicit way is a relatively new phenomenon. This sea change is partially evidenced in the plethora of books now available as practical guides to leveraging the brand in the service of human resource management (Ind, 2001; Barrow and Mosley, 2005; Sartain and Schumann, 2006; Buckingham, 2008). While tempting to see this as just another management fad, we think that the confluence of the following factors is significant in understanding this trend.

The restructuring of advanced capitalist economies has entailed massive shifts in the type and nature of employment for the vast majority of employees. In the context of this volume this is important for a number of reasons; the decline in the concept and reality of a 'job for life', for example, is crucial in framing employment issues. Under conditions of relative employment and sectorial stability, individual narratives of employment and service were sedimented by decades of employment with a single firm, currently employees are simply unlikely to spend sufficient time to learn 'what it means' to be a specific type of organizational employee by osmosis and immersion. The collapse of this kind of employment pattern, along side with the specific attack on the internal labour market structures by neo-liberal forms such as outsourcing (Rubery et al., 2002), means that the processes of identification within organizations have become far more problematic and disrupted than has been hitherto the case.

Furthermore, the growth of service work, which for the most part is brand driven, focuses attention on the employee in a much broader way than ever before. Crucially, in the case of most service work, the brand resides in the employee; employees simply are the brand. Here researchers have underlined the centrality of forms of emotional labour performed by service employees in both successfully delivering the service and perpetuating the branded experience for the customer (Hochschild, 1985). Under these conditions business success or failure is inextricably linked, not just to the productivity and material output of the workforce, but also to the way in which this work is conducted. Given what we have said previously about the collapse of sedimented forms of learning at work, we might posit employee branding as a mechanism to speed up the learning process at work in order to influence employees as they learn and internalize the behavioural rules to enable appropriate behaviour as part of a broader sense of how to conduct themselves at work in a way which is carefully aligned with the strategic objectives of the organization. The rise of the creative industries and the move towards an 'aesthetic economy' (Warhurst and Nickson, 2001; Entwhistle, 2002; Böheme, 2003; Postrell, 2003) can be set alongside such developments, wherein creativity and design are significant vehicles for competitive advantage, and jobs claiming to have a creative component are highly valued. The turn to aesthetics has significant consequences for employees in that they are encouraged to adopt specific stylized forms of embodied disposition, which are then harnessed to create value for the organization (Warhurst et al., 2000; Warhurst and Nickson, 2007). Building on previous conceptions of emotional labour, Witz et al., following Bourdieu, describe aesthetic labour as:

> the mobilization, development and commodification of embodied 'dispositions'. Such dispositions, in the form of embodied capacities and attributes, are to some extent possessed by workers at the point of entry into employment. However employers then mobilize, develop, and commodify these embodied dispositions through processes of recruitment, selection and training transforming them into 'skills' which are geared towards producing a 'style' of service encounter that appeals to the senses of the customer. (Witz et al., 2003: 36)

Against a backdrop of declining narratives surrounding work and the potential that this has for meaning making in our everyday lives, Gabriel (2005) draws attention to organizational attempts to enchant both workers and customers. In a photo essay depicting the 'Pleasures and Sorrows of Work' under contemporary capitalism de Botton (2009: 103) reflects on the tendency towards a 'crisis of meaning' in some societies where some industries have 'little connection to our sincere and significant needs' and where the banality of labour is intertwined with, and driven by, the honouring of the resulting material gains. One of de Botton's examples is United Biscuits, where (as in most organizations operating under conditions of contemporary capitalism) the work is subdivided into increasingly specialized and compartmentalized tasks. For example, workers might be involved in minutiae of designing the font for the biscuit packaging, monitoring sales in a specific region, driving delivery lorries between hubs or spotting malformed biscuits on the production line. This division of work does not only result in tedium, but further elevates the vexed question of motivation: 'whether the company could succeed in providing its staff with a sufficiently elevated set of ideals in whose name they were to exhaust themselves and surrender the greatest share of their lives' (de Botton, 2009: 82). It is in the context of the failure of work to provide sustaining and life-enhancing meaning and narrative that we think processes of employee branding are making attempts to resuscitate and rejuvenate tarnished images and ideals. In industries where both means and ends may indeed be said to be trivial, we observe, with some scepticism, that the brand could offer a medium through which sets of universally valued ideals might be made visible, thus potentially rendering work more meaningful.

A SHORT HISTORY OF THE BRAND

Dating the emergence of the brand concept is not without complexity, particularly when we consider the host of attendant activities caught up in its rise to prominence. Designers, accountants, marketers and retailers might all point to different significant events to account for its advent. Tracing the word 'brand' back to its etymological roots suggests that it is derived from brandr, an old Norse word meaning 'to burn'. In turn, this word refers to the burning of a maker's or owner's mark onto products, and this practice still endures in the branding of cattle. The meaning: 'identifying mark made by a hot iron' can be traced back to the 1550s; this was broadened in 1827 to 'a particular make of goods' but the term 'brand name' does not appear until 1922 (Online Etymology Dictionary). Very primitive examples of brands can be found as early as the Bronze Age: excavation of the Indus Valley, for example, has unearthed square seals depicting a range of animals. These seals are thought to have been used by stone and bronze craftsmen to identify the origin of their wares and therefore to signal quality. The seals have been found attached to vessels such as jars and baskets as well as documentation that would have been involved in trade (Moore and Reid, 2008).

As with most histories of consumerism, we might associate the birth of mass marketed brands with the rise of industrialism. The movement of production from artisanal, community-based industries into the factories of towns and cities put an increasing distance between the producers and eventual consumers of products. Consumers who were used to obtaining knowledge about products either from their actual producers or from their local chapman or shopkeeper, were now reliant on packaging and advertising for information about these products. Here the symbolic attributes of products, particularly their ability to compete with products of a similar type, became increasingly important. In addition, the makers of these new mass-produced products had to persuade the consumer that their products were as reliable and trustworthy, and of a comparable (if not higher) quality to the locally produced goods that consumers had long been familiar with. As Lury observes, 'the early stages of the development of the brand were intended to allow the producer to speak "directly" to the consumer through presentation, packaging and other media' (2004: 19). However, the rise of the brand is not associated solely with consumption, but more broadly with the organization of production during the industrializing period. The geographical growth of markets and increased circulation of goods produced competition on an international scale and brands were vital in competing in this new arena.

Many brands claim to be the branded 'first' in the UK, for example Bass and Company, whose red triangle was the first trademark to be registered under the UK's Trade Mark Registration Act 1875. Lyle's Golden Syrup makes similar claims to being one of the earliest brands, with their distinctive green and gold tin dating from 1885. Other examples from the late 1800s include Campbell's soup, Coca-Cola, Quaker Oats and Kellogg's cereals. These examples illustrate the inextricable relationship between the brand and wider forms of visual culture. The rise of the brand goes hand in hand with the advent and increasing sophistication of marketing activity (see Tadajewski, 2009). In terms of professional marketing, by the 1950s, a consumer-centred philosophy began to emerge among manufacturers, one that replaced the previous focus on sales. Marketing increasingly became articulated as a principal organizing function (along with innovation) whose main purpose is the creation of a satisfied customer, who consequently would reward the organization with sales (Webster, 1992).

In placing the consumer central to organizational activities, greater effort was put into marketing research in order to better understand the consumer and their needs. At this point organizations began to draw upon developing social and psychological knowledge about the consumer to input into both the design and sales processes. Indeed the use, and potential misuse, of this knowledge was not without controversy, as attested by the publication of Vance Packard's 1957 book *The Hidden Persuaders*, which offers a popularist critique of advertising manipulation.

From the 1960s onwards marketers began seriously building on the idea that consumers might have a relationship with brands (Fournier, 1998). Significant money and effort has been put into building brand images and personalities that consumers would want to, or perhaps more significantly be persuaded to, identify with. As part of this programme we have seen the rise of 'experience marketing', where the functional attributes of products are marginalized in favour of a celebration of the experience that the brand offers and this becomes the central focus of marketing activity (Pine and Gilmore, 1999; Schmitt, 2000). In the same vein 'lifestyle marketing' has become the accepted modus operandi (Michman and Mazze, 2003). This lifestyle approach attempts to reach into all areas of an individual's sense of self to include attitude, values and personality in a range of market segmentation techniques. Arguably this approach to marketing is more pervasive than ever before and attempts to address the consumer as an individual. It appeals to the individual's sense of taste and style by providing assemblages of products and attendant promotional meanings in order to resonate with, and reinforce, consumer individuality. Featherstone, in discussing the meaning of lifestyle as it relates to consumer culture, observes that:

> lifestyle… within contemporary consumer culture [it] connotes individuality, self-expression and a stylistic self-consciousness. One's body, clothes, speech, leisure pastimes, eating and drinking preferences, home, car, choice of holidays, etc. are to be regarded as indicators of the individuality of taste and sense of style of the owner consumer. (Featherstone, 1987: 55)

Thus, lifestyle marketing moves away from previous mass-marketing approaches of the 1940s and 1950s focusing on an explicit attempt to appeal to the individual and to individuality (Holt, 1997), even though such an appeal to individuality at the mass-market level is entirely paradoxical. The brand plays a central role in directing and channelling consumption meanings: the American fashion retailer Abercrombie & Fitch is a good example of a 'lifestyle brand' appealing to a very specific way of living. The company's brand promotion techniques (i.e. its store environments, advertising and clothing design) are underpinned by a very exclusionary and socially divisive set of meanings. Their stores, for example, are staffed by young 'brand representatives' who quite literally embody the Abercrombie & Fitch lifestyle: attractive, athletic, popular and enthusiastic. These employees are recruited largely on the basis of aesthetic appeal and a visual 'fit' with the brand (see also Warhurst and Nickson, 2001; Pettinger, 2004; Hancock and Tyler, 2007; Warhurst et al., 2009). Once employed, staff are instructed on how to present themselves in minute detail, as formulated in their 'Look Policy', which describes the expected 'appropriate look', including, for example, the maximum allowed length of nails.

From the 1960s onwards the visual symbolism of brands developed and strengthened to form the contemporary brand landscape where Nike's swoosh,

Mercedes-Benz' three-pointed star or McDonald's golden arches come to form their own language, condensing a complex of cultural meanings into a single symbol. Familiarity and instant recognition are prized attributes in the increasingly crowded 'brandscape' that constitutes the television adverts, supermarket shelves and streetscapes (Klein, 2000; Klingmann, 2007) of the contemporary Western world. Indeed brands have become part of the cultural fabric of contemporary commercial, but also private, life (Schroeder and Salzer-Mörling, 2006). While brands feed on popular culture for their central motifs, we also see a reverse flow of meaning with brands themselves providing the fabric for social communication, offering us a shared terrain through which to communicate meaning (Arvidsson, 2006) and around which communities might be formed (Muniz and O'Guinn, 2001; McAlexander et al., 2002; Maclaran, 2009). In this sense brands provide the context or frame for the production of meaning. As Arvidsson (2006: 8) observes, 'brands do not so much stand for products, as much as they provide a part of the context in which products are used'. While this is significant in cultural terms, in economic terms the value of this context cannot be underestimated. Focusing on the economic dimension of brands reveals the most recent turn of the wheel in a branded world. The meteoric rise of brand equity on company balance sheets reflects, in part, the objectification of brands made tangible to allow them to be leveraged and monetized (Wilmott, 2010 and in this volume). Sophisticated metrics measuring the value that a brand adds to an organization (brand equity) demonstrate in many cases brands to be the organization's most valuable asset. Brand value, and consequently the adjusted value of a company, supports and reaffirms an economic rationale, not only for brand decisions and organizational investments in branding, but also for guiding financial analysts' and investors' decisions and as such the brand is typically leveraged as a source of governance and discipline both financially and organizationally.

CASE STUDIES OF EMPLOYEE BRANDING

This collection explores both organizational and employee perspectives in investigating the 'lived experiences' of understanding, implementing and negotiating processes of employee branding. The chapters embrace both empirical and theoretical foci. The empirical case study contribution is at the core of the work (Chapters 3 to 9) and these chapters provide the 'lived' contribution to our understanding of the contemporary experience of work, and outline in detail how organizations attempt to build brands through employee relations and HRM initiatives, but also, more informally, through the nurturing of specific organizational and shop floor cultures. Chapters 2 and 10 are conceptual and theoretical reflections that seek to provide a broader contextual consideration of key aspects of employee branding and include considerations of the interstices between branding and financialization and diversity respectively. In Chapter 11 we close with a consideration of a series of themes running through this collection and offer some brief emerging theoretical perspectives in an attempt to open up ongoing debate.

The volume opens with a discussion that considers the impact of branding in the context of financialization and market capitalization. Hugh Willmott's chapter takes an ethico-political perspective to provide an analysis of branding in the wider context of capitalist reproduction where brand equity is co-produced by user-consumers. The chapter charts how, through conversion, brand value is appropriated by organizations; in doing so the chapter provides apt contextual account of the financial importance of branding to organizations and provides a useful foundation for the subsequent chapters.

Chris Land and Scott Taylor's empirical work explores branding themes in the practices of what they call 'New Age' capitalism. Their case-study organization is a retailer of fashion goods promoting an 'alternative lifestyle' which, they argue, is in tension with the capitalist values embedded within the organization. The company celebrates specific leisure activities, adopts a strong and overt ethical and environmental stance and promotes alternative lifestyles through its brand and its employees. Crucially, however, these are not necessarily reflected in the design and management of the organization's work processes in relation to, for example, the use of alternative sources of energy, employee work/life balance and the structure of organizational ownership. It is also not reflected in the views of all employees, particularly at the lower levels of the organization, and is certainly completely disconnected from the workers who manufacture their garments in the Far East (which are not directly audited by the company). These tensions are fully explored in the chapter in relation to both theory and practice and related to the notion of authenticity.

Sandra Smith and Margo Buchanan-Oliver's main concern is to unpack the processes of representation of the self, the organization and the brand from the perspective of employees. In their chapter they offer a social narrative analysis of identity construction in relation to the brand, focusing on verbal and graphical representations of the relationships between the individuals, the organization and the brand. By revealing the polysemic rather than dichotomic relation between accommodation and resistance to brand values, they argue that the experience of the brand, and the construction of branded identities, are always fragmented, complex and paradoxical, thus confirming the contested nature of employee and employer branding.

With a more specific focus on HRM practices, Jean Cushen explores the attempts of a large multinational organization, a provider of portable, high technology products and services, to engender the ideal employee through an organization-wide programme of employer branding. The chapter challenges mainstream views that soft HRM principles of unitarism, commitment and mutual fulfilment can be successful in achieving full employee commitment. In the case study presented the employer branding initiative served to direct employees' attention towards management activities that were perceived as contrary to their interests (such as cost-cutting exercises), thus creating a rhetoric–reality gap that generated anger and frustration among employees and resulted in a dramatic subvert of the initial goals of the employee branding project.

Experiences, interpretations and subversions of branding initiatives are also at the centre of Stephanie Russell's work. By focusing on training, development, aesthetic representations and organizational artefacts, this chapter explores how employees are encouraged to internalize the brand through a number of potentially invasive strategies. Stephanie explores how discourses of customer sovereignty underpin organizational attempts at employee–brand alignment within the specific case-study organization. Stephanie's contribution provides an interesting input to the labour process debate, highlighting how attempts at disciplining employee behaviour in their everyday lives, both within and outside of work, are often met by a variety of resistance tactics and behaviours through which employees' selves can be expressed.

Scott Hurrell and Dora Scholarios document the recruitment strategies of two different hotel establishments in relation to issues of person–brand fit. The two hotels studied demonstrate a different emphasis on selection procedures, leading the authors to suggest a link between HR practices, brand identification and organizational experience of skills deficit. The chapter advocates that person–brand fit-recruitment practices may be superior to standardized, competency-based procedures. Such practices would also allow applicants agency in selecting the organization, facilitating self-selection, within the decision-making processes. While a strategy based on person–brand fit could be considered successful from an HR perspective, it can also have serious implications in perpetuating specific norms surrounding appearance, background, class and gender, and operating to exclude those who do not 'fit' with these norms.

Focusing on the concept of human agency, Veronika Tarnovskaya's chapter explores ways in which employees at IKEA (the Swedish furniture store) interpret brand messages and appropriate them as part of their own identity work. Through the analysis of her empirical work, Veronika merges processes of employer with employee branding positioning the 'employee as agent' at the centre of processes of narrative construction. Framing the employer brand as a structure, and employee branding as a form of appropriation work within and upon this structure, Veronika explores the various ways in which employees both accommodate and resist the brand.

Melanie Simms takes a different perspective in her chapter: rather than exploring employee branding from an internal organizational perspective, she looks at the ways in which an outside organization (in this case a trade union) might harness the employee branding process to meet their own aims. She analyses the dynamics affecting the service brand of two charitable and two commercial organizations at the point in which trade unions are attempting to organize the workforce. In doing so she examines how the process of managing front-line service work through branding presents opportunities but also challenges for trade unions when organizing workers. The chapter explores how trade unions mobilize existing narratives of service brand values as a way to gain collective influence and frame the desired improvements to working conditions in their campaigns. The financial value attached to the positive perpetuation of the brand means that organizations may be more responsive to union requests leveraged around their brand values.

In a final conceptual contribution Martin Edwards and Elisabeth Kelan discuss processes of employer branding in relation to aspects of diversity management and question whether employer branding and diversity strategies are opposed or whether they might serve a common objective. The existing conflict between branding (as a process of value homogenization) and diversity management (as intent to acknowledge and value differences between employees) is dissected in Martin and Elisabeth's discussion. While acknowledging the challenges and contradictions between employer branding and diversity, the chapter offers some insights into ways in which these tensions can be reconciled, albeit to a point.

In the concluding chapter we seek to pull together emergent themes from the preceding chapters in an attempt to open up future discussion and commence a theoretical debate which we hope will be explored by further theoretical and empirical work on the employee branding complex practice.

NOTE

1. The term was intially used in 1997 by Steven Hankin from the consultancy firm McKinsey & Co.

REFERENCES

Andrusia, D. and Haskins, R. (2000) *Brand Yourself: How to Create an Identity for a Brilliant Career*, New York: Ballantine Books.
Arvidsson, A. (2006) *Brands: Meaning and Value in Media Culture*, Oxford: Routledge.
Barrow, S. and Mosley, R. (2005) *The Employer Brand ®: Bringing the Best of Brand Management to People at Work*, Chichester: Wiley.
Böheme, G. (2003) 'Contribution to the Critique of the Aesthetic Economy', *Thesis Eleven*, 73(1), 71–82.

Brannan, M.J. and Hawkins, B. (2007) 'London calling: selection as pre-emptive strategy for cultural control', *Employee Relations*, 29 (2), 178–91.

Buckingham, I. (2008) *Brand Engagement: How Employees Make or Break Brands*, Basingstoke: Palgrave Macmillan.

De Botton, A. (2009) *The Pleasures and Sorrows of Work*, New York: Pantheon Books.

Entwhiste, J. (2002) 'The Aesthetic Economy: The production of value in the field of fashion modelling', *Journal of Consumer Culture*, 2 (3), 317–39.

Featherstone, M. (1987) 'Lifestyle and Consumer Culture', *Theory, Culture and Society*, 4, 55–70.

Fleming, P. (2009) *Authenticity and the Cultural Politics of Work: New Forms of Informal Control*, Cambridge: Cambridge University Press.

Fournier, S. (1998) 'Consumers and their Brands: Developing Relationship Theory', *Journal of Consumer Research*, 24 (4), 343–73.

Hochschild, A.R. (1985) *The Managed Heart: Commercialization of Human Feeling*, Los Angeles: University of California Press.

Holt, D.B. (1997) 'Poststructuralist lifestyle analysis: Conceptualizing the social patterning of consumption in postmodernity', *Journal of Consumer Research*, 23 (4), 326–50.

Ind, N. (2001) *Living the Brand: How to Transform Every Member of Your Organization into a Brand Champion*, London: Kogan Page.

Klein, N. (2000) *No Logo: Taking Aim at the Brand Bullies*, Toronto: Knopf Canada.

Klingmann, A. (2007) *Brandscapes: Architecture in the Experience Economy*, Cambridge, MA: MIT Press.

Kornberger, M. (2010) *Brand Society: How Brands Transform Management and Lifestyle*, Cambridge: Cambridge University Press.

Legge, K. (1995) *Human Resource Management. Rhetorics and Realities*, London: Macmillan.

Maclaran, P. (2009) 'Building brand cultures', in Parsons, E. and Maclaran, P. *Contemporary Issues in Marketing and Consumer Behaviour*, London: Elsevier, pp. 73–88.

McAlexander, J.H., Schouten, J.W. and Keonig, H.F. (2002) 'Building brand communities', *Journal of Marketing*, 66 (1), 38–55.

McNally, D. and Speak, K.D. (2003) *Be Your Own Brand: A Breakthrough Formula for Standing Out from the Crowd*, San Francisco: Berrett-Koehler Publishers.

Merz, M.A., He, Y. and Vargo, S.L. (2009) 'The Evolving Brand Logic: A service-dominant logic perspective', *Journal of the Academy of Marketing Science*, 37 (3): 328–44.

Michman, R.D. and Mazze, E.M. (2003) *Lifestyle Marketing: Reaching the New American Consumer*, Westport, CT: Praeger.

Moore, K. and Reid, S. (2008) 'The Birth of Brand: 4000 Years of Branding History', *Business History*, 50 (4), 419–32.

Muniz, A. and O'Guinn, T.C. (2001) 'Brand Communities', *Journal of Consumer Research*, 27, 412–32.

Nickson, D., Warhurst, C. and Dutton, E. (2005) 'The Importance of Attitude and Appearance in the Service Encounter in Retail and Hospitality', *Managing Service Quality*, 15 (2), 195–208.

Noble, C.H., Bentley, J.P., Campbell, D. and Singh, J.J. (2010) 'In search of eminence: A personal brand-building perspective on the achievement of scholarly prominence in marketing', *Journal of Marketing Education*, 32 (2), 314–27.

Online Etymology Dictionary, http://www.etymonline.com/index.php.

Organisation for Economic Co-Operation and Development (2000) Science Technology Industry. The Service Economy. http://www.oecd.org/dataoecd/10/33/2090561.pdf, accessed on 21 November 2010.

Packard, V. (1957) *The Hidden Persuaders*, Harmondsworth, Middlesex: Penguin.

Peters, T. (1999) *The Brand You 50: Or: Fifty Ways to Transform Yourself from an 'Employee' into a Brand That Shouts Distinction, Commitment, and Passion!*, New York: Knopf .

Pettinger, L. (2004) 'Brand Culture and Branded Workers: Service Work and Aesthetic Labour in Fashion Retail', *Consumption, Markets and Culture*, 7 (2), 165–84.

Pine, J. and Gilmore, J. (1999) *The Experience Economy*, Boston, MA: Harvard Business School Press.

Postrel, V. (2003) *The Substance of Style*, New York: Harper Collins.

Rubery, J., Earnshaw, J., Marchington, M., Cooke, F.L. and Vincent, S. (2002) 'Changing Organizational Forms and the Employment Relationship', *Journal of Management Studies*, 39 (5) 645–72.

Sartain, L. and Schumann, M. (2006) *Brand from the Inside: Eight Essentials to Emotionally Connect Your Employees to Your Business*, San Francisco: Jossey-Bass.

Schmitt, B. (2000) *Experiential Marketing*, New York: Free Press.

Schroeder, J. and Salzer-Mörling, M. (eds.) (2006) *Brand Culture*, Oxford: Routledge.

Smith, D. (2009) 'Transforming Your Frontline Employees into Living Brand Champions', *Brand2Life: Connecting Your People to Your Brand*, Bridge Training and Events Ltd, http://www.livingbrand.co.uk/brand2life.html, accessed November 2010.

Tadajewski, M. (2009) 'A History of Marketing Thought', in Parsons, E. and Maclaran, P., *Contemporary Issues in Marketing*, London: Elsevier, pp. 13–36.

Webster, F.E. (1992) 'The Changing Role of Marketing in the Corporation', *Journal of Marketing*, 56 (4), 1–17.

Warhurst, C. and Nickson, D. (2001) *Looking Good, Sounding Right: Style Counselling and the Aesthetics of the New Economy*, London: Industrial Society.

Warhurst, C. and Nickson, D. (2007) 'Employee Experience of Aesthetic Labour in Retail and Hospitality', *Work, Employment and Society*, 21 (1), 103–20.

Warhurst, C., Nickson, D., Witz, A. and Cullen, A. (2000) 'Aesthetic Labour in Interactive Service Work: Some Case Study Evidence from the "New" Glasgow', *Service Industries Journal*, 20 (3), 118.

Warhurst, C., van der Broek, D., Hall, R. and Nickson, D. (2009) 'Lookism: the New Frontier of Employment Discrimination', *Journal of Industrial Relations*, 51 (1) 131–6.

Wilmott, H. (2010) 'Creating 'value' beyond the point of production: branding, financialization and market capitalization', *Organization*, 17 (5), 517–42.

2. Considering the 'bigger picture': branding in processes of financialization and market capitalization[1]

Hugh Willmott

INTRODUCTION

> ... brand owning companies can earn huge returns on their capital and grow faster, unencumbered by factories and masses of manual workers. Those are the things that the stock market rewards with high price/earnings ratios.
> (Akasia, 2000: 30)

> Brands are financial assets and their importance in relation to the tangible assets of most businesses continues to grow. The management of brand value is simply another aspect of managing shareholder value.
> (Batchelor, 1998: 101)

Branding has until recently been marginal to critical scholarship across business and management studies (see Arvidsson, 2006; Holt, 2002; Kornberger, 2010). Marketers, with few exceptions (e.g. Holt, 2002, 2004), have treated branding as a functional means of differentiating products or services, increasing product recognition and reputation and thereby securing or gaining market share.[2] Other students of business regarded branding as external to their domain, the principal exceptions being organization specialists interested in corporate branding (e.g. Hatch and Schultz, 2005; Schultz et al., 2000, 2005) and accounting specialists interested in the issue of accounting for brands (e.g. Tollington, 2001).

Attentiveness to branding among social scientists, whether mainstream or critical, has been muted, perhaps because it is considered too superficial to merit close or serious examination. For students of political economy, it seems that the 'soft' and intangible qualities of consumer behaviour make branding an unattractive topic. Lury's (2004) *Brands: The Logos of the Global Economy* promises to balance the account (see also du Gay et al., 1996) and yet, rooted in cultural studies (see Crane and Bovone, 2006 for an overview of culturalist approaches), her study does little to remedy the neglect of branding as an integral element of contemporary political economy. That *No Logo*, a book authored by a journalist–activist, has had such an impact by bringing the 'new branded world' (Klein, 2000: ch. 1) into some focus is indicative of a scholarly vacuum as well as symptomatic of a popular recognition of branding's contemporary significance.

Whatever the source of the antipathy or blindness to the significance of branding for capitalist expansion (see Marazzi, 2010) and, more recently, for market capitalization (see Frieder and Subrahmanyam, 2004), its comparative neglect by students of organization and human resource management is remarkable. For branding is increasingly important in shaping the identity, strategy and structure of organizations (O'Neill, 2001; Schultz et al., 2000) – in the public and not-for-profit as well as the private sectors (see Lury and Moor, 2010).

By placing branding in a 'bigger picture' of contemporary processes of financialization and the increasing involvement of consumers in the production of value, this chapter is responsive to criticism that studies of branding, and of consumption more generally, tend to be 'uneconomized' and 'oversocialized' as their predominant focus is upon 'the individual and social rewards' (Cova and Dalli, 2009: 326). A more 'economized' analysis of branding, it will be argued, must pay attention inter alia to 'the disparity in the distribution of profits arising from consumers' work' (Cova and Dalli, 2009: 326) as co-producers of brand equity where, in an era of financialization[3] this equity is ascribed a monetized, dollar value as a financial asset.

The chapter is organized as follows. In the first section a schematic history of branding is sketched as a basis for appreciating how, in the present era of financialization, brands are identified as intangible assets with a monetizable value. The second section discusses the contribution of user-consumers to the building of brand equity. The final section expands upon the relationship between financialization and branding.

A SCHEMATIC HISTORY OF BRANDING

Branding was first introduced[4] to provide assurances to customers that a product or service, such as silversmithing, could be trusted as unadulterated or reliable. In this phase, branding does not differentiate a product or service from reputable substitutes but, instead, provides a symbolic guarantee of a standardized quality. In this context, the significance of branding resides in inspiring confidence, which is a critical condition of the expansion of (impersonal, market) exchange. The assurance of a recognizable and trusted brand name, enabled through advertising and promotion, is particularly important for entry into markets where customers had previously relied upon their personal knowledge of local producers. In this phase, branding facilitates a substitution of branded for unbranded products which is a condition of possibility for enlarging sales, thereby securing an expanding, privately appropriated, surplus from the proceeds.

A second phase or layer of branding places emphasis upon elaborating a distinctive, symbolic meaning or 'personality' to differentiate a product or service from its competitors. Customers' attention and loyalty are attracted by, for example, associating products with an aspirational lifestyle. In this phase, what amounts to fetishing the brand, where customer identification and emotional attachment are induced, plays an increasingly central role in retaining market share and supporting premium pricing. As Thompson et al. (2007: 634) observe of popular music, 'what is marketed is more than music, it is the "uniqueness" of the act, its look, its "story", as well as its sound'. As they also point out, the development of these qualities – that is, elements of brand equity – 'doesn't start after but takes place during the production process' (Thompson et al., 2007: 635). What they omit to appreciate, however, and so represent the prospective consumer of pop music as a passive absorber of the brand 'story', is how consumers are actively involved, as co-creators, in interpreting and assessing this story and are active participants in elaborating and disseminating its narrative – notably, in the contemporary context, through social networking sites.[5]

During this second phase of branding, substantial resources are ploughed into styling and mass advertising by employing branding specialists and agencies (see Low and Fullerton, 1994: esp. 177 et seq.). Brand equity – in the form of brand awareness and positive associations – is thereby created through successful branding campaigns. The third phase arises with a recognition of how brand equity can, potentially, be monetized as brand value – something that becomes very apparent when a company owning a prized brand name is acquired at a price that far exceeds the value ascribed to its physical assets (see Box 2.1), thereby demonstrating how investment in brand building can produce an intangible asset capable of realizing a dollar value.[6]

Building upon the mass consumption phase of branding, and in particular the institutionalized expansion of consumption through credit, the third phase involves investment in branding, combined with outsourcing of production, as a purposeful, strategic means of increasing the return on capital invested. It was during the 1990s, as Feldwick (1996: 85) observes, that 'hardnosed business people began to notice that brands appeared to be changing hands for huge sums of money... (and) the difference between balance sheet valuations and the prices paid by predators was substantially attributed to the value of brands.' When brand equity becomes a monetized quantity, its dollar value is incorporated into market capitalization (against which cheaper lines of credit

---

BOX 2.1   THE FINANCIAL IMPORTANCE OF BRANDS: UNILEVER'S ACQUISITION OF BESTFOODS

When Unilever finally succeeded in a US\$8.6 billion takeover of Bestfoods, the primary focus of analysts and fund managers were the leading brands that this would add to the company's financial portfolio. So while institutional investors were pressuring Unilever for more than a decade to reduce its brand portfolio, the financial value attributed to Bestfoods' top brands justified the debt-financed acquisition of this company (IUF, 2006).

---

and the debt-financing of expansion or acquisition activity can be secured). As financialization becomes the driving source of capital accumulation, the contribution of branding to generating surpluses – for example, through royalties derived from subsidiaries and other companies' use of the brand name – begins to up-stage its (continuing, phase two) role in constructing symbolic value for consumers. A report discussing the emergent strategy of global food companies, such as Nestlé, Kraft and Unilever, published in 1996 was prescient in its observation that

> As income from brand royalties contributes a larger proportion of earnings growth there is a stronger motivation to direct investment into raising the value of intangible assets – especially increased expenditure on branding and marketing operations. This means that if the major food transnational corporations (TNCs) exercise control over these brands and focus on branding and marketing, food processing and packaging activities can be outsourced to subcontractors and co-packers... The fact that the major TNCs can generate a major source of revenue from intangible assets – in this case royalties paid not only by subsidiaries but eventually by co-packers – suggests that this could be the future of the global food industry. (IUF, 2006: 11)

From being an elusive quality that warrants and/or (re)enchants mundane commodities, the intangible qualities of brand equity are translated into a dollar equivalent, in the form of 'brand value'. Box 2.2 sets out the difference, and relationship, between brand equity and brand value.

From being regarded as a somewhat mysterious way of increasing sales volumes and raising price points, the value of branding is increasingly articulated in terms of its direct (brand equity), as well as indirect (market share), contribution to a company's stock price. Indeed, it has been suggested that '"brand managers" primary task is to maximise and leverage brand equity to increase brand value' (Raggio and Leone, 2007: 380; see also Raggio and Leone, 2009). To the extent that financial decision-makers (e.g. stock analysts, fund managers) assess that 'brand owning companies can earn huge returns

---

BOX 2.2   COMPARING BRAND EQUITY AND BRAND VALUE

	Brand equity	**Brand value**
Definition	'The differential effect of brand knowledge on consumer response to the marketing of the brand' (Keller, 1993: 1) (e.g. recognition, image, 'personality', etc.)	The financial valuation given to a branded product, service or company in terms of income, potential income, reputation, prestige and market value. Brand value is the valourization of brand equity
The process of translation	'Brand equity' – conceptualized as a distinctive set of assets relating to product awareness, loyalty, quality, etc. – is understood to contribute to shareholder value as it represents 'a reservoir of cash flow that has accumulated from marketing activities but has not yet [been fully] translated into revenue' (Rust et al., 2004: 78, emphasis added; see also Madden et al., 2006)	'From a financial perspective, tangible wealth emanates from the incremental capitalized earnings and cash flows achieved by linking a successful, established brand name to a product or service. These incremental earnings and cash flows came to be labelled *brand*

---

on their capital and grow faster' (Akasia, 2000: 30), corporate executives who are mindful of the fate of their share price are likely to prioritize investment in brand-building activity. The suitably inelegant term 'brandization'[7] is coined here to refer to the leveraging of brand equity to increase the contribution of brand value, as an intangible asset, to market capitalization.

'BRANDIZATION'

In a 'post-consumer'[8] increasingly financialized, world, the management of brands is increasingly about treating them as 'objects' that can be monetized and leveraged. The monetization of brand equity is significant for at least two reasons. First, it underscores how intangible assets, including brands, are important in the valuation of companies. To better understand the distinctive organization and dynamics of contemporary, financialized capitalism, it is relevant to incorporate an examination of how intangible assets, such as brands, are co-created, and how their value is calculated and realized. The process of co-production in brand-branding occurs in both industrial and consumer markets; and, today, it is most readily evident in internet-based businesses like Amazon and eBay, where user-consumers willingly provide feedback on goods and sellers that contributes to the appeal, and thus to the brand equity, of those companies.[9]

Second, the monetization of brand equity invites consideration of whether capital invested in branding can produce a higher rate of return than an equivalent investment in the production of goods and services. This becomes a 'real option' (Baldi and Trigeorgis, 2008) when it is comparatively easy, technically and politically, to outsource manufacturing and/or service delivery (see Alvarez and Stenbacka, 2007). 'Brandization' occurs as the disciplines of finance (including financial accounting) and marketing (including brand management) converge and interact with corporate strategy. In this intersection, branding assumes an increasing significance as a higher proportion of market capitalization is attributed to it. The logic is applied most vigorously by companies such as Benetton, and especially Virgin[10] and Trump, which leverage the symbolic and material equity in the brand name by applying it to an extended range of products and services[11] but, as noted earlier, this logic is also being embraced by longer established, public companies like Nestlé and Unilever. In this regard, brandization has significant implications for the (re)structuring of economic organization as companies, pressed to deliver shareholder value, concentrate upon cultivating and leveraging their intangible assets, including their brands, and outsource other activities (see O'Neill, 2001; Pike and Pollard, 2010). As Davis (2009: 35) comments on Hewlett-Packard's decision to outsource much of its manufacturing to a 'board stuffer',

> the rationale ultimately turned on the idea that the stock market values intellectual property over tangible assets… [that is why] cell phones, hot dogs, PCs, pet food and pharmaceuticals are routinely produced by contractors, leaving OEM (Original Equipment Manufacturers) to manage the intellectual property behind these products – patents, brand names, trademarks and research capabilities.' (see also Klein, 2000, esp. ch. 8)

Why are these intangibles ascribed greater value? It is because the scope for in-house, post-Fordist squeezing of value from the point of production has diminished relative to what can be achieved by contracting it out, often to offshore manufacturers or service providers operating flexible facilities with lower wage costs and/or regulatory demands. There is often greater potential for generating surplus from the unique intangible of branding – even allowing for the vulnerability of brand equity to displacement by innovation, shifts in fashion or the risk of its destruction by consumer activists. That said, it should also be borne in mind that the contribution of brandization to capital asset growth pales into comparative insignificance when compared to the asset price bubble produced by securitization (Klimecki and Willmott, 2009).[12] Nonetheless, where financial gains are privileged, branding is increasingly identified as a cost-effective means of leveraging capital invested.

BUILDING BRAND EQUITY: CONSUMERS AS CO-PRODUCERS

The business of branding involves a labour process of sign production and dissemination by stylists, packaging specialists, copywriters, media producers, etc., as well as brand managers (Wernick, 1991). In this respect, a focus upon how the contracted labour of brand specialists is harnessed within workplaces remains fully relevant. However, their labour comprises only one side of a co-creation process. When analysis is fixated upon the sphere of production, consumers are (dis)regarded as their involvement in the production of symbolic values is ignored or trivialized (see Salzer-Mörling and Strannegård, 2004). On the 'unseen' side of the production process is the labour of user-consumers who, at the very least, make assessments of the product or service and thereby actively participate in building (or destroying)[13] brand equity. This point is now developed and illustrated by considering the political economy of brand building in the most contemporary of economies – the internet – and, more specifically, the contribution of consumers, as co-producers, to the construction of social networking sites.

CO-PRODUCING BRAND EQUITY

With the advent of ICTs, and especially Web 2.0, the co-productive role of user-consumers – which can be subversive,[14] as well as constructive – becomes increasingly apparent. Consider ventures such as Facebook, LinkedIn and YouTube but also Google, eBay, TripAdvisor and Amazon. The labour of user-consumers directly builds brand equity that, when monetized as brand value, is appropriated by site owners, and not distributed to its content providers. Sites like YouTube and Tripadvisor are well known and used not because they are heavily advertised or because they employ teams of people producing videos and inspecting hotels. Rather, it is because of the uploading activity and social networking of user-consumers that such sites enjoy a degree of recognition approaching that of long-established brands like Coca-Cola or Disney.

There is, of course, no obligation to expend time and effort in uploading material or making user reviews available; and there is no monetary incentive, such as a wage or piecework payment, for participating. What, then, is to be made of this 'gift'? Arvidsson (2006, 2008, 2009) contends that it forms part of an 'ethical economy' which generates an 'ethical surplus' (Lazzarato, 1997) in the form of new relationships, meanings and a sense of belonging. This interpretation is persuasive insofar as it draws out the motivation and pleasures associated with such activity. However, in giving it this emphasis, Arvidsson's analysis follows other studies of branding in its 'uneconomised' focus upon 'the individual and social rewards' (Cova and Dalli, 2009: 326). Arvidsson's otherwise instructive analysis displaces or marginalizes consideration of how the production of such 'ethical surplus' is embedded in capitalist economies (see Bauwens, nd, 2009).

By taking time to leave feedback (e.g. Amazon, Tripadvisor) as well as by co-designing products and services (e.g. Nokia Concept Lounge, Lego's DesignbyMe; see also Stalk and Lachenauer, 2004: 119–20), the labour of consumer-users builds brand equity that becomes convertible into brand value. This value creation may be unapparent and/or of no interest to co-producers, even when the equity produced by their labour in the form of site content, or even product development, is sold for very substantial sums.[15]

Consider YouTube. Founded in February 2005, YouTube is where user-consumers upload and share their videos and music clips. YouTube was acquired by Google for $1.65 billion in 2006 when it had just 65 employees (Arrington, 2006; Helft, 2007). That is a potent illustration of how the labour of user-consumers built the brand equity of YouTube that was turned into brand value.[16] The proceeds of the sale of YouTube were shared among those legally credited with owning the site, including share-owning employees, to the exclusion of those who provided its content and built its reputation (see Coombe, 1998). The capitalist state ensured that, legally, the co-producers of YouTube's brand equity had no entitlement to the dollar value generated by their labour.

Needless to say, the appeal of YouTube to the owners of Google was not the site's design. Google staff could readily emulate what had been created by the three ex-PayPal employees who established YouTube. What Google purchased was a brand – YouTube – that had become synonymous with videos-on-the-web, and to which a large and growing population of internet users participate as content providers, and also as revenue-generating consumers, of the advertising placed on the YouTube site. The labour expended by user-consumers does not simply create 'ethical value' for site visitors, in the form of clips relevant for identity work and networking. In addition, the uploading of content delivers exchange values which take the form of advertising revenues; and it is the labour of user-consumers that (unintentionally) generates the financial value realized in the sale of YouTube to Google.

FINANCIALIZATION AND BRANDING

The context for understanding how brands have become monetized commodities is the post-1980s neo-liberal when a deregulation of markets restored a rate of profit that had been in decline during the 1970s. Reinvigorated by opportunities to trade in a variety of products and coupons (Froud et al., 2002), forms of financial liberalization – collectively conceived as financialization – became a salvationary, bust-beating driver of growth and stability (see Orhangazi, 2008: 49 et seq.). In the UK, this was signalled loudly and triumphantly in 1986 by (the) Big Bang of City deregulation. Among many others, Harvey (2005) and Dore (2008) note how, in the post-1970s era, profit-making shifted from trade and commodity production to the development and use of financial channels (see Krippner, 2005). During these decades, corporate behaviour

> became more and more financial in orientation… it has not been uncommon for corporations to report losses in production offset by gains from financial operations (everything from credit and insurance operations to speculating in volatile currency and futures markets. (Harvey, 2005: 32)

Financialization subordinates investment decision-making to one pre-eminent criterion: what will be added to market capitalization and thereby to private equity (e.g. Virgin) or shareholder value (e.g. Google)? For example, if $1 invested in building brand equity or speculating on currency and/or futures markets is anticipated to produce a higher (short-to-medium term) yield than $1 invested in new plant, then the financially defensible answer is to offshore or outsource production, and to direct the resources into coupon trading or branding. Processes of financialization unfold as corporate strategies are shaped and assessed in relation to their anticipated effectiveness in defending or raising stock prices (see Dore, 2000; Ezzamel et al., 2009).

Such financialization is, of course, nothing inherently new (Kindleberger and Aliber, 2005). It is perhaps best understood as a potential endemic to capitalism that is released when normative inhibitions (e.g. limits on share options and bonuses) and regulatory restraints (e.g. the separation of retail and investment banking) are weakened. That said, since the 'Roaring 20s', the boldest experiment with (globalized) financialization, turbo-charged by the use of information and communication technologies for trading and marketing, has occurred during the past two decades. Following the financial meltdown of 2008, the rate of expansion of financialization has been checked but, to date (mid-2011), it has not been halted, let alone reversed. Indeed, the socialization of losses arising from the reckless leveraging of paper assets and trading in exotic financial products (e.g. collateralized debt obligations and credit default swaps; see Klimecki and Willmott, 2009) has served to sustain, not to reform, an economic system that, in the absence of the political will to introduce radical reform, remains structurally geared to financialization.

FROM BUILDING BRAND EQUITY TO CALCULATING BRAND VALUE

What, then, of marketing activity? How is this redefined and restructured in an era of financialization? From a financialization perspective, its value does not reside primarily in developing or managing an appealing message about a product or service, or even in enabling consumers to interpret this message positively, thereby increasing brand equity and boosting market share. Such outcomes may be satisfying for marketers; and they may be appreciated by consumers. But when applying the discipline of financialization, simply increasing the 'brand equity' of products or services – that is, enhancing the positive symbolic meaning – provides a necessary but insufficient justification for continuing investment in marketing. This presents something of a challenge to marketers whose functional role within corporations was formed prior to the neo-liberal era of financialization. Marketers have found themselves ill-prepared for a period in which intangible assets, and brand equity more specifically, have become identified as significant sources of shareholder value. As Lukas et al. (2005: 421) note:

> Where in the past, marketing managers were seen as experts on customers, channels, and competitors, they should be seen in the future as experts on how marketing can increase shareholder value. To do this, marketers need to extend their skill base to add expertise in modern financial planning techniques.

In an era of financialization, marketers are increasingly required to demonstrate how they (and their advertising agencies, see following quote) can reshape and justify their role in terms of its contribution to developing intangible assets that 'deliver to the bottom line':

> Advertising can frequently be the difference between two products... We think of ourselves as part of the manufacturing process, building advertising properties that

fortify brands that in themselves become company assets and deliver to the bottom line. (Bartle et al., 1996: 9, cited in Nixon, 2002: 144)

Where financialization takes hold, shareholder value creation becomes a more explicit and exclusive objective of strategic decision-making, including investment in branding. Marketing and, more specifically, the value attributed to a company's brands, is then appraised according to its contribution to market capitalization. As Lindemann (2004: 37) summarizes this development:

> in the pursuit of increasing shareholder value, companies are keen to establish procedures for the management of brands that are aligned with those for other business assets, as well as for the company as a whole... Economic value creation becomes the focus of brand management and all brand-related investment decisions. Companies as diverse as American Express, IBM, Samsung Electronics, Accenture, United Way of America, BP, Fujitsu and Duke Energy have used brand valuation to help them refocus their businesses on their brands and to create an economic rationale for branding decisions and investments. Many companies have made brand value creation part of the remuneration criteria for senior marketing executives.

The body of literature connecting brand value to market capitalization is slender but developing.[17] Studies addressing the relationship between the positive valuation of brands and stock price performance point to a strongly positive relationship (for a review of the emergent literature, see Srinivasan and Hanssens (2008) and commentary by Kimbrough and McAlister (2008)); and studies in behavioral finance indicate that brand visibility directly influences the chances of a stock being bought and held. Frieder (2004: 33, 35), for example, reports that 'a preference for visible, brand-name stocks in individuals' decisions to hold stocks supports the hypothesis that individual investors exhibit a propensity towards companies with easily recognisable products'. Investment in branding to create 'brand-name stocks' can be a cost-effective means of increasing market capitalization.

SUMMARY AND CONCLUSION

Diverse literatures – marketing, accounting and finance as well as organization studies and the sociologies of work and consumption – have been drawn together to illuminate how the creation and realization of value through branding forms an increasingly significant part of a 'big picture'[18] of contemporary capitalism. The focus has been upon the co-production of brand equity by user-consumers and its translation into the monetized value that makes an increasingly substantial contribution to the dividends and capital gains enjoyed by investors.

The contemporary significance of branding as a source of value has been explored by situating the creation and valourization of brand equity within 'the full circuit of capital'. Conceived as a form of co-production occurring in the sphere of circulation (as well as production), brand-building has been connected to: the surpluses generated by the labour of user-consumers as well as the designers and producers of branded products and services; the realization of surplus through control of revenues derived from sales of these products and services; and the appropriation of surpluses, including the conversion of brand equity into brand value after deduction of costs. In this way, contemporary investment in branding is related to the financialization of brands as intangibles that make a growing contribution to market capitalization. By attending to multiple facets of the circuit of capital, including the co-production brand equity by user-consumers, some pointers have been proposed for developing a more 'joined-up' view of the 'bigger picture' of contemporary capitalist reproduction.

In this 'bigger picture', we have linked the growing importance of the production of intangible assets (e.g. brands) to processes of financialization; and we have situated the associated emergence of 'brandization' with the dynamics of neo-liberal capitalist expansion. The analysis has illuminated how the labour of user-consumers is mobilized to build brand equity which, through a process of 'brandization', is converted into privately appropriated wealth. In an era of financialization, brand equity is increasingly targeted and leveraged as a hitherto neglected source of market capitalization and shareholder value. As branding becomes financialized, attention shifts from brand building per se to how this activity can be monetized and leveraged for valourization. Whereas branding serves to (re-)enchant mundane products and services, brandization converts brand equity into brand value for investors. With the advent of 'brandization', branding becomes 'a distinctive mode of capital accumulation' (Holt, 2006: 300).

NOTES

1. This chapter is abridged and revised from 'Creating "value" beyond the point of production: branding, financialization and market capitalization', *Organization*, 17 (5), 517–42. Earlier versions were presented at the 'Re-thinking Cultural Economy Conference', Centre for Research on Socio-Cultural Change, University of Manchester, September 2007 and at seminar presentations at Cardiff, Cambridge, Lund and Nottingham Trent Universities. I am grateful for comments and conversations arising from these presentations. The chapter has also greatly benefitted from comments provided by referees and the editors of *Organization*.

2. See, for example, the Research Priorities (2006–8) of the Marketing Science Institute at http://www.msi.org/pdf/MSI_RP06-08.pdf, accessed 29 December 2007.

3. The term 'financialization' has been invoked and defined in numerous ways (Krippner, 2005). It is here taken to refer to a contemporary drive to subordinate and reconstitute all forms of economic activity – consumption as well as production – in relation to its financial

relevance and significance. A widely commended definition of financialization is offered by Epstein (2005: 3): 'financialization means the increasing role of financial motives, financial markets, financial actors and financial institutions in the operation of domestic and international economies'. The present analysis is consistent with this formulation as it gives as much attention to 'financial motives' and 'financial markets' as it does to financial institutions. Of course, financialization is not new and, arguably, is a potential inherent to capitalist accumulation (see Kindleberger and Aliber, 2005). In the post-1970s era of neo-liberal deregulation, financialization – in the sense advancing a 'pattern of accumulation in which profit-making occurs increasingly through financial channels rather than through trade and commodity production' (Krippner, 2005: 14) – became an increasingly important driver of growth. As we shall see, the monetization of brand equity is an area where 'financial channels' interact with, and increasingly condition, the (re)organization of 'commodity production' within increasingly globalized value chains.

4. For a fuller history of branding, see Moor (2007).

5. The example is given by Thompson et al. (2007). They describe a branding agency specializing in 'truly holistic identities' that was used to create an image for Keane, a British popular music band – something that is alleged to have been kept secret because it contravened conventional ideas of rock authenticity, This view assumes a touching degree of naivety and/or concern among Keane fans but it also projects upon them a set of values (e.g. about the inappropriateness of involving professional image generators) with which they may not identify. As it happens, Keane themselves clearly did take exception to the allegation and issued a spirited and stinging rebuttal of any suggestion that Moving Brands, the branding agency, had manufactured their image. See http://www.keaneshaped.co.uk/faq/#stylist. The existence of this public domain rebuttal, which would seem to cast further doubt upon the band's desire to hush it up, seems to have escaped the attention of Thompson et al. (2007), who make no reference to it.

6. The purchase of Kraft by Philip Morris in 1988 is widely regarded as a pivotal moment when most of the purchase price of $12.6 million was attributed to 'the cost of the word "Kraft"'. Instead of being regarded as an 'add-on' to the core business of production and sales, 'a huge dollar value had been assigned to something that had previously been abstract and unquantifiable – a brand name' (Klein, 2000: 7–8).

7. The neologism is intended to resonate with 'securitization', the latter being the key driver of contemporary financialized capital asset growth characterized by some as 'fictitious capital'.

8. The term 'post-consumer' does not imply that consumption stops or even declines but, rather, that it is sustained and driven on by processes of financialization, most notably by developing ingenious ways of expanding credit for purposes of consumption.

9. As a thought experiment, imagine how the brand equity, and ultimately the market capitalization, of eBay would be damaged if all feedback provided by users on sellers and buyers was erased or if the company was obliged to compensate those providing such feedback.

10. Virgin's brand-centric stratagem is particularly 'clever' as so much of the brand equity is acquired cheaply by engaging in media stunts, often ending in heroic failure, that attract global publicity.

11. Branson, the CEO of Virgin, has defined his empire as 'a leading branded venture capital organization', seeking 30 per cent internal rates of return on investments. 'The Value of Virgin', *Daily Telegraph*, 3 December 2007. Available at http://www.telegraph.co.uk/money/main.jhtml?xml=/money/2007/12/02/ccrock102.xml. See also Osborne (2007).

12. To which the growth of speculative corporate treasury activity *within* companies has significantly contributed.

13. The contingency of brand-building means that consumers may drain brands of value as well as infuse them with worth – as is evident in the (temporary?) loss of 'coolness' of brands such as Gap as well as McDonald's and Starbucks (see Thompson et al., 2006) and also in the subversive, culture-jamming activities pursued by campaigning groups like 'Adbusters' (see Holt, 2002).

14. An illustrative example is the extensive but divided involvement of a Lego 'brand community' in the development of its product Mindstorm. Its user-consumers were key initiators

and facilitators of product development but they were also resistant to aspects of it (see www.fbtb.com). The interested reader is encouraged to turn to Kornberger (in press) and Antorini (2007). Recognition of such resistance points to the emergence of other, potentially more subversive, forms of co-produced value creation (see Bauwens, 2009) – in the form of peer-to-peer production that escapes private appropriation as it is protected by a general public licence that, of course, also makes it available to commercial users.

15. As noted earlier, the chief exception to this private appropriation of the brand value generated by unpaid labour is where production is governed by a general public licence. This licence ensures that brand equity cannot be directly monetized, although, as Bauwens (2009: 125) observes, companies 'can do many things to indirectly capture the value created by peer-producing communities'.

16. It seems doubtful that the architects of YouTube ever conceived of themselves as engaging in a community service, or a charitable venture, devised to facilitate the donation of 'ethical labour' for socially beneficial purposes. If they did, then their venture did not remain charitable for long (see http://www.nytimes.com/2007/02/07/technology/07cnd-google.html?ex=1328504400&en=96fcc0326d0a7ef6&ei=5088&partner=rssnyt&emc=rss).

17. In a recent review of these studies, de Beijer et al. (2008) notes that: 'Barth et al. (1998) estimate the association between FinancialWorld brand value estimates and share prices over the period 1991 to 1996. They find a significant positive association. Kerin and Sethuraman (1998) study US consumer goods companies on the 1995 and 1996 FinancialWorld's Most-Valued Brands list and report a positive relation between brand value estimates and firm value. They also find some indications that increases in brand values are more likely to be reflected in firm value than are decreases in brand values. Custodio and Rosario (2007) and Delcoure (2008) also find a positive association between brand value estimates and firm value for US companies. Pahud de Mortanges and van Riel (2003) measure brand equity for Dutch corporate brands using Young and Rubicam's Brand Asset Valuator. They find a significant association between this brand value indicator and various shareholder value measures.'

18. Other attempts to do something similar include Thompson (2003) and Littler (2009).

REFERENCES

Akasia, J.F. (2000) 'Ford's Model E', *Forbes*, 17 July, pp. 30–34.

Alvarez, L.H.R. and Stenbacka, R. (2007) 'Partial Outsourcing: A Real Options Perspective', *International Journal of Industrial Organization*, 25 (1): 91–102.

Antorini, Y.M. (2007) 'Brand Community Innovation: An Intrinsic Case Study of the Adult Fans of the LEGO Community', Unpublished PhD, Copenhagen Business School.

Arrington, M. (2006) *Google Has Acquired YouTube* [Online]. TechCrunch. Available at: http://www.techcrunch.com/2006/10/09/google-has-acquired-youtube/ (accessed 9 October 2006).

Arvidsson, A. (2005) 'Brands: A Critical Perspective', *Journal of Consumer Culture*, 5 (2): 235–58.

Arvidsson, A. (2006) *Brands: Meaning and Value in Media Culture*, London: Routledge.

Arvidsson, A. (2007) 'Crisis of Value and the Ethical Economy' available at: http://p2pfoundation.net/Crisis_of_Value_and_the_Ethical_Economy (accessed 27 October 2009).

Arvidsson, A. (2008) 'The Ethical Economy of Customer Coproduction', *Journal of Macromarketing*, 28 (4): 326–38.

Arvidsson, A. (2009) 'The Ethical Economy: Towards a Post-Capitalist Theory of Value', *New Left Review*, 97: 13–29.

Baldi, F. and Trigeorgis, L. (2008) 'A Real Options Approach to Valuing Brand Leveraging Options: How much is Starbucks Brand Equity Worth?', working paper, available at: http://69.175.2.130/~finman/Reno/Papers/StarbucksBrandValuation. pdf (accessed 4 November 2009).

Batchelor, A. (1998) 'Brands as Financial Assets' in S. Hart and J. Murphy (eds) *Brands: The New Wealth Creators*, London: Macmillan Business/Interbrand.

Bauwens, M. (n.d.) Dornbirn Manifesto, available at http://p2pfoundation.net/ Dornbirn_Manifesto (accessed 4 November 2009).

Bauwens, M. (2009) 'Class and Capital in Peer Production', *New Left Review*, 97: 121–41.

Coombe, R. (1988) *The Cultural Life of Intellectual Properties: Authorship, Appropriation and the Law*, Durham, NC: Duke University Press.

Cova, B. and Dalli, D. (2009) 'Working Consumers: The Next Step in Marketing Theory?, *Marketing Theory*, 9 (3): 315–39.

Custodio, C. and Rosario, J. (2007) 'Corporate Brand and Firm Value', working paper, London School of Economics.

Crane, D. and Bovone, L. (2006) 'Approaches to Material Culture: The Sociology of Fashion and Clothing', *Poetics*, 34 (6): 319–33.

Davis, G.F. (2009) 'The Rise and Fall of Finance and the End of the Society of Organizations', *Academy of Management Perspectives*, 23(3): 27–44.

De Beijer, D., DeKimple, M., Dutordoir, M. and Verbeeten, F.H.M. (2008) 'The Impact of Brand Value Announcements on Firm Value', working paper, Rotterdam School of Management, The Netherlands. Also available at SSRN: http://ssrn.com/ abstract=1344535 (accessed 3 November 2009).

Delcoure, N. (2008) 'Corporate Branding and Shareholders' Wealth', working paper, Sam Houston State University.

Dore, R. (2000) *Stock Market Capitalism: Welfare Capitalism: Japan and Germany versus the Anglo-Saxons (Japan Business and Economics Series)*, Oxford: Oxford University Press.

Dore, R. (2008) 'Financialization of the Global Economy', *Industrial and Corporate Change*, 17 (6): 1097–112.

Du Gay, P., Hall, S., Janes, L. and Mackay, H. (1996) *Doing Cultural Studies: The Story of the Sony Walkman*, London: Sage.

Epstein, G.A. (2005) 'Introduction', in G.A. Epstein (ed.) *Financialization and the World Economy*, Cheltenham, UK and Northampton, MA, USA: Edward Elgar.

Ezzamel, M., Willmott, H.C. and Worthington, F. (2009) 'Manufacturing Shareholder Value: The Role of Accounting in Organizational Transformation', *Accounting, Organizations and Society*, 33 (2–3): 107–40.

Feldwick, P. (1996) 'What is Brand Equity Anyway, and How Do You Measure It', *Journal of the Market Research Society*, 38 (2): 85–105.

Frieder, L. (2004) 'Brand Perceptions and the Market for Common Stock', working paper, The Anderson School, UCLA, subsequently published in *Journal of Financial and Qualitative Analysis*, 40 (1): 57–85.

Frieder, L. and Subrahmanyam, A. (2004) 'Brand Perceptions and the Market for Common Stock', available at: http://papers.ssrn.com/sol3/papers.cfm?abstract_ id=299522, subsequently published in *Journal of Financial and Quantitative Analysis*, 40 (1): 57–85.

Froud, J., Johal, S. and Williams, K. (2002) 'Financialisation and the *Coupon* Pool', *Capital and Class*, 78: 119–51.

Gamble, A. (2009) *The Spectre at the Feast: Capitalist Crisis and the Politics of Recession*, London: Palgrave Macmillan.

Harvey, D. (2005) *A Brief History of Neo-Liberalism*, Oxford: Oxford University Press.

Hatch, M.J. and Schultz, M. (2005) *Taking Brand Initiative: How Companies Can Align Strategy, Culture, and Identity Through Corporate Branding*, San Francisco, CA: Jossey-Bass.

Helft, M. (2007) 'YouTube's Payoff: Hundreds of Millions for the Founders *The New York Times*, available at http://www.nytimes.com/2007/02/07/technology/07cnd-google.html?ex=1328504400&en=96fcc0326d0a7ef6&ei=5088&partner=rssnyt&emc=rss (accessed 3 November 2009).

Holt, D. (2002) 'Why Do Brands Cause Trouble? A Dialectical Theory of Consumer Culture and Branding', *Journal of Consumer Research*, 29: 70–90.

Holt, D. (2004) *How Brands Become Icons*, Boston, MA: Harvard Business School Press.

Holt, D. (2006) 'Toward as Sociology of Branding', *Journal of Consumer Culture*, 6 (3): 299–302.

IUF (2006) Feeding Financial Markets: Financialization and Restructuring in Nestlé, Kraft and Unilever (International Union of Food, Agricultural, Hotel, Restaurant, 1 Catering, Tobacco and Allied Workers' Associations). Available at: http://asianfood-worker.net/tnc/financializing-foodTNCs.pdf (accessed 3 November 2009).

Keller, K.L. (1993) 'Conceptualizing, Measuring and Managing Customer-Based Brand Equity', *Journal of Marketing*, 57: 1–22.

Kerin, R.A. and Sethuraman, R. (1998) 'Exploring the Brand-Value-Shareholder-Value Nexus for Consumer Goods Companies', *Journal of Academic Marketing Science*, 26(4): 260–73.

Kimbrough, M.D. and McAlister, L. (2008) 'Linking Marketing Actions to Value Creation and Firm Value: Insights from Accounting Research; A Commentary on Shuba Srinivasan and Dominique M. Hanssens' "Marketing and Firm Value: Metrics, Methods, Findings, and Future Directions"', *Journal of Marketing Research*, forthcoming. Available at: http://www.marketingpower.com/ResourceLibrary/Documents/JMRForthcoming/Linking%20Marketing%20Actions%20(COM).pdf (accessed 4 November 2009).

Kindleberger, C.P. and Aliber, R. (2005) *Manias, Panics and Crashes; A History of Financial Crises*, New York, NY: Wiley.

Klein, N. (2000) *No Logo*, London: Flamingo.

Klimecki, R. and Willmott, H.C. (2009) 'From Demutualization to Meltdown: A Tale of Two Wannabe Banks', *Critical Perspective in International Business*, 5 (1/2): 120–40.

Kornberger, M. (in press) *The Brand Society*, Cambridge: Cambridge University Press.

Krippner, G.R. (2005) 'The Financialization of the American Economy', *Socio-Economic Review*, 3 (2): 173–208.

Land, C. and Böhm, S. (2009) 'The New "Hidden Abode": Reflections on Value and Labour in the New Economy', Working Paper, Essex Business School, University of Essex.

Lazzarato, M. (1997) *Lavoro Immateriale*. Verona: Ombre Corte.

Lindemann, J. (2004) 'The Financial Value of Brands', in Clifton, R., Simmons, J. and Ahmad, S . (eds) *Brands and Branding*, London: Economist Books.

Littler, C. (2009) 'The Current Global Crisis as a Context for Labour and Industry in the Twenty-First Century', *Labour and Industry*, 19 (3): 5–28.

Low, G.S. and Fullerton, R.A. (1994) 'Brands, Brand Management and the Brand Manager System: A Critical-Historical Evaluation', *Journal of Marketing Research*, XXXI (May): 173–90.

Lukas, B.A., Whitwell, G.J. and Doyle, P. (2005) 'How Can a Shareholder Value Approach Improve Marketing's Strategic Influence?', *Journal of Business Research*, 58 (4): 414–42.

Lury, C. (2004) *Brands: The Logos of the Global Economy*, London: Routledge.

Lury, C. and Moor, L. (2010) 'Brand Valuation and Topological Culture', in M. Aronczyk and D. Powers (eds) *Blowing up the Brand*, New York, NY: Peter Lang.

Madden, T.J., Fehle, F. and Fournier, S. (2006) 'Brands Matter: An Empirical Demonstration of the Creation of Shareholder Value Through Branding', *Journal of the Academy of Marketing Science* 34 (2): 224–35.

Marazzi, C. (2010) *The Violence of Financial Capitalism*, New York, NY: Semiotext(e).

Marketing Science Institute (2007) *Research Priorities of the Marketing Science Institute* (2006–2008). Available at: http://www.msi.org/pdf/MSI_RP06–08.pdf (accessed 29 December 2007).

Martin, R. (2002) *Financialization of Daily Life (Labor in Crisis)*, Philadephia, PA: Temple University Press.

Moor, L. (2007) *The Rise of Brands*, Oxford: Berg.

Nixon, S. (2002) 'Re-Imagining the Ad Agency: The Cultural Connotations of Economic Forms', in P. Du Gay and M. Pryke (eds) *Cultural Economy: Cultural Analysis and Commercial Life*, London: Sage.

O'Neill, P. (2001) 'Financial Narratives of the Modern Corporation', *Journal of Economic Geography*, 1: 181–99.

Orhangazi, O. (2008) *Financialization and the US Economy*, Cheltenham, UK and Northampton, MA, USA: Edward Elgar.

Osborne, A. (2007) 'The Value of Virgin', *Daily Telegraph*, 3 December 2007.

Pahud de Mortanges, C. and van Riel, A. (2003) 'Brand Equity and Shareholder Value', *European Management Journal*, 21 (4): 521–27.

Pike, A. and Pollard, J. (2010) 'Economic Geographies of Financialization', *Economic Geography*, 86 (1): 29–51.

Raggio, R.D. and Leone, R.P. (2007) 'The Theoretical Separation of Brand Equity and Brand Value: Managerial Implications for Strategic Planning', *Journal of Brand Management*, 14: 380–95.

Raggio, R.D. and Leone, R.P. (2009) 'Chasing Brand Value: Fully Leveraging Brand Equity To Maximise Brand Value', *Journal of Brand Management*, 16: 248–63.

Rust, R.T., Ambler, T., Carpenter, G.S., Kumar, V. and Srivastava, R.K. (1994) 'Measuring Marketing Productivity: Current Knowledge and Future Directions', *Journal of Marketing*, 68 (4): 76–89.

Salzer-Mörling, M. and Strannegård, L. (2004) 'Silence of the Brands', *European Journal of Marketing*, 38 (1): 224–38.

Schultz, M., Hatch, M.J. and Larsen, M.H. (2000) *The Expressive Organization: Linking Identity, Reputation and the Corporate Brand*, Oxford: Oxford University Press.

Schulz, M., Antorini, Y.M. and Csaba, F.F. (2005) *Corporate Branding: Purpose/ People/Process*, Copenhagen: Copenhagen Business School Press.

Srinivasan, S. and Hanssens, D.M. (2008) 'Marketing and Firm Value Metrics, Methods, Findings, and Future Directions', *Journal of Marketing Research*, forthcoming. Available at http://www.marketingpower.com/ResourceLibrary/Documents/ JMRForthcoming/Marketing%20and%20Firm%20Value.pdf (accessed 4 November 2009).

Stalk, G. and Lachenauer, R. (2004) *Hardball: Are You Playing to Play or Playing to Win?*, Boston, MA: Harvard Business School Press.

Thompson, C.J., Rindfleisch, A. and Arsel, Z. (2006) 'Emotional Branding and the Strategic Value of the Doppelgänger Brand Image', *Journal of Marketing*, 70 (January): 50–64.

Thompson, P. (2003) 'Disconnected Capitalism: Or Why Employers Can't Keep Their Side of the Bargain', *Work, Employment and Society*, 17 (3): 359–78.

Thompson, P., Jones, M. and Warhurst, C. (2007) 'From Conception to Consumption: Creativity and the Missing Managerial Link', *Journal of Organizational Behaviour*, 28: 625–40.

Thompson, P. and Smith, C. (2009) 'Labour Power and Labour Process: Contesting the Marginality of the Sociology of Work', *Sociology*, 43 (5): 913–30.

Tollington, T. (2001) 'UK Brand Asset Recognition Beyond "Transactions or Events"', *Long Range Planning*, 34 (4): 463–87.

Wernick, A. (1991) *Promotional Culture: Advertising, Ideology and Symbolic Expression*, London: Sage.

3. Be who you want to be: branding, identity and the desire for authenticity

Christopher Land and Scott Taylor

INTRODUCTION: BRANDING AUTHENTICITY

Contemporary managers often profess concern with employees' lives outside the workplace. Mental health, physical well-being and recreational pastimes are all subjects of managerial interest and have been since before Henry Ford created his department of sociology in the early twentieth century (Clarke, 1990). As the range of counselling, coaching and employee assistance initiatives demonstrate, managers are concerned with regulating employees' behaviour in their private lives, for example with respect to alcohol and drug use (Hansen, 2004; Wray-Bliss, 2009). In the current corporate context, regulation has extended from the physical to the emotional and the metaphysical, so that even employee spiritual life is considered a fair target for managerial intervention (Bell and Taylor, 2003). In a broader social context managerial discourses and practices permeate the governance of everyday life so that in our careers, with friends, at home with family, and in our leisure time, we are encouraged to manage our selves and relationships such that life increasingly resembles a project of work (Hancock and Tyler, 2009).

The boundary between work and life is permeable in both directions, however. Just as work and managerialism leak into non-work spaces and moments, so employees' non-work lives spill over into workplaces, often using the same technologies that are associated with flexible working and the extension of work into life (Wajcman et al., 2008). While this movement can be characterized as a form of resistance if it is seen as an appropriation of time and resources, it is more often read as private lives becoming a resource for the organization. One example of this is in brand-based organizations where managers actively deploy employees' private and social lives as a resource for constructing brand identity and equity (Land and Taylor, 2010).

In managerialist discourses, bringing employees' private lives into work is usually framed as a progressive, humanizing move that overcomes the bureaucratic split between public and private; a form of 'liberation management' that avoids alienation and splitting (Bains, 2007). From such a perspective, the organization can become more humane and profitable by allowing employees to express 'real' selves at work, enabling the creation of an authentic, bottom-up corporate culture, rather than an easily resisted artificial, top-down one (Ind, 2007). Critical accounts of this management by 'authenticity' suggest there are always limits to selves that can be performed in the context of a workplace, in that only very specific performances of 'self' are acceptable, and that these managerial moves are an extension and intensification of capitalist control, rather than emancipation (Fleming, 2009).

We explore one attempt to use aspects of employees' selves – specifically, ethical values and recreational activities – to create an 'authentic' culture, with the stated aim of humanizing the workplace and establishing brand authenticity. We examine practices in one organization, Ethico, where managerial discourses suggest that work and life should be balanced by making 'work' a place where you can really be yourself and where business can be ethical, contribute to social change, save the environment, and generally make the world a better place.

The chapter is structured into three parts. First, we provide a summary of the case study organization, our research methods, and the experience of work there. We concentrate on analysis of the organization, the branding of authenticity, employment practices and labour processes. This section clarifies the 'matter' (Taylor, 1991) of what is constructed as authentic for the Ethico brand and workplace. Following this, we discuss recent analyses of authenticity and branding in organizations, noting that Ethico's managerial discourse is embedded within a contested set of developments in the political economy of contemporary capitalism. These contestations pivot around work/life balance, branding as a means of capitalizing on the immaterial labour of symbolic production and consumption, and the demands of new social movements for more meaningful employment and environmentally responsible forms of production/consumption. Finally, we draw conclusions relating to what Taylor (1991) terms the 'manner' of authenticity, how the authentic is sought within what remains a thoroughly capitalist labour process. We argue that while Fleming's (2009) account of management by authenticity as a form of 'existential exposure' explains many of the features we found in Ethico, his analysis pays inadequate attention to the kinds of shift in 'work' towards symbolic production that are found in brand-based organizations (cf. Arvidsson, 2006).

Our analysis also contributes to understanding the dynamics of control, resistance and identity within contemporary labour processes (Karreman and Rylander, 2008) by questioning Fleming's rejection (2009) of the aesthetic and expressive dimensions of critique. We also raise the possibility, with tempered optimism, that employee and customer attempts to re-imagine business and organization, however compromised at present, might contribute to a process whereby the experience of 'formal freedom' in such organizations creates conditions of possibility for the articulation of more radical demands for autonomy, authenticity and ethics at work. However, we recognize, as Ethico's employees do, that within the constraints of a capitalist business organization such freedoms and authenticity will inevitably be strictly delimited. The demands of authenticity would ultimately require the creation of a quite different set of relations of production (cf. Žižek, 2009: 142).

ETHICO: GETTING INTO THE COUNTER-CULTURE

Accessing the Workplace

Ethico inhabits a specific sector, 'New-Age capitalism' (Lau, 2000), where production and consumption are informed by a set of quasi-spiritual principles about living, working and doing business. Proponents valourize physical and spiritual well-being, holism, environmental awareness, activism, and social change through certain varieties of consumption (Heelas, 2008). Although companies in this sector appear frequently in practitioner-oriented books and newspaper articles, the organizations are largely closed to empirical academic research, perhaps as a result of a desire to protect valuable brand identity from critical analysis. We both became involved with Ethico initially as customers, and decided that it was a potentially interesting research site. We therefore began to monitor their branding activities systematically, collecting catalogues, promotional emails, and reading blogs on the company website. We made contact with Ethico's media officer in October 2006; this was the beginning of a six-month phone and email conversation leading to permission to visit the organization. In April 2007 we spent two days at Ethico's office and warehouse building, conducting eleven formal recorded interviews and the same number of unrecorded informal interviews. We also collected eight more of the quarterly catalogues produced by the company, each around 70 pages long, that we analysed along with T-shirt logos, slogans and public discussion boards relating to the company, and photos taken during our visit.

With such a diverse data set, we decided to construct an account of the organization that draws on two traditions. The first is the qualitative case study, in its three variations: intrinsic, instrumental and collective (Stake, 2005). Ethico is intrinsically interesting because it has been held up as an exemplar in the British national political context as a company that exemplifies the hopeful zeitgeist that ethical consumerism can change the world for the better. We also treat Ethico as an instrumental case to provide insight into the wider institutional field of New-Age capitalism and the 'holistic milieu' (Heelas and Woodhead, 2005). Finally, we are contributing to the development of a collective case by drawing on data and analysis from other, similar organizations, to shed light on what we suggest is a more general condition – the deployment of 'authentic' employee identities in branding in such as way as to redefine the nature of work, life and brand management.

Deciding to take a case study approach is, as Stake (2005) argues, a decision about what to study, not a methodological position relating to how to study a phenomenon. Analytically, therefore, we draw on a variety of perspectives, reflecting the range of data sources we are working with, but always with the intent of acknowledging the structural conditions of the social settings that our data were generated within. So, for example, we read identity as a performance that is the product of agency, but one that is always enabled and constrained by the social setting of its production and the formal, cultural principles or conventions of production (Atkinson and Delamont, 2005; Alvesson and Willmott, 2002). We also aim to present a reflexive account of individual and organizational branding and identity. The need to adopt this stance was reinforced when, shortly after our visit to Ethico, a photo of us appeared on Ethico's blog pages, along with an account of our visit there. The text assured readers that all of our questions about Ethico had been answered, especially the one about whether it was a 'good place to work'. We, as researchers, became part of the brand identity of Ethico as an organization that is open, reflexive, humane and 'good'.

Arriving at the Authentic Workplace

On arrival in the small town where it is based, we found Ethico surprisingly difficult to locate. We asked a man on the street who directed us towards a light industrial and storage estate on the edge of town. Wandering onto the estate we saw a man in his forties dressed in skate shoes, combat trousers and a hooded top, smoking a roll-up outside a building. He asked us if we were looking for Ethico, and pointed to an inconspicuous little logo just above his head. The man recognized us and we him – he looked like someone who would work there, we looked like people who would be looking for Ethico.

He pointed us upstairs to the office area. The vestibule and stairwell were nondescript, painted white, without decoration. On the landing halfway up the stairs, we passed two etched glass awards and an empty champagne magnum with the number '1' painted on it. At the top of the stairs, three expensive-looking bikes were parked beside the lift. The door into the office area had a couple of A4 sheets taped onto it: one read 'please keep this door closed', the other 'fail more to succeed more' followed by a little smiley face. We went into the office area and stood awkwardly looking around, while people looked back at us; then someone directed us towards the two small glassed offices to one side of the open area, and then our contact and gatekeeper appeared.

The upstairs office space at Ethico is minimally furnished with desks, chairs, PCs, phones and other office paraphernalia. Some desks are set side on to the walls, and there is a central cluster of about six in the middle of the floor. There are some quirky elements: three or four painted wardrobes are scattered around, there is a lot of paper stuck to the walls – messages, postcards, drawings, letters from customers, motivational homilies – and a couple of slogans painted in stark black lettering on the white walls (one reads 'Dick Dastardly was right, don't just stand there, do something'). To one side there is a cupboard containing the IT server, a glassed room for meetings, and an area with a two-seat sofa, small armchair, a couple of regular chairs, and a low coffee table covered in big Ethico stickers. One of the founders usually works there; an Apple power cable hanging from the wall onto the back of the sofa indicated ownership of the space.

Our gatekeeper took us on a tour of the building and introduced us to each person there, telling them who we were, where we worked, and why we were there ('to observe us'). We did a little embroidering around this, but mostly just promised to come back at some point and tried to remember names. We were then shown the sample room, the kitchen, the toilets and the 'shed'. This building featured in several Ethico catalogues, and was in the process of being converted to a short-run, environmentally sustainable T-shirt printing shop. Its redecoration and refurbishment was designed to be low-impact environmentally. It was also designed to run off-grid, generating its own power through solar panels. Recently it had become a point of conflict because of the investment required. This came to a head when people met to decide where to do a spring/summer photo shoot (in late autumn); the UK is unsuitable because weather, skies and light do not look like summer, so a plan was formulated to go to the Canary Islands. At the meeting to finalize this decision, it became clear that the company could fund either the shed refurbishment or the photo shoot. (This story was told by just about everyone we spoke to, in various forms.) One of the founders stormed out of the meeting, then came back about an hour later and announced that they weren't going to the Canaries, and that the story of the shed would be the theme of the catalogue, illustrated with photos from inside it. Although it was still not operational at the time of our visit, this would be the only space of material production that Ethico actually owned as the manufacture, and even design, of their bags and clothes was entirely outsourced.

We went back up into the office area, and were left to our own devices. We began to take photos, interview people, and hang around, initially in the warehouse area because we felt less conspicuous than in the office area. We also felt more comfortable with the men downstairs; they were friendly to us, offered tea and biscuits, and took smoke breaks, when we could talk to them.

Picking and Packing Authenticity: In the Warehouse

The warehouse was a working context that felt relatively relaxed. People could set their own break times, the music playing was loud and chosen by them, they had their own supply of tea and biscuits. Each of the four men moved around to do whatever they felt needed to be done, working hard but not sweating. We spoke to each of them over the course of the morning.

One, in his late teens or early twenties, had been advised by his tutor at college that there was a job available at Ethico, so he went there and asked if he could apply for it. The selection process consisted of someone speaking to him for a bit; he started work soon after. He was wearing baggy jeans, a long T-shirt with a prominent slogan, had shoulder-length hair and a couple of piercings. He also smoked roll-ups and seemed shy, interested in the company but not evangelical about it. He emphasized that the working environment is radically different from anywhere else he has known, and much better.

His colleague, the older man who had directed us when we arrived outside the building, had moved to the area after a very enjoyable holiday. He had been working as a removal man, so he packed up his belongings, moved them down, then drove back and left the lorry at the removal company with his resignation letter on the dashboard. He began working at the company next door, also in the warehouse, but didn't like the way he was being spoken to so gave up that job. He had seen people working at Ethico and liked the look of it, so asked them for a job, and 'hassled' them for a while. He spoke at length about how the area is his favourite place in the world.

A third warehouseman, in his early to mid-twenties, also lived locally. He spoke of how he had liked Ethico's clothes for a long time and wanted to work there because of his affinity with the ethic of the organization. He spoke knowledgeably about recycling, the politics of clothes production, and the political positions promoted at Ethico. He was also the most completely Ethico-clothed of anyone there: jeans, T-shirt, pullover, jacket and hat.

We were unable to establish a formal hierarchy in the warehouse, although the older man came across as de facto supervisor. All were keen to talk about their collage on the wall, made up of drawings and stickers and pictures that customers had sent, including a coconut that someone had sent which they had opened and drunk/eaten. The warehouse felt very well organized, tidy, compact and clean.

Administrating and Branding Authenticity

Around lunchtime we went back upstairs, which felt very different. When we got there one of the founders was leading a meeting that almost everyone was involved in. This was taking place in the meeting area that we had intended to colonize, so we had to wander around for a while. At this point, we split up to go and talk to different people.

Most of the people we spoke to had come to Ethico through contacts, friends or relatives. We were told that the majority of customers are London or south-east based; employees were also clear about the idea that customers aspire to the lifestyle that the clothes and accounts of working at Ethico represent. There was also a consensus view that most customers are in their mid-thirties and are relatively well-off professionals.

Everyone emphasized the company's roots in skating and mountain biking, and how significant that is for brand construction and customer credibility. Shortly before we visited, the founders had negotiated a partial buyout by a US multinational. That process was made public by one of the founders in an open letter posted as a blog entry on the company website. The letter empha-sizes self-belief and faith in the ideals promoted by Ethico, but also a desire for growth and the need for financial support to achieve it. The new partner company was presented as similarly idealistic, committed to environmental and social action, and an honest, values-led employer. During our visit many employees spoke about continuous financial difficulties and the limitations on making the workspaces more environmentally friendly. Employees suggested they would now be able to do more of what they wanted and that Ethico would be able to be even more true to its principles.

Organizational ambition to be more consistently authentic suddenly became something that founders, managers and employees could pursue, confident of being able to translate ideals into planning and practice. This new-found free-dom was manifest in two key areas: product sourcing and the Ethico building. Although Ethico T-shirt labels carry the legend 'Produced in a nice factory in [e.g.] Turkey', this assessment relied on ethical audits funded by other organi-zations such as Marks & Spencer. One of the founders spoke of her desire to have Ethico conduct its own audits (but not, interestingly, to make their own clothing or source from UK producers). In addition, the environmental impact of the Ethico office and warehouse produced tension with the brand ideals. The financial implications of consuming energy from renewable sources had led to compromise. Low-impact heating, for example, required capital investment three times greater than a standard system and so far had been unaffordable.

Although the employees we spoke with expressed their satisfaction with the relationship to their new owners, the buy-out led customers to question founders' actions and to impute inauthenticity. Posts on an internet discussion board for mountain-bikers mocked Ethico's proclaimed ideal of smallness by contrasting the anti-big-business messages conveyed on T-shirts to the reality of 'selling out' to a multinational corporation.

Much of this protest built on the moral ideals Ethico expresses through visual images and slogans printed onto the clothes sold. In addition, the design and production of catalogues is a key cultural representation and symbolic event. The catalogue designer, who had a background in semi-professional skating, insisted more than most on the importance of sport to the company and the people working there, reciting what each permanent employee upstairs did when not at work. Certain sports and the natural environment, he argued, define the brand image of the company, who they sell to, and what they sell. When we asked if the stories and images in the catalogue reflected the company in a broadly realistic way, he replied that the representations were broadly accurate but they had to 'juice it up a little' for the catalogue. As with the challenge to Ethico's authenticity mounted on discussion boards, this demonstrates the fragility and ambivalence of brand authenticity as a means of constructing organizational and employee identity. In order to sell, experiences have to be spiced up, but if they are seen as exaggerations, disingenuous, or in tension with the structural conditions of doing business, then the entire brand proposition is at risk.

MIND THE GAP: BETWEEN THE IDEAL MATTER OF AUTHENTICITY AND THE MANNER OF ITS MANAGEMENT

I'd Rather be Free-range...

In Western economies, many businesses are turning to a form of 'just be yourself' management in which employees are no longer expected to conform to the rigours of a creativity-stifling, managerially prescribed corporate culture. Instead, we are actively encouraged to be ourselves, 'warts and all', to have fun, express sexuality and identity, find personal fulfilment, and even rebel at work (Fleming, 2009; Ind, 2007; Ross, 2004; Frank, 1998). This managerial desire for an authentic self through which to construct a real workplace culture is primarily orientated towards increasing employees' 'existential exposure'. To work in this kind of organization, employees are expected to bring ever more of their subjectivity and put it to work producing economic value. This process is quite distinct from previous attempts at 'normative control' through the managerial imposition of a strong corporate culture (Willmott, 1993). The management of cultural meaning (Gowler and Legge, 1983; Smircich and Morgan, 1982), as promoted in the 1980s by consultants (Peters and Waterman, 1982; Deal and Kennedy, 1982), often met with cynicism and subjective distancing. At best managers elicited various forms of behavioural compliance (Ogbonna and Harris, 1998; Kunda, 1992; Collinson, 1992; Spicer and Fleming, 2007). The shift toward what the same consultants now call 'liberation management' (Peters, 1992) is a renewed attempt to capture employee subjectivity and realize complete creativity and engagement, rather than reluctant and cynical compliance. This move is based on the dubious assumption of a 'win–win' scenario in which employees can find authentic fulfilment and emancipation through employment, and the corporation can harness creativity through commitment to increase competitiveness and realize exceptional profitability (cf. Banerjee, 2007).

In his extended critique of this phenomenon, Peter Fleming (2009) challenges its basic assumptions, suggesting that liberation management represents an intensification of control where ever more of employee subjectivity is made to work for the corporation. Fleming's analysis suggests that a corporatized discourse of authenticity, mobilizing an essentialist conception of the subject as already existing outside of work, actually shapes and constructs the subject in quite specific ways, simultaneously creating possible lines of subjectivization and blocking others. The 'real' self that is brought in from the private sphere focuses particularly on sexuality, aesthetic sensibilities and consumption. There are significant absences in this, most notably class as a social identity. Class, perhaps unavoidably, evokes structural economic relations of ownership and control that would unsettle the individualistic and consumption-based expressions of 'authenticity' that underpin the managerial discourse (Fleming, 2009).

However, Fleming's focus on consumption and recreational activities also raises a limitation of his analysis. The bulk of his argument rests on empirical research in a call centre, which he calls Sunray. At Sunray, cultural management centres on the '3 Fs: Focus, Fun and Fulfilment' (Fleming, 2009: 18). The explicit intention in promoting 'fun' is to humanize work and enable it to be part of a 'fulfilling' life, but primacy is given to 'focus'. In other words, employees cannot challenge the dominant managerial ideology of performativity (cf. Fournier and Grey, 2000). Fun and fulfilment at work are legitimate only insofar as they contribute to the bottom-line by helping employees to perform otherwise tedious and routine jobs. Fleming quotes from a Sunray training manual based on a telling analogy between employees and chickens:

> Forget lone rangers – at Sunray we have free-rangers! It's hard to have fun when you're confined to a workstation like a battery hen, so we encourage you to enjoy the freedom and latitude you need in order to fulfil your obligations to Sunray. (Quoted in Fleming, 2009: 18)

To balance out the objectively tedious routine of call centre labour, employees are encouraged to express real selves at work. This expression must not affect the performance of work, but should create an organizational environment to ameliorate its worst effects. To extend the analogy, it is clear that being a free-range chicken is a better life than living in a cage; however, this empirical example neglects the more fundamental aspects of the shift in human workplaces towards immaterial labour, particularly creative and symbolic labour, rather than more routine interactive service work (Dowling, 2007; Lazaratto, 1997; cf. Thompson, 2005; Böhm and Land, 2009). In brand-based organizations both the content and location of value-productive labour have been transformed by the erosion of the boundary between work and life (Arvidsson, 2006; Land and Taylor, 2010), a point that Fleming recognizes in his theoretical exegesis but does not explore in the empirical research in which he grounds his analysis. We now turn to a consideration of the production of value through brands, and the implications of this for how we understand work.

But are You Being Authentic?

The development of the managerial discourse of authenticity is particularly significant for 'brand-based' organizations, whose value proposition depends upon being something more than just a business. For such companies:

> Value creation derives not only from the production of goods and services that extract surplus value from the labour process, but the manipulation of images that convince consumers of the firm's integrity. The sale of 'authentic' products in relation to organic foods, exotic holidays, and vegan sneakers, for example, are becoming more important for retailers as consumers desire something 'real'. (Gilmore and Pine, 2007, cited in Fleming, 2009: 3)

This observed desire for an authentic consumption experience is paradoxical, when we recall that the very idea of a commodity suggests a good or service alienated from the social relations of its production in order to circulate in a market for a price (Marx, 1976). But it is this contradiction that makes the discourse of authenticity so powerful within branding and generates its most significant organizational consequences. As the impersonal, marketized nature of commodity circulation cannot offer a guarantee of authenticity, an image must be constructed as part of branding to produce it. One way to do this, according to marketing guru Nicholas Ind (2007), is to transform an organization's members into 'brand champions' by ensuring that they really believe in the brand and serve as the embodied guarantor of the authenticity of its values.

This authenticity is necessary because, as Adam Arvidsson (2006) persuasively argues, brands are increasingly important as a resource for identity work, communication and the creation of community. This potential is the main use value of branded products, as the worth of a brand depends upon its meaning. Like all forms of communication, however, meaning is subject to contestation, translation and reinterpretation. Most of the communicational labour that goes into producing meaning is done during consumption, by those not formally a part of the organization. This creates a clear slippage between work and life, for employees and customers. In all of our 'lives', pervaded by branded consumption, we are 'working' to produce value for organizations that own the brands we deploy as communicational devices to demonstrate affiliation, taste, distinction and perform identity work.

For the brand-based organization this creates a tension. The value of their product – the brand itself – is dependent upon the free labour of consumers (Arvidsson, 2006). This labour is free in two senses: it is unpaid, as it is conducted during our free time, and it is relatively autonomous and free from direct managerial control (Terranova, 2000). The government of this free labour becomes the function of brand management:

> Brand management is about putting public communication to work under managed forms, by providing a context where it can evolve in a particular direction…

> Brand management contains a variety of techniques that all aim at controlling, pre-structuring and monitoring what people do with brands, so that what these practices do adds to its value. It is about ensuring that the means of consumption effectively become means of production…

> This is the purpose of programming. Brands evolve with the activity of the social, but in programmed ways, so that the qualities they represent stay compatible. (Arvidsson, 2006: 67; 82; 132)

In order to render it productive, consumption must be directed or 'governed' (Arvidsson, 2006) by the management of communicational protocols (Marazzi, 2010). Arvidsson offers many insights into how this government functions, and its position within the accumulation regime of late capitalism, but he says much less about its implications for the labour process within brand-based organizations. For this issue, we need to consider a more managerial text on brand management and authenticity.

Nicholas Ind's (2007) book, *Living the Brand*, opens with an account of the outdoor clothing and equipment company Patagonia. Patagonia trades heavily on its founder's life narrative. Yvon Chouinard started the company to produce low-impact pitons (devices used to secure climbing ropes to rock). As the story is told, Chouinard was equally committed to climbing as a sport and the environment, so he invented a piton that did not damage rock. For Ind, Patagonia's success can be explained through the recruitment of people similarly passionate about sports and environmentalism, so that employees and their activities become guarantors of brand authenticity. More than just ambassadors, these employees actually 'live the brand', living examples of its authenticity, making and eliciting affective investments and stabilizing brand values. Authenticity is guaranteed through employees' non-work lives, particularly their ethical commitments and recreational activities.

Rather than solving the problem of controlling the brand, however, this simply displaces it. The question for the sociologist of work is how the 'recreational labour' (Ransome, 2007) that employees conduct outside of work is managed. In this sense the question parallels that asked by Arlie Hochschild (1983) in her study of cabin crew engaging in emotional labour. While flight attendants have to manage their own emotions in order to control the emotions of customers, in the 'authentic' brand-based organization employees have to manage their own ethical and recreational behaviours in order to govern the semi-autonomous consumption processes through which the organization's main product – the brand – is produced and reproduced. This process, and its implications for our understanding of work in brand-based organizations, are made clear in our account of Ethico, a company that, like Patagonia, trades upon the commitments of its employees to environmentalism, ethical consumption and extreme sports.

Branding Authentic Identities: The Value of a Life

Ethico is clearly not alone in facing this tension. It is part of an institutional field that emphasizes the pursuit of an ideal, authentic life that promises much. The discourse is also present in British politics, as expressed in a speech made by David Cameron, the current British prime minister:

> What makes us happy, above all, is a sense of belonging – strong relationships with friends, family and the immediate world around us. That's about permanence, not change. It's about the personal, not the commercial. The most exciting and successful new businesses, the ones that capture the spirit of the age, totally understand this... [for these companies] it's about a lifestyle and attitude that celebrates hope, and hopes that through the power of ethical consumerism, business can change the world for the better. All these companies and many more besides are expressing a profound dissatisfaction with rootless, rampaging globalization and a passionate desire for capitalism with commitment, for work that has meaning and for relationships that are about more than just money and markets. (David Cameron, 2006)

The tension that Ethico and other organizations face is writ large here. They gamble that the problems capitalist businesses have given rise to – or at least the subjective effects of profound dissatisfaction and rootlessness – can be addressed by a different kind of capitalist business, one with a real soul, belief, hope and commitment to meaning and authenticity. The difficulty is that in order to communicate this, companies like Ethico have to inscribe these meanings in a brand to compete in the marketplace, removed from any direct, human-to-human relationships. The ultimate criterion for success is not whether this ersatz community actually changes the world – as it might be for a social movement – but whether the brand sells products. Without sales, the company will go out of business and will not have the resources to communicate these dreams and meanings.

As the quote from David Cameron's speech indicates, the key to establishing authenticity lies outside the marketplace and the workplace. Like other organizations in this milieu, Ethico employees work hard to make this happen. A similar but larger organization, Fat Face, also trades on the construction of authenticity through slogans like 'better a bad day on the beach than a good day in the office', 'life is out there', and 'kit for an active lifestyle', all suggesting that we should be outside doing some kind of sporting activity rather than sitting in a workplace earning money to consume goods. To experience 'real' life and to be ourselves is only possible, in these brand narratives, outside of work, in our recreational activities, whilst work figures as tedious and alienating. (Unless, of course, you work somewhere like Fat Face, where you will find ways of combining making a living with doing what you really love.)

Ethico also builds on the idea that it does business in a new and different way into its brand narrative. Promotional materials contain a very clearly articulated anti-hierarchical, anti-work and anti-authoritarian set of ideas. Concerns about maintaining quality of life in the face of alienated workplaces and unsatisfying jobs are expressed through T-shirt slogans such as 'Time not cash'. These might be interpreted as a recuperation of anti-capitalist sentiment that attracts thoroughly disillusioned followers of Jean Baudrillard's philosophy, taking pleasure in the paradoxically secure knowledge that all meaning, language and symbol is ultimately free-floating and has no connection to an external 'real' that might anchor it. For the majority of consumers, however, we would suggest that buying into the Ethico version of authenticity is not a cynical exercise, but driven by the desire to believe that there is really something other than the anomie of rootless, rampaging globalization.

To secure such representations as authentic, there is a further step. They must be supported by the reflexive incorporation of Ethico into its own brand narrative in two ways: first, by suggesting that the business itself and the promise that it holds out is a genuinely different way of organizing and doing business; and second, in support of this, through the inscription of individual employees into the brand by establishing their authentic commitment to the company's values and sports outside of work. To illustrate this, we return briefly to Ethico, exploring the construction of organization and employees as carriers of brand identity as part of the labour process.

BRAND/WORK

Organization as Brand

Ethico catalogue stories and corporate blog posts suggest that commitments outside of work enable employees and organization to be authentic. The impression given by images of twenty-somethings skating, surfing and biking, is that this is the lived reality of working at Ethico. Similarly, by incorporating stories such as the construction of the low-impact printing shed into the brand narrative, the company is inscribed as genuinely committed to the environment. This message is reinforced by the commitment of 1 per cent of turnover or 10 per cent of pre-tax profits to social and environmental causes.

This idea of a commitment to the values expressed in the brand is also developed through the founding narrative of Ethico, in which the original owners are characterized as disaffected city workers striving for something more real. The choice to relocate to a more rural setting and find a calmer pace of life reinforces the matter and manner of developing authenticity against the hyper-reality of life as an advertising executive in a large city. The commitment is further underpinned by recurring motifs of sacrifice in the founding narrative. This is sometimes expressed through stories of heroism, when members of the organization put in extremely long hours, working in difficult conditions, to get orders out and keep the company afloat. A second recurring theme is financial investment; the founders tell how they repeatedly re-mortgaged their family home to ensure cash flow. These sacrifices are framed in terms of the company being 'too good' to give up on, creating an almost spiritual space within which work is elevated from the normal profane world of financial instrumentality and accumulation to partake of the sacred (Grint, 2010). The narratives inform customers that the company's primary purpose is not profitability, as personal financial wealth and security are regularly sacrificed for it, but an unspecified 'good' related to the values and ideals that the brand represents. In some accounts this 'good' is explicitly placed above conventional business logic, as when the founders describe a 'crisis' in which the business was failing. Rather than giving up on an unsuccessful business model, the founders marshalled their energies to save their company, which was 'too good' to give up on. These narrative devices ensure that the organization is represented within its own brand as an egalitarian place where people work not mainly for profit or wage, but because of their ethical commitment to the company and belief in its values.

Employees as Brand

As well as the organization appearing as a character in the brand narrative, employees are regularly mobilized to contribute to the story. One of the founders was quite explicit about this, suggesting that recruitment and selection at Ethico involved assessment of what an employee could bring to the brand narrative as much as competence in performing the actual work. In this way the organization recruited lives as much as workers. Once recruited, employees found that the need to perform in private life according to the requirements of the brand narrative was ongoing. One young woman who worked in the 'call centre' – a small group of three desks at which the employees, all young women, sat answering the phones and processing internet orders – rather apologetically told us that she was 'learning about the environmental stuff' and clearly felt a pressure to at least understand the corporate values. Like the young men working in the warehouse, however, the main appeal of Ethico for this woman was the pay and relatively humane working conditions.

This dynamic also became clear when we asked about the 'too nice to work day' voucher system. This initiative began as a reward for exceptional performance; employees who worked particularly hard during sales or Christmas periods were given a voucher for a day off over and above the standard annual leave entitlement. A number of people opened their desk drawers to show us little bundles of unused vouchers, implying either that they had not yet found a valid reason to take a day off or that they had not been able to negotiate the time away. Shortly after we visited Ethico, an entry appeared on the blog from an employee who had 'cashed in' a voucher to go sea kayaking. This activity was then validated through writing a blog entry, implying that the day off had been anything but. While she had not been at her desk that day, her activities certainly contributed to the brand identity of Ethico as a humane workplace and authentically invested in sports and progressive employment practices. A nominally extra-mural activity was reinscribed as work to contribute towards brand and image as key sources of value. We did wonder what would happen if an employee took a day off to lie in bed, smoke, masturbate, watch day-time TV, or organize a trade union branch, a thought that clearly occurred also to the workers, one of whom told us quite explicitly that the catalogues were targeted at employees: 'The catalogues… quite a lot of it is for us, to tell us how to work and live our lives and stuff. So it's not just saying "We're this great company, we're doing all these things." It's for us really to tell us how we should be doing things' (Sales employee, interview). In other words, the production of the brand was quite explicitly a co-production aimed at managing employees' lives in accordance with brand values.

CONCLUDING DISCUSSION: FREEDOM TO IMAGINE THE POLITICS OF AUTHENTIC ORGANIZATION

The account we provide in this chapter can be read in a variety of ways. One reading suggests there may be varieties of organizational authenticity. In the call centre at the core of Fleming's (2009) analysis, the content of the actual labour process is left unchanged by the managerial discourse of authenticity. The brand of the company can be seen as relatively independent of the 'authentic' performances of the employees. The development of an authentic, 'just be yourself' management style is, in that case, more concerned with recruitment, retention and motivation than with establishing brand authenticity. For Ethico, on the other hand, the authenticity of employees at work and outside is essential to the production of brand value. If consumers experience the brand as inauthentic, then value will be lost as the functionality of the product is secondary to its semiotics and the identity work that it enables a consumer to perform (Arvidsson, 2006).

This shift in the production of value is significant. Fleming's (2009) empirical work remains focused on matters of control and resistance within a spatially bounded, modernist labour process. His discussion of managing authenticity is concerned with the use of private lives to control or enhance performance at work. However, Arvidsson's analysis and our account of the practices at Ethico suggest that work – the labour of producing economic value – is no longer located exclusively in what the employee does at the point of production. Rather consumption, communication and therefore the labour process are distributed and immanent to the process of social production itself. In this sense the lives of consumers are branded, but not in a hylomorphic stamping of 'brand' upon 'life'; instead, a relatively autonomous process of communication and co-construction of brand takes place.

Arvidsson (2006) recognizes that this creates a unique challenge for brand management. Those responsible for it must find a mode of governance that can guide the communicative labour of consumption; managers tend to recognize that they cannot directly control this, even though the production of brand value and economic wealth is dependent upon it. While Arvidsson recognizes this challenge, he has little to say about how it is resolved in practice. Our case goes some way towards explaining managerial practices. Brand management is a precariously achieved process of narration in which personal ethical commitments and values of organizational members, owners and employees, and the business model itself, are incorporated into the brand as indicators of authenticity. This creates an ongoing requirement for employees to live according to these principles and contribute to the brand by narrating life activities as an embodiment of brand values. Of course, this must be done in such a way that it does not appear to be a top-down exercise of cultural control, but instead as emerging from an organizational space in which employees' real selves can be expressed. The authenticity of employees in the social and communicative circuits that consumers seek to locate themselves within through consumption of the brand becomes productive of value for consumers and therefore the organization. To establish the authenticity of employees' affective expressions, the workplace is represented as a humanized sphere of authentic expression, contrasted with the traditional workplace defined by alienated conformity. The humanization of work as a space to express one's authentic self is the practice through which the organization can appropriate the autonomous, private lives of its employees and valourize them through the brand, understood as a space for the accumulation of immaterial capital (Arvidsson, 2005). As Fleming's (2009) analysis demonstrates, however, this practice is predominantly productive and performative rather than expressive. The performances of 'life' that can be inscribed within the organization are limited to expressions of particular lifestyles related to specific recreational activities or values.

This perspective challenges managerial, unitarist claims of encouraging authenticity as progressive, allowing employees to express themselves at work when in the past they were bureaucratically repressed, alienated and forced to conform (Bains, 2007). It reflects the position developed by Boltanski and Chiapello (2005), suggesting that the 'artistic critique' of capitalism formulated in the late 1960s has been recuperated and mobilized to reinvent management. By apparently enabling the subjective expression of creativity and an essential self found outside of work in ethical and recreational commitments, this discourse lays claim to a solution to alienation without changing or even acknowledging the underlying structural features of the employment relationship. This echoes Walter Benjamin's reading of Fascist politics:

> Fascism attempts to organize the newly created proletarian masses without affecting the property structure which the masses strive to eliminate. Fascism sees its salvation in giving these masses not their right, but instead a chance to express themselves. The masses have a right to change property relations; Fascism seeks to give them an expression while preserving property. (Benjamin, 1973: 130)

In a similar way, the right of an employee to express themselves at work, a right that is being recast as an imperative, leaves the underlying property relations of capitalist ownership and the employment relationship unchanged. From this perspective, the move to management by authenticity, and the extension of branding into the management of employees' private lives, at best reproduces the status quo and at worst expands and intensifies capitalist power and control.

However, we also want to raise another possibility, to address the question of whether we should dismiss moves towards expression and the idea of authenticity so completely. From the time we spent at Ethico and in subsequent data analysis, it is clear that employees there are not passive 'dupes', ceding their private lives to an organizational brand without any sense of agency. All employees we spoke to were extremely articulate about the advantages of working at Ethico, the limits of their freedom within the organization, and the compromises that working in a business involved for their other activities. However prejudiced, the ideal of work as freedom, as potentially authentic, constructed through the Ethico brand, was interpreted as positive in some respects.

So perhaps the pursuit of authenticity in life and the workplace is a reasonable ideal? Organizations like Ethico can be read as part of a wider movement to re-introduce meaning into the processes of production and consumption. This may be experienced as re-enchantment, as re-construction of purpose, and as participation in the micropolitics of local activism or the macropolitics of global social movements. However, analytically there is a need to again acknowledge the distinction between form and content in the pursuit of authenticity. Returning to Taylor's (1991) terms, the manner or form of our pursuit of authenticity may be separable from the matter or content of that being pursued. For Taylor, the manner is less significant than the matter; this means that the significance of this organizational movement lies in the idea (1) of authenticity that we can read into Ethico and other organizations. Most readings of this dynamic in contemporary work organizations suggest the attempt to practise authenticity in profit-oriented, rational, modernist work organizations is fated to fail – or at least to be so riddled with contradictions and tensions that it lacks any credibility, leads inevitably towards disillusionment, and results in the creation of identity and brand that destroy hope and faith rather than sustaining them. Authenticity is carefully circumscribed through commodification, specifically excluding variations considered immoral or socially damaging, and the pursuit of any form of 'New-Age' style authenticity represents the shift from collective to individual, from shared activist politics to a narcissistic identity ethic.

As we have suggested, the strategy of authenticity and the ideology surrounding working practices at Ethico may be read in this way. T-shirt slogans, employees contributing stories from sports activities to support the brand narrative, commodification of moral and ethical positions, sourcing products from lower-wage economies – surely all of this indicates an instrumental, rational, exploitative approach to authenticity of experience, feeling and identity? However, these actions may be seen as the manner of approaching authenticity at Ethico. The matter, on the other hand, may remain a moral ideal – as Taylor (1991) argues, even a debased ideal provides a picture of a better way of living, a moral standard that can remain desirable and accessible. The contemporary forms of authenticity that companies such as Ethico draw on are considerably more accessible and tangible than pre-modern articulations; the possibility of moral, ethical or subjective perfection has descended from being the preserve of angels to being embodied in either people or commodities. The language we use to describe ideals of authenticity is articulated through reference to humanity or human activity in common idioms, rather than through reference to deities or 'a human-independent ontic order' (Taylor, 1991: 94) that can only be described through specific theological or philosophical idiom. Nonetheless, these contemporary idioms still refer to something beyond the everyday or commonplace, not easily achievable, and not within the self, and are hence part of a struggle to retain 'higher and fuller modes of authenticity' (Taylor, 1991: 94) in settings of production and consumption.

To conclude, then, we would suggest that Ethico and similar organizations offer two versions of employee identity in the construction of branded authenticity. The first is as an extension of managerial attempts to harness employee subjectivity, incorporating leisure activities, political ideals and metaphysical beliefs to produce competitive advantage and distinction. This is commodified authenticity, where the tensions and contradictions involved in 'being yourself' in a social setting ultimately severs valuable identities from their transcendent or immanent ideal selves to produce brand equity, and returns us to a vision of work and workplaces with little or no meaning or magic in which any sense of collective, any idea of enchantment, has gone. This is a truly bleak vision, alleviated only by the possibility of complete mental and physical escape – leaving work, pursuing a life based on either individualistic or communal freedom from work. According to Fleming (2009), such a flight would result in people occupying a 'plane of immanence' and living a 'life of full positivity' in which divisions such as work/life, public/private, and authentic/inauthentic, are overcome, rendered meaningless in a society founded on the idea of the commons.

The second position involves engaging more closely with the philosophical idea of authenticity, in such a way as to develop more nuanced sociological questions. If we do this, the key question becomes whether the representation of production and consumption as holistic, ethical, spiritual or transformative, is valid for anyone involved in the process. It is easy to identify inconsistencies, exploitation, commodification and managerial wickedness. There are self-indulgent consumers, for sure, interested only in branding themselves and acquiring social or environmental credentials to impress; there are also managers making entirely instrumental use of aspects of authentic life or belief in its possibility to increase productivity. Reducing complex selves to ciphers of production and consumption is however to assume a simplicity of action and subject that is unsupportable empirically or theoretically (Heelas, 2008).

This is not to present an argument for small-scale tempered radicalism, but rather to recognize the potential for change that is found in even the expression of freedom and authenticity – a tempered optimism, perhaps. As Žižek (2009) (a radical theorist not well known for his temperance) has suggested, the experience of formal freedom is an insufficient but necessary condition for the pursuit and creation of real freedom. Without the experience of apparent freedom that capitalism offers, recognition of its limits would not be possible; nor would the affective investments in realizing true freedom make sense. The same might be said of the ersatz form of authenticity offered by Ethico and similar organizations. In allowing only a very constrained form of freedom and demanding new patterns of conformity, they also inevitably hold out an ideal image as a mirror to capitalism and its associated practices. Rather than simply rejecting the compromises that such organizations necessitate, we may, following Žižek, see in them the potential for a more radical form of ethical, authentic organization. Of course, realizing this potential is then the task of a more political form of emancipation; but in critical analyses of these developments we should be wary of throwing the authentic, ethical baby out with the branded, recuperated bathwater.

REFERENCES

Alvesson, M. and Willmott, H. (2002) 'Identity regulation as organizational control: Producing the appropriate individual', *Journal of Management Studies*, 39: 619–44.

Arvidsson, A. (2006) *Brands: Meaning and Value in Media Culture*, Abingdon: Routledge.

Arvidsson, A. (2005) 'Brands: A critical perspective', *Journal of Consumer Culture*, 5(2), 235–58.

Atkinson, P. and Delamont, S. (2005) 'Analytic perspectives', in Denzin, N. and Lincoln, Y. (eds), *The Sage Handbook of Qualitative Research*, London: Sage.

Bains, G. (2007) *Meaning Inc: The Blue Print for Business Success in the 21st Century*, London: Profile Books.

Bannerjee, B. (2007) *Corporate Social Responsibility: The Good, the Bad and the Ugly*, Cheltenham, UK and Northampton, MA, USA: Edward Elgar.

Bell, E. and Taylor, S. (2003) 'The elevation of work: Pastoral power and the New Age work ethic', *Organization*, 10 (2), 331–51.

Benjamin, W. (1973) *Illuminations*, London: NLB.

Böhm, S. and Land, C. (2009) 'The 'Value' of Knowledge: Reappraising Labour in the Post-Industrial Economy', in Jemielniak, D. and J. Kociatkiewicz (eds) *Handbook of Research on Knowledge-Intensive Organizations*, Hershey, PA: Information Science Reference.

Boltanski, L. and Chiapello, E. (2005) *The New Spirit of Capitalism*, London: Verso.

Cameron, D. (2006) Speech made in 2006 to the Google-sponsored 'Zeitgeist Europe' conference. The full text can be found here: <http://www.guardian.co.uk/politics/2006/may/22/conservatives.davidcameron>

Clarke, S. (1990) 'New Utopias for old: Fordist dreams and Post-Fordist fantasies', *Capital & Class*, 14 (3), 131–55.

Collinson, D. (1992) *Managing the Shopfloor: Subjectivity, Masculinity and Workplace Culture*, Berlin: de Gruyter.

Deal, T.E. and Kennedy, A.A. (1982) *Corporate Cultures: The Rites and Rituals of Corporate Life*, Reading, MA: Addison Wesley.

Dowling, E. (2007) 'Producing the dining experience: Measure, subjectivity and the affective worker', *Ephemera: Theory & Politics in Organization*, 7 (1), 117–32.

Fleming, P. (2009) *Authenticity and the Cultural Politics of Work: New Forms of Informal Control*, Cambridge: Cambridge University Press.

Frank, T. (1998) *The Conquest of Cool: Business Culture, Counterculture and the Rise of Hip Consumerism*, Chicago: University of Chicago Press.

Fournier, V. and Grey, C. (2000) 'At the critical moment: Conditions and prospects for critical management studies', *Human Relations*, 53 (1), 7–32.

Gilmore, J. and Pine, B. (2007) *Authenticity: What Consumers Really Want*, Cambridge, MA: Harvard University Press.

Gowler, D. and Legge, K. (1983) 'The meaning of management and the management of meaning: A view from social anthropology', in Earl, M. (ed.), *Perspectives on Management: A Multidisciplinary Analysis*, Oxford: Oxford University Press.

Grint, K. (2010) 'The sacred in leadership: Separation, Sacrifice and Silence', *Organization Studies*, 31 (1), 89–107.

Hancock, P. and Tyler, M. (2009) *The Management of Everyday Life*, Basingstoke: Palgrave.

Hansen, S. (2004) 'From "common observation" to behavioural risk management', *International Sociology*, 19 (2), 151–71.

Heelas, P. (2008) *Spiritualities of Life: New Age Romanticism and Consumptive Capitalism*, Oxford: Blackwell.

Heelas, P. and Woodhead, L. (2005) *The Spiritual Revolution: Why Religion is Giving Way to Spirituality*, Oxford: Blackwell.

Hochschild, A. (1983) *The Managed Heart: Commercialization of Human Feeling*, Berkeley: University of California Press.

Ind, N. (2007) *Living the Brand*, London: Kogan Page.

Kärreman, D. and Rylander, A. (2008) 'Managing meaning through branding: The case of a consulting firm', *Organization Studies*, 29 (1), 103–25.

Kunda, G. (1992) *Engineering Culture*, Philadelphia: Temple University Press.

Land, C. and Taylor, S. (2010) 'Surf's up: Work, life, balance and brand in a New Age capitalist organization', *Sociology*, 44 (3), 395–413.

Lau, K. (2000) *New Age Capitalism: Making Money East of Eden*, Philadelphia: University of Pennsylvania Press.

Lazaratto, M. (1997) 'Immaterial labour', in Virno, P. and M. Hardt (eds), *Radical thought in Italy: a Potential Politics*, Minneapolis: Minnesota University Press.

Marazzi, C. (2010) *The Violence of Financial Capitalism*, Los Angeles: Semiotext(e).

Marx, K. (1976) *Capital*, Volume One, London: Penguin.

Ogbonna, E. and Harris, L.C. (1998) 'Managing organizational culture: Compliance or genuine change?', *British Journal of Management*, 9 (4), 273–88.

Peters, T. (1992) *Liberation Management: Necessary Disorganization for the Nanosecond Nineties*, London: Pan.

Peters, T. and Waterman, R. (1982) *In Search of Excellence*, New York: Harper and Row.

Ransome, A. (2007) 'Conceptualizing boundaries between "life" and "work"', *International Journal of Human Resource Management*, 18 (3), 374–86.

Ross, A. (2004) *No Collar: The Human Workplace and its Hidden Costs*, Philadelphia: Temple University Press.

Spicer, A. and Fleming, P. (2007) 'Intervening in the inevitable: Resistance to globalization in a public sector organization', *Organization*, 14 (4), 517–41.

Smircich, L. and Morgan, G. (1982) 'Leadership: The management of meaning', *The Journal of Applied Behavioural Science*, 18 (3), 257–73.

Stake, R. (2005) 'Qualitative case studies', in Denzin, N. and Lincoln, Y. (eds), *The Sage Handbook of Qualitative Research*, London: Sage.

Taylor, C. (1991) *The Ethics of Authenticity*, Cambridge, MA: Harvard University Press.

Terranova, T. (2000) 'Free labor: Producing culture for the digital economy', *Social Text*, 18 (2), 33–57.

Thompson, P. (2005) 'Foundation and empire: A critique of Hardt and Negri', *Capital & Class*, 29 (2), 73–98.

Wajcman, J., Bittman, M. and Brown, B. (2008) 'Families without borders: Mobile phones, connectedness, and work-home divisions', *Sociology*, 42 (4), 635–52.

Willmott, H. (1993) 'Strength is ignorance: Slavery is freedom: Managing culture in modern organizations', *Journal of Management Studies*, 30 (4), 515–52.

Wray-Bliss, E. (2009) 'Over the limit: The management of drug and alcohol use', in Hancock, P. and Tyler, M. (eds), *The Management of Everyday Life*, Hampshire: Palgrave Macmillan.

Žižek, S. (2009) *First as Tragedy, Then as Farce*, London: Verso.

4. The branded self as paradox: polysemic readings of employee–brand identification

Sandra Smith and Margo Buchanan-Oliver

INTRODUCTION

In this chapter[1] we unpack the brand experience by investigating employee representations of the self, organization and brand, from a social narrative perspective. Using a range of techniques, such as group and individual interviews, participant-generated visual texts and narrative analysis, we frame employee portraits of the brand as reflections or mirrors of the branded self. We assert that how the employee represents the brand is central to not only the branded identity of the employee but also, collectively, to that of the organization. This chapter outlines how employees may either accommodate or resist, to varying degrees, identification with the organizational brand. However, we add to this view by also exploring instances where the brand constitutes the self beyond the professional realm. We also uncover post-structuralist complexity which confounds notions of the branded self as unitary, predictable or complete. Our findings mirror the post-structuralist perspective of organizational identity expressed by Alvesson and Willmot (2002). Consequently, we represent and hold in tension competing portrayals of the self–brand–organization, thereby confirming the branded self as contingent, frequently paradoxical and 'the nodal point of intersecting subject positions' (Harding, 2008: 45).

ORGANIZATIONAL CONTEXT

Using a single case approach allows us to provide a rich, narrative portrayal of one organizational context. One key rationale for using a case study approach is that it is an effective way of linking theory and real-life experiences (Gummesson, 2007). Also, using this approach provides the opportunity for narrative analysis given that case studies often contain 'a substantial element of narrative' (Flyvbjerg, 2007: 399). Furthermore, this methodology: 'allows the brand, which in its very nature is different from one organization to the next, to be explored in-depth, and "in the round"' (King and Grace 2005: 293), thereby providing detail that might otherwise be overlooked if another methodology was used.

The organization we selected[2] is a long established, large financial services provider, the brand name of which is well known within the markets it serves. Our selection of this organization was based on three main factors. First, the chosen organization's business model creates opportunities for employees to interact with each other, with external consumers and with other stakeholders in a number of ways (e.g. face-to-face, email, telephone, website, and intranet), thereby creating a rich organizational environment within which to explore the brand–employee interaction. Second, the organization has a very strong brand culture and depends on a high degree of employee alignment to, and engagement with, this culture to deliver on its brand promises. Third, we had the ability to access employees for the purpose of our research; gaining access to large corporations can be difficult given the competitive environments many organizations operate within.

FRAMING THE EMPLOYEE–BRAND RELATIONSHIP

While it has been established that there is a service component in all product offerings (Vargo and Lusch, 2008), the employee–brand relationship is, it could be argued, more central to a product offering which is service-dominant. Thus we decided to explore a service brand. Branding has gained increased recognition as a major contributor to the value of service organizations. It is recognized that having a strong brand creates a competitive advantage for the firm by increasing customer loyalty and therefore brand equity (Berry, 2000). According to O'Cass and Grace (2004), experience with the service brand provides a strong basis upon which consumers attach meaning to the brand, and ultimately brand attitudes emerge through consumption.

The employees of a service firm become crucial players in the enactment of the brand promises. There is clear recognition of the importance of the employee–brand relationship when it comes to service delivery (Gapp and Merrilees, 2006; King and Grace, 2005; Prasad and Steffes, 2002). Also, the concept of service quality has been gaining increased attention in the marketing literature (Parasuraman and Grewal, 2000). While the employee's role as enabler of brand promises has been, and is increasingly, acknowledged, Vallaster (2004) points to a gap in our empirical knowledge of how this occurs, and Vallaster and de Chernatony (2006) call for further research into understanding how corporate branding structures are (re)produced in group interactions. De Chernatony (2002) has also asked for consideration of how external and internal brand promises can be 'orchestrated' to provide employee–brand value alignment. Yet other researchers have established the process by which employees internalize the desired brand image and then project this image to other stakeholders (Miles and Mangold, 2007; Heskett et al., 1997), while Mohtashemi (2002) frames the employee brand as the external face of the brand where employees are encouraged to connect with the brand in the same way external consumers do, usually by internalizing brand values.

Much of the research around brand experiences has focused on the external consumer of the brand. Meanwhile, internal branding has been more thinly covered, and according to Vallaster (2004), has been a relatively recent focus in the branding literature. Research focusing on internal marketing and branding issues includes an exploration into the criteria for service brands to be successful (de Chernatony and Segal-Horn, 2003), the link between internal marketing, relationship marketing and service quality (Barnes et al., 2004), the relationship between organizational structures and individual brand supporting behaviour (Vallaster and de Chernatony, 2006), the issue of building an internal brand in a multicultural organization (Vallaster, 2004) and internal marketing programmes (Papasolomou and Vrontis, 2006).

While research does exist in the context of uncovering organizational identity by first looking at the internal members of an organization (e.g. Bronn et al., 2006), there are gaps in the literature around the issue of the brand experience within an organization, and in organization and individual identity construction arising from that experience. Thus, we have turned the lens upon employees (the internal consumers of the brand), their experiences and the meanings they attach to these experiences. Our aim has been to further explore the employee–brand interaction by considering the employee–brand experience within one large organizational setting. We particularly focus on the way employees either accommodate or resist being aligned to or engaging with the brand. Accommodation and resistance are concepts often associated with identity formation in organizational contexts (e.g. Collinson, 2003), and in a post-structural world, the accommodation–resistance dichotomy reveals opposing subject positions.

Internal marketing and internal branding are linked to corporate identity since projecting a uniform and positive identity is claimed to be a common aim of business leaders (de Chernatony, 2002). Creating a common, shared vision of the corporation is connected to the notion of there being a unitary self on both an individual and corporate basis. Corporate identity management authors such as Simões et al. (2005) position management as being key in the development and maintenance of corporate identity; paying particular attention to the internal and controllable aspects of the process. The corporate identity management approach, like the internal marketing and internal brand-ing approaches, has a desire for organizational unity and alignment as a main goal. However, we explore the organization from a post-structuralist perspec-tive in order to reveal the multiplicity and complexity of internal organiza-tional culture, communication streams, informal as well as formal dialogues, and the co-creation of 'the marketing message' and lived experience of the internal consumers of the brand.

Markets are framed by Penaloza and Venkatesh (2006) as social construc-tions, and, as a consequence, they call for work that focuses on studying consumers, marketers and firms in social groups. For them, viewing markets as social constructions creates an understanding of the relationship between market beliefs and practices. In addition, Muniz and O'Guinn (2001) see brand meaning as being socially negotiated. More specifically, they view brands as social entities which are created as much by consumers as by marketers in a complex social dance: 'This intersection of brand – a defining entity of consumer culture – and community – a core sociological notion – is an impor-tant one' (Muniz and O'Guinn, 2001: 428).

Thus we frame the brand as a socially constructed phenomenon. In addition to the view that brands can be framed as social constructions, we also assert that the brand can be viewed as text (Hatch and Rubin, 2006). Our rationale for framing the organizational brand as a socially constructed text is that this fram-ing reflects the complexity of organizations by acknowledging the multiple narratives that exist within any particular brand context.

We chose to explore employee texts in order to move beyond studies of organization that centre on the way things ought to be rather than how they actually are. We employ certain assumptions. First, organizations are socially constructed and constituted as discursive, rather than being independent enti-ties, and within this framing the complexity of the organization is more fully expressed (Brown and Humphreys, 2006). Second, within the context of orga-nizational-level studies, collective self-narratives are likely to be fractured, contested and multilayered, given the pluralism and polyphony that character-ize organizations (Humphreys and Brown, 2002). Third, the organization is a site of multiple communities that each negotiate meaning through narratives, and identities can be traced within the organizational worlds that these narra-tives construct (Hopkinson, 2003).

As well as viewing brands and organizations in this way, we employ the metaphor of the mirror in relation to the branded self since the mirror reflects the self as an image. Lacan (1998) has presented the self in relation to the mirror in which the subject deceives itself into coherence through phantasmic relation to the Other; in other words, the subject misrecognizes a coherence that represses its fragmented character, and it is in the Other that the subject finds its unity. Harding (2007) highlights Lacan's view that:

a subject comes into being enacts the ways of being a subject in the world. The shock of identity experienced before the mirror serves as the highly particularized foundation for a universal structure of human existence. In looking at each other, two material entities experience recognition, identification, alienation and aggression. This occasion, this look, is repeated until death. This reflexive recognition demonstrates the need, the desire, for an Other. Reciprocal reflexivity enables intersubjectivity. (Harding, 2007: 1769)

Using this metaphor, the self can only ever, therefore, be represented, reflected, portrayed in some way but never known in completion:

I am neither the eye which sees, nor the reflection seen; rather I am the very process or movement between the two, an identity produced in a structure of alienation. (Easthope, 1983: 39)

Furthermore, as well as including the visible, that which is mirrored can include the invisible, disavowed, and even impossible (Muller, 1985).

Closely aligned to the mirror metaphor is the metaphor of the portrait. The portrait is used to represent corporate or organizational identity in Guthey and Jackson's (2005) analysis of CEO portraits. Their work highlights a growing trend to visualize that which is not visual, and to construct via a seemingly stable and authentic format that which resists stable or authentic representation. They suggest that authenticity is paradoxical and call for further exploration into the social and symbolic construction of business leadership. We argue here that closely aligned with the social and symbolic construction of business leadership through portraiture, is the social and symbolic construction of the employee, and, therefore, organizational identity through portrayal of the branded identity.

We employ the term 'portrait' to incorporate both illustrative and transcribed representations of the branded identity. The treatment of visual representations as texts has a rich tradition within advertising research; namely, Stern's (1993) deconstruction of advertisements such as the Dakota Woman; Scott's (1994) casting of advertising images as visual rhetoric; and McQuarrie and Mick's (1999) examination of stylistic elements in advertising. In addition, Schroeder (2005) asserts that branding is a powerful representational system that produces knowledge through discursive practice. Thus, with reference to this rich tradition, we cast the illustrations and verbal representations generated by participants in our study as textual representations which portray the branded identity through a representation of the self, organization and brand.

In the tradition of Fournier's (1998) exploration into the consumer–brand relationships of three women in diverse life situations, we extend the consumer–brand interaction into the realm of service branding and from the perspective of three employees' brand portraits. We read these portraits as texts that can be unpacked, untangled but never truly deciphered.

The assumption here is that our reading is just one reading. We hold to the notion that the birth of the reader begins with the death of the author (Barthes, 1977). Thus the true place of writing is reading; the reader is inscribed through the reading process just as the reader inscribes that which is read. In addition, these employee-generated brand portraits are framed as representations of reality, a construction we cannot test or control for, 'but only allude to through the use of alternative and competing signs' (Christensen and Askegaard, 2001: 300). Thus we allow the texts to speak for themselves, thereby presenting a contested, complex and paradoxical picture of the branded identity within an organizational setting.

Within this negotiated, fractured, narrative organizational landscape the employee can no longer be considered as having an essentialist, 'core' self. Drawing on a post-structuralist perspective on identity which rejects essentialist notions of a unitary self (Alvesson and Willmott, 2002) we look towards the work of not only Lacan, but also Derrida and Foucault. As Harding (2007) asserts, the self (and therefore organization) is always becoming, never complete. However, constructs of the self appear in individual's narratives of themselves, and in the case of our research, we argue, in the individual's narratives of their branded selves.

METHODOLOGY

For the purpose of foregrounding our research approach, we use Crotty's (1998) four-tiered model of identifying and constructing a research methodology. The metatheoretical perspective we have chosen through which to lens this study is a social constructionist one. We chose to use this perspective because it provides a basis for exploring 'how meaning is constructed in the social world in order to be meaningful in and to the social world of marketing' (Hackley, 1998: 130). Using a constructionist epistemology means that we need to recognize the different meanings and therefore 'realities' people live within and among. This assumption of differing realities maps, therefore, onto an interpretivist approach, which, according to Haigh and Crowther (2005), remains uninterested in realistic assumptions of measuring observable behaviour; instead, this approach assumes that each interactional text is unique, shaped by the individual who created it.

We adopted an interpretivist framing for this study using Labov's (1997) dictum about having continual engagement with the discourse as it was delivered, and Braun-La Tour et al.'s (2007) view that such an approach may uncover the social nature of the text. We chose discourse analysis (Hepburn and Potter, 2004; Fairclough, 1993) as a methodological approach because it allows language to be treated in a way which highlights its physicality and lack of transparency as an object, its complexity as a vehicle for constructing worlds within worlds, and its use as a social text.

Narrative analysis is positioned here as a subset within the wider frame of discourse analysis. We decided to adopt a narrative approach because narrative is a powerful way we can understand the human experience (individual and collective) that is not directly open to other forms of analysis, given that people have a natural propensity to create meaning about their worlds through stories (Padgett and Allen, 1997). For example, Stern et al. (1998) use narrative text in order to contribute to an understanding of the consumer's perspective. In their study they used an interview technique which encouraged participants to contextualize a marketing relationship in their life histories, thereby facilitating a phenomenological study of 'lived meaning'. Using the assumptions we have outlined around language in relation to discourse analysis as a methodological approach, we have adopted Riessman's (1993) view that the researcher does not have direct access to another's experience, but can only know ambiguous representations of it. Ultimately, by abandoning any attempt to treat participants' accounts as 'true' pictures of 'reality', we open ourselves up to understanding the culturally rich methods through which interviewers and interviewees generate 'plausible accounts of the world' (Silverman, 2000: 823).

In order to generate interview data, we purposively selected employees on the basis of role, tenure, gender and ethnicity. For practical reasons, only employees from one geographic region were considered. Our aim was to speak to a range of people who represented the diverse population that constituted the organization within this regional context. Interviews were generated in a three-stage process. This process is depicted in Table 4.1.

Table 4.1   Three-phase interview process

Phase one	Phase two	Phase three
Nine focus groups of 2–8 participants (n=53)	Six focus groups of 2–6 participants (n=23)	Fifteen individual interviews (n=15)

In phase one, we grouped those who agreed to participate in this study into role-based groups. For phase two, however, we mixed up the groups in order to explore any role-based differences. Lastly, in phase three we explored the employee–brand relationship on an individual basis. We designed the data generation process in this way in order to: (1) explore the employee–brand relationship in depth (that is, beyond just a single one hour group interview); (2) build trust and a sense of knowing with participants who took part in each phase; and (3) increase the trustworthiness of our findings by employing both group and individual interviews. In this account we focus on the third stage of this larger study, and in particular we focus on three dissimilar participant narratives to reveal both the similarities and differences, the paradoxes and complexities which typify the larger body of data.

We used a combination of interview and visual data[3] in order to enrich our exploration of the branded self. Specifically, we requested that participants illustrated the relationship between themselves, the brand and the organization. Participants were given the freedom to draw whatever they chose (e.g. shapes, words, pictures), and to show any kind of relationship between the three elements, that is, whether they saw the elements as being separate, connected, the same. For example, the following excerpt shows how the interviewer typically introduced the notion of drawing the brand, organization and self:

> Interviewer: I would like you to depict how you perceive the relationship between the brand, you and the organization. You can draw absolutely anything... Take your time, there is no time limit.

Our rationale for employing this method is because drawings provide the researcher with a different perspective of human sense-making compared to written and spoken texts in that drawings represent that which may ordinarily be difficult to put into words (Kearney and Hyle, 2004; Weber and Mitchell, 1995). Furthermore, we would suggest that visual text is much more than just an adjunct to the interview data we obtained, but instead forms an integral part of the narrative experience, and therefore if woven into the verbal narratives serves to create new meanings (Pink, 2004).

HOLDING UP A MIRROR TO THE BRANDED SELF?

In this section, we provide a reading of three brand portraits.[4] We briefly discuss, compare and analyse these portraits for resistant, accommodating and constituting verbal themes and visual elements. The usual criteria for trustworthiness and reliability were applied during the analysis. We achieved this through a process of hermeneutical analysis in which we explored texts (verbal and visual) to determine recurrent themes to the point of theoretical saturation (Spiggle, 1994). During the third phase individual interview participants were asked to illustrate the self, organization and brand. The brand portraits consist of what participants said and what they drew. These portraits are not presented in any particular order and we reiterate that this reading of them is just one lens through which they can be viewed. We selected these three participant portraits in order to illustrate the diversity found within the larger participant population. First, these participants have quite different roles and are therefore likely to have different perspectives of the brand due to their relative organizational positions (both to each other and also to front line staff). Second, their portraits are reflective of the larger body of visual texts that were generated by the final fifteen interviewees.

At the time of the interview, Participant A was employed in a front-line role; her illustration of the brand, self and organization (Figure 4.1) is reminiscent of traditional managerial branding models (viz., de Chernatony, 2002)

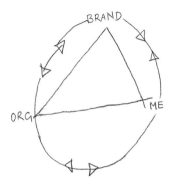

Figure 4.1   Illustration by Participant A

However, Participant A admits it was not her first instinct to draw what is shown here:

> But when you mentioned it the first time the first thing that came into my head was people hugging each [other] or kind of one of those... holding hands around the world images, but I think this [referring to what she has drawn] would be more accurate, kind of a triangle and a circle.

Participant A's dissonant views reflect a tension between conforming to that which she deems is accurate and that which is more instinctual. Paradoxically, her initial view which highlighted the notion of fellowship ('people hugging each other') could be read as acculturation into the expressed, intentional organizational vision of being supportive, communal and familial (this theme was strongly indicated in the initial phases of the interview process); however, the final version the respondent decided on could be read as resisting this symbolic aspect of the organizational culture.

The participant's drawing represents a two-way flow between each element (self, organization and brand). The brand is positioned at the apex of the triangle and is therefore in the most dominant position. However, the circle reflects a degree of equality between the three elements and her explanation establishes the existence of a circular relationship:

> [The brand] leads into the organization and then the organization leads into me, and then in turn I lead back into the brand.

This illustration also shows separateness; namely, the brand and organization can link into each other or the self can link into either the organization or the brand. The paradox of being separate and yet connected is reflected in her description of movement:

> it goes both way[s]..., it links everything together and also links everything separately, and [there is]... a slight separation, I'm not sure why [I think like that] but I do.

The words 'slight separation' show resistance. However, she also claims that 'together they make a more powerful entity', suggesting that a oneness or synergy occurs when all three are linked. The synergistic nature of the relationship is also represented when she states:

> The organization would be fine on its own but it gets more power from the brand and I would be fine on my own but I get more power from the brand.

The brand is textually privileged in this statement, and also visually privileged as it is positioned at the top of the apex.

Participant A provides two reasons for being detached. First, the respondent asserts that one can maintain a level of detachment while still demonstrating loyalty to the organization. Such detachment can offer a more reasoned evaluation of the organization. The respondent tells the story of another worker within the organization who is nicknamed 'the evangelist':

> One guy at the [organization] is called 'the preacher' or something like that, of the [organization].... He's always proclaiming about how good it is. Evangelist, that's the word... because he believes in it so much, which is quite incredible, and maybe after I've spent as many years in it I may feel the same way.

However, she distances herself from that kind of relationship. Second, she explains that she resists a close relationship ('people hugging in a circle') because:

> you never know what is going to happen; [it] could be like breaking up with a partner or something where you have the emotional disability afterwards.

Thus, Participant A's need to be separate is also about protecting herself emotionally. In this respondent's portrayal of the branded identity there are tensions between the urge to conform and to remain connected, and yet remain separated. There is accommodation with the brand (conforming but not believing too much), but there is also resistance to the brand (separateness), and there is also dissonance (different visions, connected but separate).

Participant B was performing a support (back office) role when interviewed. Her verbal explanation of her relationship with the brand emphasizes pride, belonging and being known:

> It comes back to the pride of the brand and the feeling that you belong sort of, like it's like a family and... you kind of go the extra mile because you do belong and there's this community feel about the place and basically we're everywhere and it's so well known, the brand is so well known, and you feel proud to be part of that brand.

However, this story of pride and belonging could be read as being dissonant to her geometrical illustration of the self, organization and brand (see Figure 4.2), which betrays a hierarchical and fragmented view. Participant B depicts the organization as being larger than both herself and the brand. This respondent uses a rectangle because: 'It's got a very solid base.'

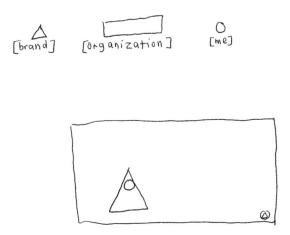

Figure 4.2   Participant B

On the other hand, she represents the brand using a triangle shape and draws it smaller because while she admits it is part of the organization, 'it's not the be all and end all'. Participant B describes why she has represented herself and the brand as occupying two different spaces and as two different sizes:

> I think there's more than one place to put me, but I just have to work out the size... and I also don't know how big to make the circle that represents me; when I'm part of the organization I'm really little in the corner here, but when I'm inside

the brand I'm a little bit bigger. I appreciate that the organization is [several thousand] employees and I'm only one of those, but I put myself near the base probably because of my experience and expertise. I'm part of the foundation, and I think I'm inside the brand triangle because I help to portray the brand rather than it being in me, but you could argue that there's a little brand inside me.

This respondent represents the organization as rectangular and stable, enclosing both the brand and the self. She sees her main role as portraying the brand but concedes that the brand to a lesser extent (depicted as such because of the smaller size), also portrays her/him. There is resistance in this statement ('but you could argue') but also accommodation ('there's a little brand inside me'). For this participant, the brand is largely about the external appearance: 'I think the brand is the products and the services, the actual physical things you can see.' However, she also includes: 'the philosophies of the organization itself... so to me it is physical, the connotations behind it are service... good customer service'.

This classification of philosophies as being part of or at least connoted by the tangible aspects of the brand suggests the brand is not merely that which is seen, but is also constituted by intangible properties. Also, despite Participant B's attempt to represent the brand and her branded identity in a state of containment (the dual selves within the organization), there is a spilling over of the brand into her life outside the company: 'I wear [the brand name] socks to golf, and use [the brand name] golf balls.'

Thus, while she resists allowing her identity to be completely aligned with or subsumed by the brand it does become part of the visible signs of her identity when she is outside her professional sphere. Paradoxically, this admission of the brand being part of her private as well as work-based identity reflects her feelings of pride in belonging to such a well known brand.

Participant C occupied a middle management role at the time of this interview. For this participant the brand is an extension of herself:

I do consider it part of my family..., it's an extension of me... and I talk to people often that talk about going to their job and going to work and they've separated [them] quite distinctly, and I possibly don't, it is part of me, it's part of my family.

The participant's words suggest a close identification with the brand. Her dependence on the brand is reflected in the following:

I think we ask a question of our customers, can you imagine a life without [the brand name] or something along those lines and I think about that myself and I [pause], I can't.

In keeping with this portrayal of dependency, Participant C's representation of the brand is rather child-like (Figure 4.3).

Figure 4.3   Participant C

She explains the illustration as follows:

> We have me and, in my lovely warm sunny house, with the sun, so I guess that's me, the house is I guess it's partly the organization and then the sun is the bank, growing, light… the brand is the sun, the house is [partly] the safe aspect of the organization.

The house simultaneously represents the respondent's life outside the organization and also represents the organization as a type of home. For this participant the house, the sun and the representation of herself coalesce. Therefore, while these elements may be separate, they are connected by the participant's interpretation of the structural requirements of the picture, which, as with Participant A's illustration, reflects a synergistic relationship between the three elements:

> [T]hese three elements are all in one, it's one picture, it's all one picture, one… separate structures but they all go together, you need the people and the sun with the house.

For this participant, the brand is vital for her life (without the sun life perishes) and is a persistent feature in her life: 'It's taken me through different stages in my life… from childhood to adulthood and to [parent]hood.'

She represents the organization as being protective. When asked to comment on her experience in the group interview, she was shocked that some people didn't know what the brand mission and values were, she was also surprised that they could not relate to the brand: 'why they don't believe it, I don't know'.

Participant C's devotion to the brand is evident:

> I don't always want to be a [manager] but I always want to work for [the brand name].

Her devotion to the brand is further emphasized when she represents herself as being 'indoctrinated by the brand'. She explains that through her belief in the brand she has found the freedom to grow as a person, to make mistakes and learn from those mistakes:

> [P]eople do make mistakes and I think that, the brand doesn't represent human error, the brand represents how they resolve mistakes, I guess, whether internally or externally, so that's no different if we made a mistake with a customer it's how we deal with that mistake going forward and that we learn from that mistake so that, that's a brand philosophy. The mistake itself is a human error.

However, when this comment is compared to the illustration, there is agreement between what is said and what is drawn; that is, the brand is represented by the sun as being an integral part of the picture (connected to the self) and yet far away and powerful (separated from the self). Moreover, the brand, like the sun, constitutes Participant C's world beyond organizational boundaries, and in fact blurs these boundaries, thereby possibly representing a conflation of the respondent's organizational and personal worlds.

DISCUSSION AND CONCLUSIONS

A summary of the various elements or attributes of each illustration is provided in Table 4.2. There are common features, such as the use of shapes such as squares, circles or triangles (Figures 4.1 and 4.2) to signify relationships. Figure 4.3 uses a building to represent the organization/home. Movement is shown by arrows in Figure 4.1. Fragmentation of the self and brand is depicted in Figure 4.2. Figure 4.1 shows the self–organization–brand in a circular relationship, while in Figures 4.2 and 4.3 the self is enclosed within either a building or shape. Lastly, while not necessarily the largest elements in these representations of self–organization–brand, the element that is most salient for and elaborated on by participants in each illustration is the brand in Figures 4.1 and 4.3, and the organization in Figure 4.2.

Table 4.2   Summary of visual elements

Participant	Shapes	Buildings	Movement	Split	Circular	Inside	Strong
A	×		×		×		Brand
B	×			×		×	Organization
C		×				×	Brand

This montage of visual texts, when seen together, demonstrates some commonalities but also reveals complexity, fragmentation and paradox. These visual texts also reveal a mirrored world which, as Muller (1985) states, includes the invisible, disavowed, and even impossible. These employee representations also illustrate elements of resistance to, and accommodation of, the brand. Brand resistance is shown when the self and brand are visually separated (Figure 4.1). Accommodation is shown when the self and brand are visually connected (Figures 4.1 and 4.2). Being constituted by the brand is shown when organizational–personal boundaries are conflated (Figure 4.3) or when the brand is placed within the self (Figure 4.2).

Participants' visual and verbal representations demonstrate both assonance and dissonance. Not only, therefore, do these portraits reveal competing views of the branded identity which highlight the pluralism and polyphony that characterize organizations, noted by Humphreys and Brown (2002), but they also reveal affirming and/or competing views within each individual portrait. Branded identity has been shown to simultaneously be a product of resistance of (Participants A, B, and C), of accommodation to (Participant A and B), and of being constituted by, the brand (Participant C). Not only is there complexity between the three sets of narratives but there is also complexity between the modalities (visual and verbal) and within each narrative account. Thus our findings reveal a branded self that is contingent, mutable and located 'at the nodal point of intersecting subject positions' (Harding, 2008: 45), is multifaceted, rather than unitary (Alvesson and Willmott, 2002), and a self that is always becoming but never complete (Harding, 2007).

This selection of visual and verbal texts reflects the brand experiences of three employees of a large financial services organization. In this reading of the participants' brand portraits we view the branded self from their perspective and read their narratives through a post-structuralist lens. We argue that brands are necessarily contextualized in a post-structuralist world, which reveals complexity, contestation and contingency. Thus, we hold a mirror up to one organizational context through the lens of these participants' brand portraits. In doing so, we extend the accommodation–resistance dichotomy common to organizational studies' framing of the corporate brand to include polysemic readings of employee brand identity, and we also contribute to new knowledge by revealing that employees can also be constituted by the brand. In addition we show that not only is the conceptualization of the brand contested by participants but there is also dissonance between the ways the brand is pictorially and verbally represented. The brand in this organizational and narrative context reveals itself as fragmented. Thus representations of branded identity mirror the fragmented character of the self (Lacan, 1998) as it attempts to see itself in relation to the Other and confirm the contested paradoxical and complex nature of the brand experience.

NOTES

1. This chapter is based on Smith's (2011) unpublished PhD thesis, which explores more broadly how participant (employee) narratives construct a service brand.
2. We have omitted any details from our description of the organizational context which might reveal the organization's identity.
3. In order to project the anonymity of our participants we have depicted them all as female, using 'she' to describe them in the text.
4. In order to further preserve each participant's anonymity, which in some cases could have been compromised through recognition of participant handwriting samples, drawings have been traced over and any handwriting reproduced in a more neutral style.

REFERENCES

Alvesson, M. and Willmott, H. (2002) 'Producing the appropriate individual: identity regulation as organizational control', *Journal of Management Studies*, 39 (5), 619–44.

Barnes, B., Fox, M. and Morris, D. (2004) 'Exploring the linkage between internal marketing, relationship marketing and service quality: a case study of a consulting organisation', *Total Quality Management*, 15 (5–6), 593–601.

Barthes, R. (1977) *Image, Music, Text* (trans. Stephen Heath), New York: Hill and Wang.

Berry, L.L. (2000) 'Cultivating service brand equity', *Academy of Marketing Science*, 28 (1), 128–37.

Braun-La Tour, K., LaTour, M. and Zinkhan, G. (2007) 'Using childhood memories to gain insight into branding meaning', *Journal of Marketing*, 71 (April), 45–60.

Bronn, P., Engell, A. and Martinsen, H. (2006) 'A reflective approach to uncovering actual identity', *European Journal of Marketing*, 40 (7–8), 886–901.

Brown, A. and Humphreys, M. (2006) 'Organizational identity and place: a discursive exploration of hegemony and resistance', *Journal of Management Studies*, 43 (2), 231–57.

Christensen, L. and Askegaard, S. (2001) 'Corporate identity and corporate image revisited', *European Journal of Marketing*, 35 (3–4), 292–315.

Collinson, D. (2003) 'Identities and insecurities: selves at work', *Organization*, 10 (3), 527–47.

Crotty, M. (1998) *The Foundations of Social Research*, Leonards, NSW: Allen and Unwin.

de Chernatony, L. (2002) 'Would a brand smell any sweeter by a corporate name?', *Corporate Reputation Review*, 5 (2–3), 114–32.

de Chernatony, L. and Segal-Horn, S. (2003) 'The criteria for successful service brands', *European Journal of Marketing*, 37 (7–8), 1095–118.

Easthope, A. (1983) *Poetry as Discourse*, London: Methuen.

Fairclough, N. (1993) 'Critical discourse analysis and marketization of public discourse', *Discourse and Society*, 4 (2), 133–68.

Flyvbjerg, B. (2007) 'Five misunderstandings about case-study research', in C. Seale, G. Gobo, J. Gubrium and D. Silverman (eds), *Qualitative Research Practice*, London: Sage Publications, pp. 390–404.

Fournier, S. (1998) 'Consumers and their brands', *Journal of Consumer Research*, 24 (4), 343–53.

Gapp, R. and Merrilees, B. (2006) 'Important factors to consider when using internal branding as a management strategy: a healthcare case study', *Brand Management*, 14 (1–2), 162–76.

Gummesson, E. (2007) 'Case study research and network theory: birds of a feather', *Qualitative Research in Organizations and Management*, 2 (3), 226–48.

Guthey, E. and Jackson, B. (2005) 'CEO portraits and the authenticity paradox', *Journal of Management Studies*, 42 (5), 1057–82.

Hackley, C. (1998) 'Social constructionism and research in marketing and advertising', *Qualitative Market Research*, 1 (3), 125–31.

Haigh, J. and Crowther, G. (2005) 'Interpreting motorcycling through its embodiment in life story narratives', *Journal of Marketing Management*, 21 (5–6), 555–72.

Harding, N. (2007) 'On Lacan and the "becoming-ness" of organizations/selves', *Organization Studies*, 28 (11), 1761–73.

Harding, N. (2008) 'The "I", the "me" and the "you know": identifying identities in organisations', *Qualitative Research in Organizations and Management*, 3 (1), 42–58.

Hatch, M. and Rubin, J. (2006) 'The hermeneutics of branding', *The Journal of Brand Management*, 14 (1–2), 40–59.

Hepburn, A. and Potter, J. (2004) 'Discourse analytic practice', in C. Seale, G. Gobo, J. Gubrium and D. Silverman (eds), *Qualitative Research Practice*, London: Sage Publications, 168–84.

Heskett, J., Sasser, W. and Schlesinger, L. (1997) *The Service Profit Chain: How Leading Companies Link Profit and Growth to Loyalty, Satisfaction and Value*, New York, NY: Free Press.

Hopkinson, G. (2003) 'Stories from the front-line: how they construct the organization', *Journal of Management Studies*, 40 (8), 1943–69.

Humphreys, M. and Brown, A. (2002) 'Dress and identity: a Turkish case study', *Journal of Management Studies*, 39 (7), 927–52.

Kearney, K. and Hyle, A. (2004) 'Drawing out emotions: the use of participant-produced drawings in qualitative inquiry', *Qualitative Research*, 4 (3), 361–82.

King, C. and Grace, D. (2005) 'Exploring the role of employees in the delivery of the brand: a case study approach', *Qualitative Market Research*, 8 (3), 277–95.

Lacan, J. (1998) 'The mirror stage as formative of the function of the I as revealed in psychoanalytic experience', in J. Rivkin and M. Ryan (eds), *Literary Theory: an Anthology*, Oxford, UK: Blackwell Publishers, 178–83.

Labov, W. (1997) 'Some further steps in narrative analysis', *The Journal of Narrative and Life History*, http://www.ling.upenn.edu/~labov/sfs.html, accessed 4 May 2010.

McQuarrie, E. and Glenn, M. (2003) 'Visual and verbal rhetorical figures under directed processing versus incidental exposure to advertising', *Journal of Consumer Research*, 29 (4), 579–87.

Miles, S. and Mangold, W. (2007) 'Growing the employee brand at ASI: a case study', *Journal of Leadership and Organizational Studies*, 14 (1), 77–85.

Mohtashemi, A. (2002) 'Why companies should brandish their 'Internal Brand', *European Business Forum*, 9 (Spring), 65–70.

Muller, J. (1985) 'Lacan's mirror stage', *Psychoanalytic Inquiry*, 5, 233–52.

Muniz, A. and O'Guinn, T. (2001), 'Brand community', *Journal of Consumer Research*, 27 (4), 412–32.

O'Cass, A. and Grace, D. (2004) 'Service brands and communication effects', *Journal of Marketing Communications*, 10, 241–54.

Padgett, D. and Allen, D. (1997) 'Communicating experiences: a narrative approach to creating service brand image', *Journal of Advertising*, 26 (4), 49–62.

Papasolomou, I. and Vrontis, D. (2006) 'Building corporate branding through internal marketing: the case of the UK retail bank industry', *The Journal of Product and Brand Management*, 15 (1), 37–47.

Parasuraman, A. and Grewal, D. (2000) 'The impact of technology on the quality-value-loyalty chain: a research agenda', *Journal of Academy of Marketing Science*, 28, 168–74.

Penaloza, L. and Venkatesh, A. (2006) 'Further evolving the new dominant logic of marketing: from services to the social construction of markets', *Marketing Theory*, 6 (3), 299–316.

Pink, S. (2004) 'Visual methods', in C. Seale, G. Gobo, J. Gubrium and D. Silverman (eds), *Qualitative Research Practice*, London: Sage Publications, pp. 391–406.

Prasad, A. and Steffes, E. (2002) 'Internal marketing at Continental Airlines: convincing employees that management knows best', *Marketing Letters*, 13 (2), 75–89.

Riessman, C. (1993) *Narrative Analysis: Qualitative Research Methods Series, 30*, Newbury Park, CA: Sage Publications.

Schroeder, J. (2005) 'The artist and the brand', *European Journal of Marketing*, 39 (11–12), 1291–305.

Scott, L. (1994) 'Images in Advertising: the need for a theory of visual rhetoric', *Journal of Consumer Research*, 21 (2), 252–73.

Silverman, D. (2000) 'Analyzing talk and text', in N. Denzin and Y. Lincoln (eds), *Handbook of Qualitative Research* (2nd edition), Thousand Oaks: Sage Publications, pp. 821–34.

Simões, C., Dibb, S. and Fisk, R. (2005) 'Managing corporate identity: an internal perspective', *Journal of the Academy of Marketing Science*, 33 (2), 153–68.

Smith, S. (2011) 'Brand stories: an exploration into how employee narratives construct a service brand', Unpublished doctoral dissertation, University of Auckland, New Zealand.

Spiggle, S. (1994) 'Analysis and interpretation of qualitative data in consumer research, *The Journal of Consumer Research*, 21 (3), 491–503.

Stern, B. (1993) 'Feminist literary criticism and the deconstruction of ads: a postmodern view of advertising and consumer responses', *Journal of Consumer Research*, 19 (4), 556–66.

Stern, B., Thompson, C. and Arnould, E. (1998) 'Narrative analysis of marketing relationship: the consumer's perspective', *Psychology of Marketing*, 15 (3), 195–214.

Vallaster, C. (2004) 'Internal brand building in multicultural organisations: a roadmap towards action research', *Qualitative Market Research*, 7 (2), 100–13.

Vallaster, C. and de Chernatony, L. (2006) 'Internal brand building and structuration: the role of leadership', *European Journal of Marketing*, 40 (7–8), 761–84.

Vargo, S. and Lusch, R. (2008) 'The transition from product to service in business markets', *Industrial Marketing Management*, 37 (3), 254–9.

Weber, S. and Mitchell, C. (1995) *That's Funny You Don't Look Like a Teacher!: Interrogating Images, Identity, and Popular Culture*, London: Falmer Press.

5. The trouble with employer branding: resistance and disillusionment at Avatar

Jean Cushen

INTRODUCTION

Employer branding appears to be emerging as the human resource management (HRM) practice 'de jour' promoted by respected HRM professional bodies such as the Chartered Institute of Personnel and Development in the UK, numerous management consultants, and leading business schools. An employer brand can be understood as 'The identity of the firm as an employer. It encompasses the firm's value system, policies and behaviours toward the objectives of attracting, motivating, and retaining the firm's current and potential employees' (Ainspan and Dell, 2001: 3). Employer branding entered the HRM toolbox amidst a discourse of universal 'best practice' and 'institutional isomorphism' (DiMaggio and Powell, 1983). In other words, it is argued that implementing employer branding should yield positive results in all instances as it has been claimed to be successful in other locations.

For human resource practitioners, the cited potential of employer branding is enticing as it appears to encapsulate the hallmarks of 'good' human resource management (Boxall, 1992; Guest, 1987). For example, employer branding seeks to create a unitary cultural framework of commitment by making explicit the binding, positive, social characteristics that are supposedly common to the organization. It is, as one commentator states, 'marketing for your corporate culture' (Ferdinandi, 2010). The message of unitarism is promulgated through claims of mutual interests, that is, that living the brand is the route to achievement of both organization goals and individual fulfilment. In addition to creating a unitarist frame of reference, the practice of employer branding also promises to deliver on a second fundamental HRM objective, that of creating people management practices that support achievement of the business strategy. Increased business alignment enhances HRM's relevance and legitimacy, an issue many HRM departments struggle with (Martin et al., 2005; Sisson, 2001). Employer branding is understood to be particularly suitable for organizations that have a strong brand presence in the external consumer market and for whom the brand is a key source of competitive advantage (Anon, 2001, 2002). By appropriating the external brand to create an internal normative, behavioural framework, HRM can contribute to ensuring the ongoing sanctity of the brand. Ultimately, employer branding represents the latest step in the range of soft, cultural HRM practices that seek to galvanize employee commitment through a discourse of unitarism, mutual interests and business alignment.

In recent years, numerous commentators have claimed that considerable tensions and contradictions can arise between the unitary ideals associated with soft HRM and the harder actions required to achieve financial targets (Hodson, 2001; Keep and Rainbird, 2000; Legge, 2005; Marchington and Grugulis, 2000; Sisson, 1993; Thompson, 2003). In fact, there is an emerging perspective that within fast-changing, liberal financial markets, organizations are placing so much emphasis on achieving financial targets that soft HRM, and its unitary rhetoric of commitment and mutual fulfilment, is rendered irrelevant (Kunda and Ailon-Souday, 2005; Mintzberg at al., 2002; Peters, 2003; Ross, 2004; Thompson, 2003, 2005). In an environment of ongoing change and financial short-termism, strong cultures of commitment are portrayed as neither feasible nor desirable as they constrain the flexibility required to survive. Liberal markets, it is argued, set the rules so thoroughly that an organization 'apparently does not have time for culture and is more interested in reducing than transforming the workforce' (Thompson, 2005: 168). In fact, some 'management gurus' who once heralded the value of strong corporate cultures claim that ongoing organizational change is so endemic that, in order to survive, employees should be self-promoting and individualistic (Peters, 1999). An organization with a strong corporate culture has been described as 'an inward looking, conformist, complacent organisation, sunk into a morass of groupthink, rigid rather than flexible in its outlook' (Legge, 2005: 237).

This tension exposes the complexity of achieving alignment between HRM and the business strategy. Strategic HRM is 'about how the employment relationships for all employees can be managed in such a way as to contribute optimally to the organization's goal achievement' (Legge, 2005b: 223). This begs the question whether optimistic rhetoric of mutual, unitary interests is appropriate in cases where achievement of strategic financial targets has negative consequences for employees, particularly as 'organizational disloyalty fuels employee self-loyalty' (Kunda and Ailon-Souday, 2005: 213). Interestingly, despite the novelty associated with the concept of employer branding, the problems surrounding its implementation and impact remain caught up in the dilemma that emerged with HRM itself, namely the difficulty in balancing the soft and hard elements of people management.

This chapter[1] will explore one organization's efforts to fashion an ideal employee identity through internally disseminating an employer brand. In this case, an employer brand was designed and launched amidst continuous organization change and a range of cost-cutting initiatives, both of which were deemed to be critical to achieving financial targets. Perspectives on the role and impact of the employer brand will be provided from three stakeholders. These include the 'Brand Purveyors', namely directors and HR; 'Brand Implementers', namely line managers; and 'Brand Recipients', namely employees. Particular attention will be paid to the extent to which the employer brand succeeded in creating a unitary environment that drove employee commitment towards achievement of the business strategy. What this case demonstrates is how soft rhetoric and management claims of unitary interests, far from extracting commitment, can be counterproductive. In this case the employer branding initiative only served to direct employee attention towards the management activities that ran contrary to employee interests. In other words, organizations who claim their employer brand rests on soft HRM principles of unitarism, commitment and mutual fulfilment can actually create a rhetoric-reality gap that generates anger and frustration among employees.

THE CASE

Avatar Corporation (pseudonym) is an instantly recognizable global, market-leading provider of portable, high-technology products and services. It has made repeat appearances in listings which rank the world's top twenty most valuable brands.[2] The Avatar Ireland (Avatar) workforce consists primarily of white-collar workers in roles such as IT, engineering, marketing, sales, customer management, finance, project management, strategy, law and HR. It can be characterized as a knowledge-intensive firm as 'most of the work is said to be of an intellectual nature and... well-educated, qualified employees form the major part of the work force' (Alvesson, 2001: 863). It is largely assumed that soft cultural HRM practices, such as employer branding, are more suitable for managing knowledge workers than, for example, hierarchy and bureaucracy (Flood et al., 2001; Legge, 2005: 11; Newell et al., 2002). This is because of a second assumption, namely that knowledge workers must possess a positive affective commitment to the organization if they are to orient their discretionary, tacit abilities towards the achievement of organization goals (Alvesson, 2001). This notion has gathered so much credence that it is claimed that the hierarchical, iron cage stereotype is being replaced by another cliché, namely 'that organizations are becoming increasingly network based, organic, and flexible, and mainly knit together through bonds in the imaginary realm: values, ideas, mutual adjustment, community feelings or identity' (Kärreman and Alvesson, 2004: 163).

In 2007 I conducted an ethnographic study within Avatar which was the Irish subsidiary of Avatar Corporation. This involved working for six months within the HR department. Seventy-five in-depth, semi-structured interviews were conducted. A wide range of documentation and processes pertaining to the organization's business and people management strategies were reviewed. Formal observations were undertaken through attending 25 meetings. During the interviews and meetings all individuals were aware of my status as a PhD student conducting research.

Top management claimed the Avatar brand was a key strategic asset that accounted for much of Avatar's success in consumer markets. Therefore maintaining the sanctity of the brand was of fundamental concern. The core tenet of the Avatar brand was that Avatar did not just provide certain products and services; instead, Avatar products and services provided consumers with a certain experience, a feeling that they were living each moment to its fullest potential. While it was accepted that products, services and technologies evolved, the one constant exchange between Avatar and its consumers was this brand experience.

Each day I took the employee bus to Avatar. Stepping onto the bus was the first act of entering Avatar's branded world. The outside of the bus contained bright vivid brand imagery of young people having fun alongside statements describing how exciting, action-packed and high energy the bus journey should be. The journey itself was supposed to be part of the Avatar brand experience. The Irish headquarters of Avatar were compelling and described by Avatar as a 'state of the art corporate village'. The internal decor of the atrium-style building was a prominent reflection of the brand. The primary colour was light beige and the main variation of that came from the colourful and often dramatic wall hangings describing the brand through vibrant imagery and text. Ultimately the physical setting was a combination of bright, spacious, minimalist, branded decor populated by smartly dressed individuals carrying high-tech accessories. Entering the building for the first couple of times was compelling, as there was a sense of entering an intoxicating microcosm of branded glamour, success, creative, high-energy youthfulness. Avatar overtly called for all employees to 'live' the brand through an initiative termed 'brand essence'.

BRAND ESSENCE

Brand essence originated in the Avatar Corporation marketing department following an exercise with a consulting firm to explore consumer's perception of the brand. Avatar Corporation decided that what consumers claimed was positive and unique about the brand in the external market could be harnessed internally to create a normative behavioural framework. Brand essence consisted of three brand characteristics, the enactment of which was positioned as essential to organization and individual success. The unitary premise and strategic importance of brand essence was emphasized by the Avatar CEO, who stated:

> You need an organization that is fully aligned with what you're trying to do so that people have a common purpose and you need to have embedded the brand value and culture into the organization such that what [Avatar] is giving the customer is a very seamless and consistent experience.

For the purposes of anonymity the exact language will not be used; in general terms, however, the three characteristics called for employees to be passionate, dependable and innovative. Ultimately, branding logic of extracting additional value through positive association was applied internally to stimulate desired employee behaviours. This was described by the HR director, who stated:

> The whole [brand essence] concept was saying in order to be an ongoing successful company we had to differentiate ourselves in the eyes of our customer and in order to deliver that 'wow' customer experience we needed to be a certain way ourselves, to live the brand from the inside out. And the way we're going to describe that brand or that customer experience from an internal perspective is that we want to be [passionate, dependable and innovative].

A HR manager described the importance of aligning the external and internal brand in order to portray the organization in a certain light:

> I think externally we get pressure that [brand essence] is what the culture is like in here because that's what our external brand says. It does come down from the corporate literature and from the top. You'd have the Corporation CEO having to talk to the [financial markets] about us being very innovative.

All employees completed brand essence training. A senior manager described the initial launch of brand essence, stating:

> There were whole road-shows done on it. So it kicked off with the larger scale management team where there was full day workshops on it off-site, but done in like a really cool way where you sat in beanbags rather than sitting in chairs and stuff like that. That launched the whole idea and the reasons behind it; what it would mean to us, how we were going to work. And then that theme was rolled throughout the rest of the business where managers came back and did de-briefs on it. But then everybody got to go to some sort of workshop or some sort of a session where it was the same sit on a bean-bag type of experience.

Employees at all levels completed these brand essence workshops. Employees were provided with reading materials and DVDs outlining how to feel and behave in a way that was consistent with brand essence. A director, quoted in the reading materials and DVD, stated 'Every strong brand has its own unique personality. The characteristics that set it apart from the rest... Our brand essence is who we are; it's how we behave and how we make people feel.'

The ideal employee identity was portrayed as being a direct reflection of the brand. It was the brand manifested in embodied feelings and behaviours. Avatar top management were featured in the DVD heralding the importance of each individual in espousing brand essence; as one director stated, 'Each one of us plays an important part in making [the brand] live and creating an evermore unique and inspiring experience for our customers.

This message was delivered to employees in overtly unitary rhetoric with the overriding message being that 'living' the brand was the route to organizational and individual success. Below is a typical excerpt from brand essence material distributed to inductees:

> Imelda is Head of a Department in Avatar Ireland and she's passionate about the Avatar Brand. 'I [Imelda] live and breathe it, and try to bring it to life in everything I do. And once you've got everyone else around you doing it, and it's an innate part of your organization, it can be an amazingly powerful thing... It's all about being passionate, enquiring and creative in what you do. You just have to believe it and make it part of you – the rest will follow.'

The brand essence materials provided to employees contained lengthy definitions of the three brand characteristics. Terms such as warmth, honesty, humanity, empathy, integrity, life's journey, best in class, challenging, inspiring, creative and optimism were all tied to what the Avatar brand essence experience was all about. There was also extensive use of dramatic, colourful, high-energy imagery to bring the three characteristics to life and convey the message that each moment should be understood as an experience.

Ultimately the training materials explicitly communicated to employees how they were supposed to feel and subsequently behave. In terms of feelings, employees were required to feel inspired to see each moment as an experience and an opportunity to be passionate, dependable and innovative. The guidelines around behaviours focused primarily on communications. For example, to help employees 'live' brand essence, specific tips were provided on how to write, talk and manage one's body language. During the training, sample emails were distributed and videos of conversations and meetings were shown. These sample communications were then labelled 'on brand' or 'off brand' depending on the extent to which the language and tone of the communications were deemed to be passionate, dependable and innovative. There was no subtlety regarding the need to self-regulate in order to behave and communicate in a manner that was 'on brand'.

The brand essence characteristics also guided work as if they were the premise for decision-making. For example, proposals for new products and services, and even internal initiatives, were assessed against the three specified characteristics to ensure they were 'on brand'. This meant that employees had to communicate their ideas in terms of the characteristics. In fact, to be labelled 'off brand' signalled the death knell for any idea. As such the brand operated in a political sense to legitimize some ideas and delegitimize others. Ultimately, brand essence was the dominant official normative paradigm running through Avatar positioned as key to achieving financial success and the delivery of return to shareholders.

AVATAR IRELAND FINANCIAL TARGETS

Avatar Corporation is a 'Fortune 500' company and categories of Avatar Corporation's 'high technology' shares are listed on some of the world's major stock exchanges. The shareholder relationship was managed by Avatar Corporation, which pursued a high dividend payout ratio. This meant that a higher proportion of earnings were paid to shareholders than what was retained and reinvested in the organization. As a profit-and-loss subsidiary of Avatar Corporation, Avatar Ireland experienced considerable financial pressures to achieve the financial targets set with Avatar Corporation. Avatar Corporation wielded firm control over subsidiary financial performance and the parent–subsidiary budgetary exchanges were the primary mechanism facilitating this control. Specifically, Avatar Ireland was targeted with maximizing revenue while reducing costs. The need to maximize revenue by staying strategically competitive while reducing costs was described by a director in Avatar Ireland who stated:

> The only way you can compete in a competitive world is by having the lowest cost base because if you don't, you're just not going to be competitive, regardless of what you do on the top. So, that's a message to the organisation. 'You have to reduce costs, have to be more lean, have to be more efficient, have to be more process oriented, have to be more boring,' because reducing costs is boring. At the same time as that's happening, we are driving a need to make a new world happen and to make sure that Avatar is playing a key part in new business models that will be the business models of the future. Which requires innovation... I think the cost saving together with the innovation is sending two messages to people at the same time and it's putting people under a lot of pressure and constraints.

During the period of the ethnography a range of cost reduction initiatives had either recently been completed or were ongoing. These included redundancies, outsourcing and centralization of a number of functions to other subsidiaries. There was also a range of miscellaneous measures that impacted employees such as reduced bonus payments, shutting off the air conditioning system at 5 p.m., switching to cheaper office supplies, providing fewer beverages at coffee stations throughout the building and reducing canteen menu options. In addition to the cost cutting, Avatar went through continuous organization restructuring in order to deliver the constantly evolving suite of products and services. This involved taking apart and changing the organization structure. Teams and roles would cease to exist and new ones created. Affected individuals often had to apply for one of the newly created roles, work within a newly formed team and work for a new manager. During the course of the six-month ethnography, three re-organizations were conducted that significantly changed the organization structure.

Ultimately, within Avatar, the initiatives undertaken to achieve financial targets often resulted in job insecurity and/or change for employees. As will be highlighted in the remainder of this chapter, the combination of the brand essence, cost cutting and job insecurity created considerable tensions for managers and employees.

THE BRAND PURVEYORS

The purveyors of brand essence in Avatar Ireland, namely the directors and HR, recognized that Avatar frequently went through periods of change and uncertainty. However, they claimed that brand essence had been designed with this in mind and the characteristics of being passionate, innovative and dependable could be adapted to stimulate the different behaviours required for different situations. For example, certain situations might call for an individual to focus primarily on being dependable whereas another might require greater innovativeness. However, it was important for individuals to ensure that all three characteristics were being displayed in some way. This was described by an HR manager, who stated:

> The idea of brand essence is you dial up and down depending on need but you have to have all three [brand essence characteristics]. It's what we were calling the 'Bloody Mary' effect, it's not a Bloody Mary if it doesn't have vodka, or it has vodka and it doesn't have tomato juice; it's that kind of thing.

Regardless of how the change or cost cutting initiatives affected employees, brand essence was used to inject a positive, optimistic tone into the communications surrounding such initiatives. This was described by an HR manager, who stated:

> I think the culture likes good news. Probably everybody does. I think to a degree [Avatar] finds bad news, or not good news, difficult. So we find it hard to say that things are not going as well as we thought they would. Whereas we love saying things are going well, we find that easy to do and happy to do it and great. But we

find it more difficult I think when things are not going well... We try and put a gloss on it. We'd say 'Well actually this is good news that we're going to outsource the IT department.'

The brand purveyors claimed brand essence was a tool designed to absorb the financial pressures. Brand essence was supposed to take the emphasis off the substantive issue of what was being done and place it on how it was being done; it was a normative tool for all situations.

This was perhaps most starkly evidenced by the manner in which some directors and some HR personnel claimed the recent redundancy programme had been executed in an 'on brand' manner. As stated by one director:

> Restructures and redundancies and things like that you know, it's a big big deal for people... It was funny because we did talk about when we were doing it that we would do it in a brand essence way and the funny thing about it is I think, no matter what you say, they [HR] did an incredible job of this because it could have been a hell of a lot worse than it was but I think the actual process from beginning up to actually going through with it and migrating to the new structure was really, really good, really people-centric... So actually, funnily enough it was probably one of the best kind of expressions of brand essence.

At first glance, brand essence appears to be a compelling optimistic, unitary people management tool that overtly regulates behaviours, is unique to the organization, facilitates changing business environments, and absorbs harsh business decisions. If this was the case, brand essence should have been an invaluable tool for line managers who were tasked with implementing the change and cost reduction while meeting targets at the team level. However, for line managers, it became quickly apparent that employee resistance was so strong that using brand essence was counterproductive.

THE BRAND IMPLEMENTERS

Managers were supposed to use brand essence as a tool to communicate to their teams in order to bring about change and guide their team towards achievement of targets. Elaborate communication materials were provided to managers for this purpose. However, most managers claimed they were faced with instant resistance from employees when they attempted to integrate brand essence into daily working life. Managers reported that the main problem was how the optimistic rhetoric required employees to view all business decisions in a positive light regardless of the actual consequences. In this case, the soft rhetoric of brand essence, far from soothing the harsher business messages, only served to focus attention on the plurality of interests. A middle level manager described his team's reaction to brand essence, stating:

People really hate [brand essence]. I was surprised because the way these things come down, as a manager you're sort of told you've got to feed this to your team and fine OK, I'll roll in, I'll do the job and I'll pass it out, it's fairly innocuous, we can ignore it at a reasonable level; and you sort of pass it out. Then you get this whoosh, 'will you shut up about that bloody thing, it's awful'. People were sort of saying 'well they [Avatar] don't tell the truth, they don't do this, they don't do that'. So you've got a list of all these things that you want people to do, but you're not doing them yourself, now that came down strongly.

A senior manager whose area had been impacted by redundancies and outsourcing claimed brand essence was:

one of the craziest things that was brought in. I understand and I agree with the sentiments of it, but I think the way it's being rammed down our throats is crazy... given everything else that was going on in the company; it was the last straw for people... throwing in something like that when they were after doing [redundancies].

Another middle level manager discussed how the unitary premises of the framework actually served to irritate employees:

It would be seen probably by a lot of people as, as being a little bit sort of fake... If you're not together as a company, putting out a poster saying 'We're all together as a company' is bad rather than good. It's not seeming to address the issues that are over there. And people would say 'Well, you know, we can see the problems, we know the problems are there. Why doesn't the company do something about addressing them instead of putting out posters?'

Some managers took a more critical stance towards organizational attempts to shape personal attitudes, values and feelings and interpreted the resistance as employee aversion to having their subjectivity managed:

That [brand essence] was universally slammed in the department I worked in. The key reason I can think of is that inherently I just think it's very patronising from a corporate perspective to dictate to people how they should feel as a company. I just feel that they're treating us a little bit like we're a bit immature or something. That's the overriding sense I get is that people are going 'Why are you telling me to be dependable, because if I wasn't dependable, I wouldn't be here or I wouldn't be doing the job I'm doing?' I don't think [Directors/HR] have really understood that that's the sense that people get. I think they just think it's a 'rah rah Avatar!' kind of thing. But I think the deeper reason is that people are just turned off and go 'you're just really patronising me'. And I sense that as well. I must say I was thinking it. But again you play the game, if that's what Avatar want you to do, you put it on the end of your emails and it's no skin off my nose but it ain't gonna motivate me or make me work any differently. I think they're a bit naive if they think it does.

While line managers attempted to roll out brand essence, they claimed that far from being a unitary, galvanizing force it actually became counterproductive.

The brand essence claims that Avatar represented certain optimistic ideals only drew attention to the decisions and behaviours of top management that employees felt ran contrary to these ideals. Furthermore, the perception that top management were requesting employees to work according to a higher value code than they set themselves caused a significant level of vitriol. This sentiment was further explained by employees.

BRAND RECIPIENTS

Employees corroborated managers' accounts of instant resistance to brand essence. Almost all employees interviewed professed to have a strong negative reaction to it. The most common explanation for this adverse reaction was the gap between soft rhetoric and their harsher reality. This was explained by an employee who stated:

> It's very hard to swallow, extremely hard, they're telling you one day how important you are to them and the next day they're making more redundant. They're telling you there's not enough people to do the job, and they're agreeing that they're trying to do something about it. Then they're letting all these people go and they're not taking people on to replace them. It's just hypocrisy after hypocrisy; they don't eat their own dog food basically.

The unitary premises of brand essence were directly attacked by another employee who stated:

> I suppose they want to sell their brand to you so you can go and sell it on, they want you to understand what you're trying to achieve and what they're trying to achieve and how you fit in to that big plan. But drawing it up and saying this is what we do really well is bullshit... When they're ignoring I suppose some of the core issues... It [the brand essence workshop] was about three hours long, and it was about three hours at some ridiculously busy time of the year as well and I thought 'I don't need to be sitting here making Avatar feel good about itself.'

So, far from being a unifying framework the extent to which it was deemed to create a rhetoric–reality gap served to invoke a collective adversarial reaction from employees, as stated by one:

> I think [brand essence] is actually good in that it forms a common enemy. It has banter around it do you know what I mean, like a bad boss can do that as well, can get a whole team together to slag them behind their back... everyone clings together a bit better.

A similar perspective was offered by an employee who claimed that brand essence was actually detrimental to achieving work-related goals as 'It probably has a bad effect as people start bitching about it for about half an hour every time somebody says it.' Another employee commented, 'The purpose of it from high above would be I suppose to try and get their staff to be more motivated and efficient, but I think what it does in Ireland anyway is just it's annoying. I wouldn't say a single person is a percent more efficient.'

The rhetoric–reality gap was not the only reason employees rejected brand essence. Many simply resisted such overt attempts of normative control. Many employees expressed surprise that Avatar would attempt to regulate subjectivity through a construct that was as blatantly artificial and vacuous as a brand. Employees had experience of creating brand-related materials for products and services in order to extract higher value from consumers. Consequently they were keenly aware of the manufactured, contrived nature of branding and how it was used as a tool to shape beliefs. Ultimately employees were not willing to be duped by their own propaganda. Interestingly, although HR and the directors launched brand essence in Avatar Ireland, most employees intuitively guessed it came from an external marketing agency and referred to it as marketing speak that they prided themselves on seeing through. For employees, usage of brand essence became an indicator of falseness: as one employee described:

> The managers were always using it but we'd always shoot 'em down... You kind of scratch your head and say 'Oh come on, we're sitting here and we're having a discussion about something... we can be frank with each other and be blunt.'

This idea that Avatar employees were sufficiently savvy to see through was keenly evident as described by one employee:

> For professionals like me or relatively intelligent people it really is insulting... massively negative, it's like 'where's my school uniform?' when I'm getting up in the morning. I'm a professional you know, I've been to college and I've done all these things and I've qualified and you know there's people even more qualified than me and they're suffering this.

Another employee put it more simply, stating 'I think [brand essence] doesn't give people enough credit for having a brain.'

CONCLUSION

The asserted potential of employer branding is indeed enticing for any HR department looking to unleash that 'Holy Grail' of extra functional, discretionary effort through a 'best practice' unitary discourse of commitment that directly reflects broader business goals and activities. However, the failure of the Avatar brand essence to have the desired effect is symptomatic of two broader challenges that have consistently dogged the practice of HRM.

Firstly, the story of employer branding in Avatar Ireland highlights the difficulty of adopting a soft, high road rhetoric of unitarism and mutual commitment amidst an environment of financial short-termism. Reducing costs and continuously changing the organization structure represents a turn to harder HRM practices associated with headcount resource management (Torrington and Hall, 1987; Tyson and Fell, 1986). Employees felt that Avatar top management paid more heed to the hard principles of headcount resource management than they did to upholding the softer values of brand essence. Employees specifically resented that they were expected to feel and demonstrate their 'passion, reliability and innovativeness' about all decisions no matter what the consequences were for employees. Ultimately the effect of brand essence was to draw attention to a gap between what top management preached and what they practised.

The second challenge the Avatar case study highlights are the problems associated with the universal notions of 'best practice' human resource management. The Avatar case particularly highlights the need for HR practitioners to reflect more on the validity of 'best practice' claims by HR professional bodies and consultants, particularly as such parties are likely to have vested interests in appropriating notions of best practice (Alvesson, 1990). For example, among such respected HR institutes Avatar's brand essence was celebrated and publicized as a success story. This dichotomy between how HR present their initiatives and how these initiatives are received in the organization raises the need for more in-depth analysis that go beyond the viewpoint of those whose own legitimacy is dependent on these practices being seen in a positive light.

Despite employees' negative reaction, brand essence in Avatar remained the overarching normative rhetoric that, on the surface, espoused the social characteristics that bound the organization for the purposes of delivering business goals. However, brand essence made no real inroads into the working life of employees and certainly did not serve to overtly regulate behaviours. The obvious question this raises is why the purveyors opted to persist with implementing a practice so far removed from the reality of the employment experience. The answer appears to be that the other option for HRM, that is, a pluralistic, adversarial and harsher truth, was simply unbecoming of a market-leading firm.

Ultimately the Avatar case raises questions about the feasibility of unitarism and the validity of best HR practice. The Avatar case also highlights how, when an organization makes normative behavioral claims, it creates a rhetoric–reality stick with which it can be beaten. Employees in Avatar were fully cognisant of the prescribed role of brand essence and for them it became a standard by which they measured not just their own behaviours but the behaviours of top management. Perhaps then, before business executives and HR call upon employees to 'live the brand', they need to stop and ask whether they are capable of doing it themselves.

NOTES

1. This chapter has been developed from an earlier article from the same author, 'Branding Employees', *Qualitative Research in Accounting and Management*, 6 (1/2), 2009.
2. http://www.millwardbrown.com/Sites/Optimor/Content/KnowledgeCenter/BrandzRanking. aspx.

REFERENCES

Ainspan, N. and Dell, D. (2001) *Engaging Employees Through Your Brand*, New York: The Conference Board, Inc.

Alvesson, M. (1990) 'On the Popularity of Organizational Culture', *Acta Sociologica*, 33 (1), 31–49.

Alvesson, M. (2001) 'Knowledge work: ambiguity, image and identity', *Human Relations*, 54 (7), 863–86.

Anon (2001) 'Building employer brands', *Business Europe*, 41 (10), 1–3.

Anon (2002) 'The 100 top brands', *Business Week*, (5 August), 77–80.

Boxall, P.F. (1992) 'Strategic Human Resource Management: Beginnings of a new Theoretical Sophistication?', *Human Resource Management Journal*, 2 (3), 60–79

DiMaggio, P. and Powell, W. (1983) 'The iron cage revisited: institutional isomorphism and collective rationality in organizational fields', *American Sociological Review*, 48 (2), 147–60.

Ferdinandi, C. (2010) 'Employer Branding through Social Media'. http://renegadehr. net/employer-branding-through-social-media, accessed 20 January 2010.

Flood, P.C., Turner, T., Ramamoorthy, N. and Pearson, J. (2001) 'Causes and consequences of psychological contracts among knowledge workers in the high technology and financial services industries', *International Journal of Human Resource Management*, 12 (7), 1152–65.

Guest, D.E. (1987) 'Human resource management and industrial relations', *Journal of Management Studies*, 24 (5), 503–21.

Hall, P. and Soskice, D. (eds) (2000) *Varieties of Capitalism: The Institutional Foundations of Comparative Advantage*, New York: Oxford University Press Inc.

Hodson, R. (2001) *Dignity at Work*. Cambridge: Cambridge University Press.

Karreman, and M. Alvesson, D. (2004) 'Cages in tandem: Management control, social identity, and identification in a knowledge-intensive firm', *Organization*, 11 (1), 149–75.

Keep, E. and Rainbird, H. (2000) 'Towards the Learning Organization?', in Bach, S. and K. Sisson (eds) *Personnel Management*, Oxford: Blackwell, pp. 173–94.

Kunda, G. and Ailon-Souday, G. (2005) 'Managers, Markets and Ideologies – Design and Devotion Revisited', in Ackroyd, S., R. Batt, P. Thompson and P. Tolbert (eds) *Oxford Handbook of Work and Organization*, Oxford: Oxford University Press, pp. 200–19.

Legge, K. (2005) *Human Resource Management: Rhetorics and Realities*, Hampshire: Palgrave Macmillan.

Legge, K. (2005b) 'Human Resource Management', in Ackroyd, S., R. Batt, P. Thompson and P. Tolbert (eds) *Oxford Handbook of Work and Organization*, Oxford: Oxford University Press, pp. 220–41.

Marchington, M. and Grugulis, I. (2000) 'Best practice' human resource management: perfect opportunity or dangerous illusion?', *International Journal of Human Resource Management*, 11 (6), 1104–24.

Martin, G., Beaumount, P., Doig, R. and Pate, J. (2005) 'Branding: A New Performance Discourse for HR', *European Journal of Management*, 23 (1), 76–88.

Mintzberg, H., Simons, R. and Basu, K. (2002) 'Beyond Selfishness', *MIT Sloan Management Review*, 44 (1): 67–74.

Newell, S., Robertson, M., Scarborough, H. and Swan J. (2002) *Managing Knowledge Work*, Basingstoke: Palgrave Macmillan.

Peters, T. (1999) *The Brand You 50: Fifty ways to Transform Yourself from an 'Employee' into a Brand that Shouts Distinction, Commitment, and Passion!*, New York: Knopf Inc.

Peters, T. (2003) *Re-Imagine! Business Excellence in a Disruptive Age*, London: Dorling Kindersley.

Ross, P. (2004) *No Collar: The Humane Workplace and its Hidden Costs*, Philadelphia, PA: Temple University Press.

Sisson, K. (1993) 'In search of HRM', *British Journal of Industrial Relations*, 31 (2), 201–10.

Sisson, K. (2001) 'Human resource management and the personnel function – a case of partial impact?' in J. Storey (ed.) *Human Resource Management: A Critical Text* (3rd edn), London: Thomson Learning.

Thompson, P. (2003) 'Disconnected Capitalism: or why employers can't keep their side of the bargain', *Work Employment and Society*, 17 (2), 359–78.

Thompson, P. (2005) 'Part II – Introduction' in Ackroyd, S., R. Batt, P. Thompson and P. Tolbert (eds) *Oxford Handbook of Work and Organization*, Oxford: Oxford University Press, pp. 165–75.

Torrington, D. and Hall, L. (1987) *Personnel Management, A New Approach*, London: Prentice-Hall.

Tyson, S. and Fell, A. (1986) *Evaluating the Personnel Function*, London: Hutchinson.

6. Internalizing the brand? Identity regulation and resistance at Aqua-Tilt

Stephanie Russell

INTRODUCTION

This chapter explores empirically the process of employee branding and seeks to explore the various ways in which employees are encouraged to internalize the brand. In particular it examines the ways in which the brand can be harnessed to encourage individual–organizational identification. The data are drawn from an ethnographic investigation of Aqua-Tilt, a global manufacturer in the passive fire industry. This industry covers the manufacturing and installation of fire protection products, such as ceiling panels, fire doors and cavity wall barriers. The headquarters of Aqua-Tilt are located in the north of England, where I undertook research as part of a wider investigation into the impact of deregulation and voluntary compliance in the private sector. The concept of employee branding highlights how organizations seek to shape employees' behaviour so that they are more inclined to externalize the organization's brand through their everyday work behaviour. The increase in interest surrounding the process of employee branding is widely considered to include a range of aspects such as work on training and development (Miles and Mangold, 2004; Callaghan and Thompson, 2002) and décor and artefacts (Chugh and Hancock, 2009; Hancock and Tyler, 2000). Acknowledgement has also been made to the role of customer-orientated discourses on encouraging organizational identification (du Gay and Salaman, 1992) and how this can result in increased forms of control which employees actively seek to resist (Wallace and de Chernatony, 2009).

The account provided in this chapter will seek to acknowledge the ways in which cultural techniques have been used to harness the brand at Aqua-Tilt. Specifically, the focus will be on exploring these through the lens of ethnographic data sources, including interviews, non-participant observation and documentary analysis. I aim to contribute to existing literature on this topic by shedding light on how the different techniques used to communicate the brand are shrouded and underpinned by a discourse which is focused primarily on customer sovereignty. Attention is also paid to how employers come to regulate and modify employees' behaviour through these practices and how subsequently this can lead to individuals' resisting as they seek to claim back an, arguably more authentic, sense of 'self'. The chapter is organized as follows. First, background details of the case study organization are provided. This is followed by a theoretical insight into the concept of employee branding which contextualizes the account this chapter will provide. This is followed by an account of the methodology adopted in the research. The subthemes of training and development and décor and artefacts are then explored and analysed with a view to examining the ways in which the organization encourages identification with the brand. Interwoven throughout this chapter is a consideration of the notion of customer sovereignty as the underlying discourse through which employees are encouraged (and indeed coerced) into buying into the brand. In the latter part of the chapter the employee branding process is examined as a form of organizational control which produces tactics of resistance among employees. Concluding comments are then provided.

AQUA-TILT

Aqua-Tilt is a global organization located in the north of England and it is actively involved in international sales operating in more than 120 countries worldwide. The company is a world leader in developing, manufacturing and marketing top-quality products for professional customers in the construction industry. It specializes in products used in drilling and demolition, diamond coring and cutting, measuring, fire-stopping and screw fastening.

Aqua-Tilt was founded in 1941 by two brothers who established the first factory in Liechtenstein. After World War II, the organization became directly involved in international sales and during the 1970s the organization consisted of 420 employees and had sales worth €27.3 million. This growth continued until 1980 when, despite four plants having been built around the world which constituted the hub of Aqua-Tilt, sales stagnated at €817.6 million. Changes were implemented in not only cost structure and sales, but this also initiated the first culture development process and emphasis was more directly placed on improving the organization's brand and advertising techniques. Over the last decade, Aqua-Tilt has directly addressed these initial concerns, leading to more focus being placed on the desired brand image and a strongly branded organizational culture, which sought to enhance its competitive advantage. The organizational structure consists of four main 'team roles' which emerged from the attempts to re-engineer the culture. These consisted of the 'Strategic Sherpa Team'; 'Culture Journey Sherpa Teams'; The 'Leadership Sherpa Team' and 'Team Member Sherpa Team'. The latter two groups are both situated at Aqua-Tilt headquarters. The 'leadership' group is allocated to each team in order to facilitate the branding process and rectify misaligned issues, while the 'Team Member Sherpa Team' consists of employees who are subject to the branding process and are expected to share the experience with customers when applicable.

EMPLOYEE BRANDING: REGULATION AND CONTROL

Branding has been long established in the marketing literature as a means by which to classify, identify and distinguish organizations from one another and enhance their competitive offerings (Kotler et al., 2005). The mechanism through which this process occurs draws upon external promotion devices such as advertising (Keller, 1993). Branding has not only been applied to tangible products but also more recently to intangible products (Krishnan and Hartline, 2001) which provides the point of departure in considering how branding also involves employees. Employee branding extends the traditional perspective, which was largely limited to the branding of products, as it seeks to utilize the internal organization's practices and techniques to align employees with the brand, thereby increasing organizational commitment and loyalty. According to Kapferer (1997), brand identity includes externalized and internalized features as it involves the relationship between sender and receiver. Externalization refers to the process whereby the brand is projected outwards in a tangible and visible format, while internalization involves how the receiver is influenced by the brand's attributes in terms of its effect on self-identity and meaning (Kapferer, 1997). The latter includes incorporating facets of the brand's 'culture' in terms of a 'set of values feeding the brand's inspiration' (Kapferer, 1992: 101). It is through externalizing a brand's attributes that employees and customers can adopt it as their own, thus internalizing it. By internalizing, they can therefore externalize; it becomes a benign circle.

The essence of employee branding within this chapter can be explored through the lens of regulation and control. Branding can regulate individuals' identities and behaviour, and in doing so, act as a form of disciplinary control (Foucault, 1977). As Alvesson and Willmott (2002: 622) identified, employees are required to 'buy in' to the culture and act in ways which meet the organization's norms and values; this can result in them suppressing their individuality. This is supported by Willmott (1993), who explored the darker side of culture and identity regulation by arguing that it prevents employees from expressing critical thought due to the homogenization created by the norms and values. Relating this to branding, employees who subjugate themselves to the culture can reduce feelings of insecurity and anxiety, which reinforces the extent of control which such branding practices may have. As Willmott (1993: 540) stated:

Employees' willingness to subjugate themselves to the corporate culturalism is procured by the sense of identity, security and self-determination that devotion to corporate values promises to deliver.

Recent theorists have also contributed to this topical literature by arguing that specific brand practices can be enacted which aid employees in communicating the brand to customers. These have ranged from the importance of training and development procedures (Miles and Mangold, 2004: 540; Callaghan and Thompson, 2002) to décor and artefacts (Warren, 2008; Hancock and Tyler, 2000).

Miles and Mangold (2005) found in their employee branding study of Southwest Airlines that training and development was designed to clarify and reinforce the values of the organization, thus influencing employee behaviour. It took place at the company's 'University For People' (2004: 540), which provided knowledge of the organization's culture, values and skills for the job. Other training also involved videos such as 'Keeping the Spirit Alive', which was meant to orient employees to the 'Southwest Spirit' (Miles and Mangold, 2004: 540). As Callaghan and Thompson (2002) argue, companies often seek only those employees who demonstrate the 'right' attitudes on arrival. This saves them having to invest in training employees as they already have the necessary qualities. Training and development therefore help employees to deliver brand values by motivating them to enact brand-supporting behaviour.

Awareness of the correct attitude is only one aspect of employee branding: ensuring that it remains consistent is also important. The internal forms of communication regarding décor and artefacts of the building are just as essential. Hancock and Tyler (2000) found in their study of flight attendants that employees were expected to embody the desired aesthetic of the company. This included speaking in the organizational tone of voice and having a flexible personality; in fact employees' bodies were required to become artefacts in the same way as any other object. Moreover, Chugh and Hancock's (2009) study of two hairdressing salons in the UK found that artefacts contributed to the 'landscaping' (Gagliardi, 1992: 13 cited in Chugh and Hancock, 2009: 464) of the salons as they generated responses among employees which aligned them to their place of work. This was in order to ensure that an inter-relationship existed between artefacts and employees; for instance, the salon's colour scheme of black and white interior was matched to the organizational dress code. This similarity spread as far as the furniture and other branded items (Chugh and Hancock, 2009).

Studies of employee branding appear to have been driven by a focus on either how organizations can enhance their brand and the strategies required to achieve this (Mitchell, 2002), or alternatively how employees are exposed to the brand and the effects this has on their working practices (Warhurst and

Nickson, 2007). What seems to be missing is acknowledgement of how the practices associated with communicating the brand are underpinned by a series of dominant discourses. This chapter explores one such discourse, that of consumer sovereignty. The programmes associated with employee branding may appear to be separate from one another, but they are in fact interlinked and driven by a discourse whose aim is to enchant customers. Moreover, when explored ethnographically, employees' 'lived experience' of these processes can be brought to the fore.

METHODOLOGY

I initially gained access to Aqua-Tilt through a number of contacts I had made with employees, having met them at corporate events and been introduced to them through other respondents. I then revisited the organization on numerous occasions, having maintained contact with some individuals. The fieldwork took place between February and April 2009 and consisted of employing a variety of ethnographic methods, including interviews and non-participant observation (Van Maanen, 1988). I formally interviewed ten individuals from a range of job positions, including the cultural team leader, fire engineers, sales consultants and call centre employees. Opportunities also arose which enabled me to conduct impromptu chats with other employees, such as during lunch, or as I waited for my other interviewees to arrive. Non-participant observation was also possible when I was left to sit and observe as I waited for respondents to return from a meeting. A tour of the building also drew my attention to the artefacts that were being utilized to communicate the brand.

Regarding documentary analysis, I was provided a copy of the 'Team Camp Guide', which is a booklet given to newly recruited employees. It is used as a communication and socialization device to orient individuals to the company. The values and mission statement are discussed in the booklet and activities are also provided which employees are expected to undertake. These include tasks such as answering questions about themselves and the company. For example, 'What is a personal goal of mine that will fulfil the organizational value of integrity?' (Team Camp Guide, 2004: 56). Additionally, the company website provided access to the annual company reports, the history of the company and leadership documents. Such documentary methods reinforce what the organization expects of its employees and enhances knowledge and understanding of the company's values and cultural principles.

During my time at Aqua-Tilt I was only able to gain access to two groups responsible for communicating the brand (Leadership Sherpa Team and Team Member Sherpa Team); therefore I interviewed individuals representative of these groups. This chapter draws on the interview transcriptions and the material recorded in a fieldwork journal. Adopting these various methods encouraged sensitivity to the 'lived experience' of those individuals involved in the research. All of the interviews at Aqua-Tilt's headquarters took place in conference rooms as opposed to the open plan offices where the majority of employees worked.

'GETTING THE RIGHT PERSON ON THE BUS': ATTRACTING THE RIGHT EMPLOYEES

Attempts to encourage employees to internalize the organizational brand (Miles and Mangold, 2004) began before they were even employed at Aqua-Tilt. The companies' recruitment advertisements typically refer to Aqua-Tilt's mission statement: 'We passionately create enthusiastic customers and build a better future!' (Team Camp Guide, 2004). Each job advertised on the company's website typically begins with a paragraph outlining the mission statement and the core values which are 'integrity'; 'courage'; 'teamwork' and 'commitment' (Team Camp Guide, 2004). This is followed by a short description of the jobs' responsibilities, titled 'Your Responsibilities', before a 'Your Profile' section, which outlined the necessary skills expected. These often included 'good communication, presentation and negotiation' skills and the need to be 'enthusiastic, proactive and self-reliant'. The close connection between the skills required for the job and the organizational values and mission statement reflects a desire on the organization's part to 'recruit the right people', individuals who will already be aligned with the brand and have the 'correct attitude' prior even to joining the organization.

Prospective employees are carefully assessed during their interviews by being asked to provide examples of situations they had experienced which showed their utilization of Aqua-Tilt's values. For instance, one employee explained, 'in my interview I was asked to describe situations which showed the core values, so where I showed courage, teamwork, commitment... I used some examples from my previous job.' By assessing employees on this basis, it was possible to clarify and reinforce the brand's values and individuals' behaviour prior to employment. Clearly, this helps to ensure that individuals working in the organization will be committed and driven to embody the brand image; employers are concerned about employees performing effectively and having qualities commensurate with the organization's image (Warhurst and Nickson, 2007).

This led to an individual–organization fit whereby individuals could align themselves with the organization and in some respects use it as a 'mirror' to reflect their own identity and vice versa (Dutton and Dukerich, 1991: 551).

As Scott and Lane (2000: 48) stated, organizational and individual identity is explicitly intertwined, as constructed organizational images not only enhance individuals' identity, but also contribute to organizational goal attainment. Attempts to determine employee attitudes are regarded as legitimate management practices as they contribute to ensuring the desired service encounter. Employers were concerned with the relationship between customer-focused employees, promoted through a discourse and their recruitment, training and development processes. In a January 2009 press release, the Human Resource Director stated:

> our brand represents premium and quality; therefore our people are the foundation of our brand. We recruit on our core values of integrity, courage, teamwork and commitment.

This was reinforced by an informal discussion with a newly recruited employee, where it became clear that alignment was an essential part of the selection process. In the process, applicants also have a choice to self-select out if the goals/values of the organization are not consistent with their own. Hannah, sales co-ordinator, commented that:

> I know the HR department are heavily involved in recruitment and I think [if] you start at that point and look for values in the individuals... before they come into the organization, there must be a really small chance that you get somebody that comes in that maybe it doesn't sit quite right with, and they don't end up believing in it.

The priorities of recruitment emerge strongly from this quote. Hannah's interpretation of the recruitment process clearly indicates that employers attempt to only employ individuals who will continue to 'believe' in the values. These cannot be trained; they have to already be part of the individual. This supports Callaghan and Thompson's (2002) work, who found that companies aim deliberately to recruit and mould individuals who already have the 'correct' attitude on entry. This is part of a wider strategy which ensures that attitudes relating to customer service and quality are reinforced, rather than skill or qualification levels. A tension exists between exhibiting 'quality' customer service and ensuring 'quantity' of goods sold (Callaghan and Thompson, 2002). A similar approach has been adopted by Southwest Airlines, who hire individuals based on attitude and values: prior to recruitment, the organization encourages employees to appreciate the values associated with the brand and this continued into the induction and orientation programmes (Miles and Mangold, 2005). The aim is therefore to reduce the dissonance between the employees' values and the organization's brand.

GOING THE EXTRA MILE: CONSUMER SOVEREIGNTY AND THE SELF-GOVERNING SUBJECT

Once employees have been selected and passed through the recruitment stage, their exposure to Aqua-Tilt's brand and organizational values becomes ever more pervasive. This was particularly evident in the 'Team Camp Guide', which new recruits receive. It was presented in the same red and white colours as the company logo and consisted of 150 pages. There were few words as the information was mainly in pictures, diagrams and symbols. The booklet was described as an 'employees' bible' as it detailed the culture of the organization and the working practices required of employees; it was carefully designed to present a consistent message to employees about what Aqua-Tilt represents and what is expected of individuals. One example was a visual articulation of required behaviour regarding 'direction' and 'change'; these were seen through the use of two pyramids. 'Change' was achievable once individuals had faced the 'brutal facts' and rectified their own behaviour in order to improve the organization. This is supported by the associated discourse in the Team Camp Guide, where it is stated that one should 'Change the organizational/team structure to [the] upside down pyramid. We are here to be responsive to our team members and customers.' Such statements are conceptually interesting and indicate that, despite the organization promoting the autonomy of employees, they are still heavily monitored and regulated.

Clearly, the training and development practices were also orientated towards affirming the discourse of customer sovereignty. Employees explained this to me in relation to their participation in a two-day induction programme that took place outside of Aqua-Tilt; this was designed to reinforce the purpose of the organization, while covering aspects of the organization's products, services and sales management. It was here that they learnt about customer service and how best to ensure that customer needs would be met and delivered appropriately. Role plays were used where individuals had to measure themselves and others on a 'DISC' behavioural scale (an acronym for 'dominance, influence, steadiness and conscientiousness'). This was used to identify each employee's strengths and weaknesses and indicated which specific attributes could be modified to improve team and customer effectiveness. The classification of the DISC profile was provided in the Team Camp Guide, along with questions such as: 'Using the DISC instrument, what specific behaviours do you wish to modify in order to increase your effectiveness on the team?'

This induction is followed up with a structured development programme consisting of a series of team camps. Employees informed me that they participated in six team camps throughout the duration of their career in the organization. These team camps were facilitated by an individual existing in the 'Leadership Sherpa Team'. The events involved team working and problem-solving activities as well as encouraging the development of trust between colleagues. These were based on 'soft' skills (Warhurst and Nickson, 2007: 105) with the emphasis on social interaction. This was specifically focused on enhancing communication between colleagues, which was subsumed within the management discourse of 'internal' customer sovereignty (du Gay and Salaman, 1992). Controlling the activities employees were involved in helped to 'create' employees who would direct their actions towards improving and enhancing the delivery of the brand's attributes in line with the customer service encounter. From the perspective of Bob, a team leader, all employees, from board members to those in the warehouse, were addressed using the same techniques. He said:

> it is all based around self-responsibility... I see people when they come on our team camps being out of their environment and I'm asking them to do things which are a bit different. They always come up with solutions and if I ask them to decorate a car or design one, it doesn't matter if they're from the board room or the warehouse, they all come up with solutions... but the point is we're not telling them how to do it.

Bob's comment that 'we're not telling them how to do it' reveals the extent to which this type of organizational control relies on subjects' self-governing practices (du Gay and Salaman, 1992).

There are several further structural examples of the (re)production of this discourse of consumer sovereignty in company initiatives. Perhaps the most obvious of these is the 'customer perfect order' (CPO). Here employees are expected to show commitment to achieving and sustaining relationships with customers and communicating the brand attributes to them. It is stated at the front of the Team Camp Guide that one of the targets that employees should strive for is 'The goal for CPO – Customer Perfect Order' – is 95%'. While of course achieving excellent levels of customer service is central to organizational competitiveness, and therefore profits, the Camp Guide instead appeals to a 'higher purpose' which 'goes beyond products and services'.

Such prioritizing of customer satisfaction, however, resulted in employees feeling that they had to put more into their work than was expected. Kim (sales co-ordinator) demonstrated this using an example where a customer rang to ask for advice on repairing a tool. Rather than simply providing only what the customer wanted, Kim asked the customer whether they would benefit from her personally arranging for one of the company representatives to visit the site in question. This would ensure that the tool was repaired correctly but also that product upgrades and safety advice could also be provided at the same time. Kim explained the result by saying 'I could have just given what the customer wanted, a tool repaired, but I went the extra mile.' It appeared that employees were expected to assume the status of servant in relation to the customer, who was always the master (Bolton and Boyd, 2003). Offering additional support and advice in the expectation that customers may report back to the company about their behaviour reflects the pervasiveness of the discourse of customer sovereignty. In this respect, the recent introduction of an annual 'Customer Opinion Survey', the results of which are published in the company magazine *Filter*, acts as a significant disciplining tool.

This resulted in immense pressure on employees and was felt by some to be an incessant process of 'trying to make customers like you' (notes from an informal discussion). Again, Kim provided an interesting example of this when she explained that two managing directors of a purchasing company were 'rude and arrogant' when she first began dealing with them. They told her 'it will take four years to get business out of us' which led her to think 'I will make you like me' and she explained to me 'that was my challenge of getting them to like me'.

IT'S TOTALLY IMBEDDED IN OUR LIVES: INTERNAL DÉCOR AND ARTEFACTS

Inside Aqua-Tilt employees experience 'everyday brand exposure' (Casteel, 2006) through the internal décor of the building. On arrival at Aqua-Tilt, one enters through automatic sliding glass doors at the front of the building and immediately encounters the reception desk. Behind the desk, on the wall, are the mission statement and core values in the organization's colour scheme along with the brand name and logo, which is displayed with white, bold lettering against a red background. As you face the reception desk, behind you are soft leather chairs separated by a small glass table which holds the latest product catalogues and in-house company magazine *Filter*. The documents are laid out in the shape of a fan with each one slightly overlapping the other. Directly adjacent on the left-hand-side wall are 'excellence' awards presented to the organization relating to customer service, delivery speed and consistency. All of these artefacts made the reception area into an exhibition suite where old and new comers alike are exposed to the brand and the image of the organization on arrival. The display of the brand continued throughout the building as the mission statement and core values had been placed on every floor and outside every lift. This was supported by photos of the winners of various awards and articles/newspaper clippings which conveyed stories and comments regarding Aqua-Tilt's success. There was also evidence of the organization having been placed in the *Sunday Times* 'top ten companies', which was an important means to convey the desirability of working for the organization as well as acting as an external public relations technique (Miles and Mangold, 2004).

The interior layout of the building included offices for four or five staff as opposed to individual offices. This arrangement was explained to me in an informal discussion I had with individuals during a lunch break. They said that it encouraged 'teamwork' and 'commitment' as it stimulated openness, creativity and sparked off ideas. In addition, clipboards and pens are available in every workspace. The team leader, Bob, explained to me that this 'encourages employees to discuss ideas and help each other. Writing things down can reinforce what is said, so it does have the potential to improve working practices.' On peering in to offices through the open doors my eye was drawn to display boards which held the mission statement and core values pinned at different angles, and posters which had been strategically chosen to emphasize values such as 'courage' or 'integrity'. These were supplemented with items such as cups, pencil holders and paper weights all bearing the company logo scattered on individuals' desks. Aesthetically, the interrelationship between Aqua-Tilt's internal colour scheme and the layout of the company meant that the communication of the brand was actively reinforced, allowing the aesthetic displays to add meaning as well as influence employees who used them. For example, Gary, a fire engineer, commented that: 'going on site with our products acts as a reminder to customers that they're working and buying from us. You know, they come to remember us through the visual products we use.'

The reception area décor was replicated throughout the building with small tables and soft comfy leather chairs being located in various places dotted around the different floors which were used as waiting areas; these were covered with copies of *Filter*, which all employees received quarterly. The magazine reinforced the values of the organization by displaying individuals who had espoused them and indicated what others could do to match their success. For example, in one case an employee had been rewarded for supporting a customer whose order had been misplaced; she maintained constant contact with him throughout and took full responsibility for the process. This is just one example of many where individuals are rewarded for authentically embodying and communicating the organizational brand.

A second example of employee reward and recognition is the scheme referred to as 'World Aqua'. Part of the scheme involved a 'Spontaneous Award' designed to 'boost morale and make employees feel valuable and worthwhile' and 'provide an opportunity for internal customers to recognize one another' (Reward and Recognition Scheme, 2009). The award was based on recognizing individual members of the organization who had contributed something such as 'making others smile', 'being helpful' or 'contributing significantly to the achievement of goals' (fieldnotes from an informal discussion). The individual concerned would be nominated by their peers and given tickets which could be used to purchase branded gifts such as a laptop bag, rucksack, drinks container or a watch. The significance of these products was exemplified when I noticed their presence in offices and on employees' desks. Individuals appeared to value these gifts displaying them prominently on their desks. To some extent they may represent a tangible reminder of individual's success in internalizing the brand; on a more basic level they may symbolize achievement.

Branded artefacts then appear to play a key role in employees' socialization into the brand as indictors of reward and recognition. Importantly in some small way these objects also act as 'carriers', carrying the brand beyond the walls of the company into employees' homes. One employee, Sarah, recalled a recent corporate event where employees all received a toy van bearing the Aqua-Tilt brand logo:

> we all got a van, you know, a miniature van and that's something which you know goes into families and stuff and it kind of filters into your home life. They are put in prominent places.

Interestingly, later on in the interview Sarah observed her feeling that the organization actively encouraged a work–life balance. Aqua-Tilt involved the family and demonstrated that 'you're not just an employee number, you're a person with a family at home as well' (comments in fieldnotes). With another member of her family also working for Aqua-Tilt, Sarah described the organization as being 'totally imbedded in our lives' (interview comments).

INTERNALIZING THE BRAND: IDENTITY REGULATION AND RESISTANCE

With the above discussion in mind, and despite the fact that some employees might be enthusiastic about employee branding, it might be argued that it is essentially a means of 'identity regulation' (Alvesson and Willmott, 2002: 625). It regulates employees' identities by encouraging them to present themselves in a way that is valuable for the organization and supports its core beliefs, norms and mindsets. Arguably this process has the potential to prevent full expression of individuality (Alvesson and Willmott, 2002; Willmott, 1993). As Kapferer (2004: 52, cited in Kärreman and Rylander, 2008: 106) commented:

> Within the company, people must recognize the brand values as their own. The internalization process is crucial.

Accommodating the brand into one's behaviour was the first step to projecting the brand to customers and colleagues. This was positively reinforced at Aqua-Tilt through the expressed need to 'exercise your passion to create "Aqua-Tilt fans"' (Team Camp Guide, 2004). Rather than just a subset of core employees who had direct contact with customers (salespeople, customer service), it was deemed necessary that every employee should represent the brand through their behaviour. The scope for employees to see their work as contributing to excellence and reinforcing Aqua-Tilt's brand and values was significant. This was further reinforced by Sarah when she explained humorously to me about how she borrows elements used in the team camps to discipline her young son. In doing so it suggests the internalization of values which she then utilizes in situations outside of Aqua-Tilt. She said:

> Those sessions can be intense but you can take aspects of it into your home life and find ways of dealing with little people... it's about using the exercises to teach your children a certain amount of self-responsibility so you don't have to chase around after them... I think in that context it's good to be used in family life. (Interview comments)

Sarah appears to be justifying the infiltration of the culture beyond the walls of the company. She admits that the sessions are 'intense' but we sense she tries to mitigate the effects of this by arguing that in particular contexts, such as teaching children self-responsibility, then the exercises can be useful. Underlying this, however, is an intense regulation of employees' internalization of the brand values which relates back to the training and development programmes where the team leader used a mirror to encourage new employees to constantly think about their personal and organizational attributes (Team Camp Guide, 2004). Using the mirror encouraged employees to identify strengths and weaknesses, to articulate action plans, and align their behaviour more directly with that of customers. It individualized employees by 'making it possible to measure gaps' (Foucault, 1977: 184) and defining 'what counts' (Fournier, 1998: 66) by identifying individuals' distance from the core elements. Talking to Sarah, it also became clear that there was a relationship between the branding process and the ways in which employees were assessed. Sarah stated:

> there's a standard throughout the company... it means that you can make sure everybody is kind of doing it in the same way and that we're all sort of having the same sort of development discussions with people. So it kind of makes sure that it does work all across the board. You will set targets that relate back to the company's values and then obviously that evaluates how you're performing in your role.

The emphasis placed here on how the company's values were part of assessing employees' behaviour and achievement indicates that it was a key strategic approach by management. This ensured that there was no incongruence between individuals and the organization. Employees were arguably attracted to the company by its ability to confirm who they are as employees and what they stand for. There were often comments about how the appraisal schemes were 'excellent' and 'brilliant' with a great deal of emphasis placed on the ability to 'learn new skills' and 'be seen as successful' (comments from field-notes). This organization was viewed as consisting of individuals who were bright and ambitious. Kim, one of the many employees who appeared to have wholeheartedly internalized Aqua-Tilt's brand values, stated:

> People have said to me that 'you are Aqua-Tilt' as you represent fully the company's values. I think that once you embody it, you begin to love it. (Discussion from fieldnotes)

Thus Kim reflected a 'conformist' self (Collinson, 2003: 536), shaping her own identity wholly in line with the brand and conforming to what was expected by the organization. However, despite Kim being classified on a core competency framework as a 'people person', this identity was challenged when a customer referred to her as 'dominating' and 'like a Rottweiler' (fieldnotes made from conversation). This raised feelings of uncertainty and insecurity as she said 'That's not who I am and that's not how I wanted to portray myself' (fieldnotes from conversation). Tied into this is the omnipresence of the customer discourse whose authority is central to employees' efforts to project desirable brand behaviour. The discourse acted as a form of control. Employees were expected to self-regulate, suppressing emotions and attitudes which risked them being perceived as not having the appropriate attributes to respond to customer sovereignty; such as failing to be empathetic or being too 'pushy'.

Employees were being encouraged to have the 'freedom to act and show initiative' (Team Camp Guide, 2004) but this was coupled by ongoing forms of control. The tour of the customer service department highlighted that performance targets and surveillance of individuals were pervasive, with a large black box showing flashing digital green headphones on screens above each team's work desk. This indicated how many calls were waiting to be answered and how long each employee had spent on the phone. Although the calls had to be dealt with effectively in order to increase customer satisfaction, this had to be undertaken in the shortest possible time in order that other customers were not left waiting. Employees working in this section of the company had more direct contact with customers and so appeared to be under more pressure consistently to display the brand's attributes and fulfil the customer orientated discourse. It was also discovered that the headquarters had recently established a global computer system which enabled control to be enhanced at the individual level. It was expressed by Bob that:

> we have a global system which gives you lots of control so our boss sitting in [head-quarters] can see what Jimmy did yesterday, during his day, can look at the number of calls he made, who he went to see, and what he said.

The discussion of employee branding so far does not acknowledge the extent to which it can range in intensity from a superficial accommodation to something which is more meaningful and internalized. This ignores the extent to which individuals can engage in 'role distance' (Goffman, 1961: 107) and the mechanisms sometimes employed to attempt to subvert the intensity of normative control devices (Willmott, 1993; Kunda, 1992). Viewing employee branding techniques as simply mechanisms that are inevitably accepted by individuals implies determinism, ignoring the underlying fractures and tensions.

In Aqua-Tilt, despite employees expressing an unquestioning acceptance about the brand's values, there were instances of 'backstage' (Goffman, 1969: 115) practices. Informal discussions identified a sense of camaraderie pervading the organization and this not only defined the essence of the brand image which brought in ideas of fun and humour, but also led to 'teamwork pranks'. For instance, two individuals I spoke to commented that the core principles underlying the reward and recognition scheme 'World Aqua', which was discussed earlier, are often jeopardized as are the supporting brand values. Teams decide among themselves to nominate all members for a reward, regardless of whether appropriate behaviour has occurred or not. Bob commented that:

> integrity is the golden one really you know... if we're sitting round in our team (looking at the table)... well there's eight of us and we say look at these [World Aqua] tickets, we've all got four each... now the idea is that you give them to people that have done something for you OK, but we could sit round here and say look, you give me your four, I'll give you my four... I know there will be some teams that do that.

Here, Bob identifies an occasion when the majority of the brand values of Aqua-Tilt are challenged; employees do not show 'integrity' or 'commitment' to the brand as they are being dishonest about their teams' performance and while teamwork is evident it is not being utilized in the 'correct' manner. This also challenges the essence of the discourse associated with customer delivery because of the lack of consistency regarding the messages being portrayed. The messages emanating from the organization regarding the emphasis on customer sovereignty, achieved through the mission statement, values and brand image, fail to be consistent. Ind (2004: 74 cited in Wallace and de Chernatony, 2009: 198) describes such employees who fail to conform to effective service delivery as 'brand saboteurs' who are 'working actively against the brand idea'. Wallace and de Chernatony (2009) contend that brand sabotage is the result of fear, overwork or excessive compliance requirements and it can be argued that Aqua-Tilt employees face similar issues. During the time of the research, Aqua-Tilt was experiencing financial constraints which had led to a stringent regime of performance monitoring. Compliance offers structure and conformance around brand values but it can also be rigid and diminish empowerment; this may explain why employees seek to resist against these constraints by engaging in deviant acts.

Despite the pervasive attempts to create a clear alignment between individuals, the brand and customers there was the potential for employees to create 'unmanaged spaces' (Bolton and Boyd, 2003: 297). By branding employees as representatives of the organization, both inside and outside the building, it appeared to prevent them from ever expressing their own sense of identity. When a situation did arise where specific organizational frameworks and guidelines were more relaxed, fleeting moments of individuality were possible. Individuals created the opportunity to subvert conventional boundaries of acceptable behaviour, thus challenging the overarching principles which branding techniques embodied.

CONCLUSION

This chapter has sought to expand understanding of two distinct practices associated with harnessing the adoption of a brand in a global manufacturer referred to as Aqua-Tilt. The chapter has recognized that employee branding is a topical and increasingly researched area of study. Consequently, it has been argued that to enhance understanding of the employee branding process, one can emphasize more directly how certain factors which individuals are exposed to, such as training and development and artefacts and décor, can in fact contribute to the mobilization of their behaviour. This subsequently leads to reinforcing the associated discourse of customer sovereignty, which is promoted and underpins the articulation of the brand. This research has indicated that employers seek to create congruence between employee attitudes at the point of entry into an organization and reinforce this through cultural practices.

In many respects, my findings have largely supported many of the conclusions from other studies cited earlier in this chapter. For instance, the emphasis placed on training and development discussed by Hancock and Tyler (2000) in terms of the regulation of body language was, although not fully explicit at Aqua-Tilt, still evident in terms of ensuring employees monitored their behaviour in line with the brand and the customer. The findings also echo Chugh and Hancock (2009), who fruitfully provided an insight into the inter-relationship between artefacts and employees, finding that colour schemes, dress codes and furniture were all consistent with enhancing the meaning of the brand. This study has attempted to contribute to the advancement of understanding surrounding these issues by firstly employing an ethnographic approach. This enabled a more in-depth insight into organizational practices while also bringing to light the pervasiveness of the customer discourse. This was an underlying thread of all the employee branding practices within Aqua-Tilt and acted as a basis from which to measure, control and modify employees' behaviour.

The chapter raises questions and debates particularly relating to the extent to which employee branding practices result in the internalization of organizational values. This process operates not only inside the company, but also outside of it as it infiltrates into domestic life. These conceptual links therefore have the distinct consequence of regulating employees' identity and can be seen operating as a form of control. By encouraging individual and organizational alignment through the discourse of consumer sovereignty, employees are expected to suppress their individuality. However, as the empirical data have demonstrated, this does not mean that individuals are mere passive subjects who simply accept the control enacted onto them. Instead, moments of resistance at Aqua-Tilt were still possible when organizational values were used to meet ends which were not in the company's interest. This provided the opportunity to challenge and ridicule the brand image. Exploring these issues in greater depth during future research could enhance understanding of how employee branding can enhance commitment, but also control, while simultaneously providing avenues for resistance and conflict.

REFERENCES

Alvesson, M. and Willmott, H. (2002) 'Identity Regulation as organizational control: Producing the appropriate individual', *Journal of Management Studies*, 39, 423–44.

Bolton, S.C. and Boyd, C. (2003) 'Trolley Dolly or Skilled Emotion Manager: Moving on from Hochschild's managed heart', *Work, Employment and Society*, 17 (2), 289–308.

Callaghan, G. and Thompson, P. (2002) '"We Recruit Attitude": The Selection and Shaping of Call Centre Labour', *Journal of Management Studies*, 39 (2), 233–54.

Casteel, J. (2006) 'Jump on the Brand Wagon: Extending Corporate Culture and Brand Identity to an Outsourcing Provider', www.brandchannel.com/brand_speak.asp?bs_id=153Original accessed 1 February 2010.

Chugh, S. and Hancock, P. (2009) 'Networks of aestheticization: the architecture, artefacts and embodiment of hairdressing salons', *Work, Employment and Society*, 23 (3), 460–76.

Collinson, D. (2003) 'Identities and Insecurities: Selves at Work', *Organization*, 10 (3), 527–47.

du Gay, P. and Salaman, G. (1992) 'The Cult[ure] of the Customer', *Journal of Management Studies*, 29 (5), 615–33.

Dutton, J.E. and Dukerich, J.M. (1991) 'Keeping an Eye on the Mirror: Image and Identity in Organizational Adaptation', *Academy of Management Review*, 34 (3), 517–54.

Foucault, M. (1977) *Discipline and Punish; The Birth of the Prison*, London: Penguin Books.

Fournier, V. (1998) 'Stories of Development and Exploitation: Militant Voices in an Enterprise Culture', *Organization*, 5 (1), 55–80.

Goffman, E. (1961) *Encounters*, Indianapolis: Bobbs-Merrill.

Goffman, E. (1969) *Presentation of the Self in Everyday Life*, London: Penguin.

Hancock, P. and Tyler, M. (2000) 'The Look of Love: Gender and the Organization of Aesthetics', in Hassard, J., Holliday, R. and Willmott, H. (eds) *Body and Organization*, London: Sage, pp. 108–29.

Kapferer, J.-N. (1992) *Strategic Brand Management*, London: Kogan Page.

Kapferer, J.-N. (1997) *Strategic Brand Management: Creating and Sustaining Brand Equity Long Term*, 2nd edn, London: Kogan Page.

Kärreman, D. and Rylander, A. (2008) 'Managing Meaning through Branding – the Case of a Consulting Firm', *Organization Studies*, 29 (1), 103–25.

Keller, K.L. (1993) 'Conceptualizing, Measuring, and Managing Customer-Based Brand Equity', *Journal of Marketing*, 57 (1), 1–22.

Kotler, P., Wong, V., Saunders, J. and Armstrong, G. (2005) *Principles of Marketing*, Harlow: Pearson Education Ltd.

Krishnan, B.C. and Hartline, M.D. (2001) 'Brand Equity: Is it more important in services?', *Journal of Services Marketing*, 15 (April/May), 328–42.

Kunda, G. (1992) *Engineering Culture. Control and Commitment in a High-Tech Corporation*, Philadelphia: Temple University Press.

Mitchell, C. (2002) 'Selling the brand inside', *Harvard Business Review*, 80 (1), 99–105.

Miles, S.J. and Mangold, W.G. (2004) 'A Conceptualization of the Employee Branding Process', *Journal of Relationship Marketing*, 3 (2/3), 65–87.

Miles, S.J. and Mangold, W.G. (2005) 'Positioning Southwest Airlines through Employee Branding', *Business Horizons*, 48, 535–45.

Scott, S.G. and Lane, V.R. (2000) 'A Stakeholder Approach to Organizational Identity', *Academy of Management Review*, 25 (1), 43–62.

Van Maanen, J. (1988) *Tales of the Field, On Writing Ethnography*, Chicago: Chicago University Press.

Wallace, E. and de Chernatony, L. (2009) 'Exploring brand sabotage in retail banking', *Journal of Product and Brand Management*, 18 (3), 198–211.

Warhurst, C. and Nickson, D. (2007) 'Employee experience of aesthetic labour in retail and hospitality', *Work, Employment and Society*, 21 (1), 103–20.

Warren, S. (2008) 'Empirical challenges in Organizational Aesthetics Research: Towards a Sensual Methodology', *Organization Studies*, 29 (4), 559–80.

Willmott, H. (1993) 'Strength is Ignorance; Slavery is Freedom: Managing Culture in Modern Organizations', *Journal of Management Studies*, 30 (4), 515–52.

7. Recruitment and selection practices, person–brand fit and soft skills gaps in service organizations: the benefits of institutionalized informality

Scott A. Hurrell and Dora Scholarios[1]

INTRODUCTION

Brand management is usually associated with how organizations present themselves to customers or develop product brands (Aaker and Joachimsthaler, 2002), but recent interest in employer branding draws attention to employees and potential recruits as important stakeholders (Gapp and Merrilees, 2006; Lievens et al., 2007; Van Hoye and Lievens, 2005). Identity-based brand management is suggested as essential if employees are to behave in ways that are consistent with a brand philosophy and remain committed to this brand (Burmann and Zeplin, 2005). Within the human resource management (HRM) literature, research has shown employers' increasing emphasis on recruitment as a vehicle for building an employer brand (CIPD, 2007) and 'brand image' is regarded as part of a signalling process which informs potential employees of an organization's attributes and reputation (Cable and Turban, 2006; Lievens and Highhouse, 2003).

In this chapter, we focus on the hospitality industry, which is widely accepted to suffer from high levels of skills deficits and employee turnover, especially in the 'soft skills' that are essential for customer service. Within this sector, businesses often distinguish themselves through the creation of service brands. Contrasting two hotel establishments with distinct brand identities and different degrees of reported soft skills deficits (e.g. in social and self-presentational skills), we propose that recruitment and selection practices which lead to closer person–brand fit will result in fewer skills deficits. Based on evidence linking recruitment and selection strategies with person–organization fit, we argue that person–brand fit can also be shaped in these early stages of the developing employment relationship.

SOFT SKILLS DEFICITS, RECRUITMENT AND SELECTION: PERSON–BRAND FIT IN THE HOSPITALITY INDUSTRY

A number of commentators have noted the shift from purely technical and cognitive notions of skill to include 'soft' interpersonal and social qualities (see for example Grugulis et al., 2004; Payne, 1999). These are especially important for customer-facing employees in interactive services, such as retail and hospitality (Korczynski, 2005). Indeed, research indicates that for customer-facing workers, social skills, the ability to deal with customers and self-presentation are the most important skills sought by employers in recruitment, rather than technical skills or work experience (Nickson et al., 2005).

Employers have consistently reported deficits in these soft skills (Baum and Odgers, 2001; Baum, 2002; Hurrell, 2009). The most commonly reported problems relate to skills gaps in current employees, although problems also exist in skills shortages in potential recruits. Within Scotland, the focus of the present study, nationally representative Employers' Skills Surveys conducted annually between 2002 and 2004 showed that 16–25 per cent of employers reported skills gaps in current employees, typically in soft skills areas such as oral communication, customer handling and team-working (Hurrell, 2009). The Scottish hospitality sector was disproportionately affected by these soft skills gaps (Hurrell, 2009).

The hospitality industry is notorious for its ad hoc approach to HRM as well as its persistent problems with poor image, high turnover and skills shortfalls (see for example Hoque, 2000). Although evidence of 'best practice' can be found in the hotel industry (Hoque, 2000), informal or unreliable HR approaches – for instance, the reliance on brief interviews, references or an 'arms and legs' approach to hiring – seem to dominate, especially among small, single-establishment employers with limited resources (Lockyer and Scholarios, 2004). Other findings show that structured 'situational' interviews are at least espoused as an ideal tool for assessing customer service competencies (Brannan and Hawkins, 2006), while less prescriptive approaches argue that the HR requirements of the hotel industry depend on their service processes (Schneider and Bowen, 1993). Thus, selecting for service contexts may involve the matching of employee qualities with the expectations and needs of the customers in the targeted market (Schneider and Bowen, 1993). In such a differentiated model, the fit between the employee and the organization will be essential if the organization is to meet its service goals.

A person–organization fit perspective promotes effective communication of organizational attributes to job applicants to shape their perceived value congruence with the organization. Rather than emphasizing technical (or psychometric) qualities of recruitment and selection methods, the primary interest here is their social or interactive qualities (see, for example, Herriot, 1989). In particular, some methods are thought to have 'socialization impact' (Anderson, 2001). The interview, for instance, allows two-way communication and a richer environment for both employer and candidate to establish congruence in job expectations. Furthermore, work sample tests or job simulations are perceived by candidates as being salient, providing realistic job previews and amongst the fairest methods of assessment (Anderson and Witvliet, 2008; Schuler, 1993). Such methods are, therefore, more likely to result in positive evaluations of the employer, and stronger commitment to the recruitment process.

Pre-entry experiences thus build relationships between the organization and future employees. Early interactions shape individuals' identification with the employer, job and whether to remain with the hiring process. Schneider et al.'s (1995) attraction–selection–attrition model, for example, indicates how individuals self-select out of recruitment processes, or later the organization, if they believe it does not match their values or expectations. This perspective seems particularly apt for describing a value-based relationship based on a brand philosophy. Moreover, this emphasis on person–organization fit is appropriate for understanding the high levels of skills deficits and turnover that have plagued hospitality establishments. Methods which allow both parties to establish 'fit' will lead to employees who are more likely to be satisfied in their jobs, more committed to the goals (or brand) of the organization, and less likely to leave (Derous and de Witte, 2001; Schneider et al., 1995).

Conceiving the process in this way provides considerable practical benefit for both parties. Applicants are able to make informed decisions about whether to remain within the selection processes and subsequently join and remain with the organization. For service establishments, success may depend on building and maintaining a strong employer brand. Distinctive branding has been proposed as a vehicle for dealing with competitive labour markets and attracting and retaining talent in service-based organizations (e.g. de Chernatony and Segal-Horn, 2003; Knox and Freeman, 2006). Burmann and Zeplin's (2005) institutionalized approach to 'internal brand management', so called because it is strategically recognized and encouraged by senior management, draws from organizational behaviour concepts in emphasizing the importance of brand citizenship behaviours and brand commitment amongst employees, especially within service organizations. These behaviours and attitudes are developed through brand-centred human resource activities, communication and leadership, including recruitment and selection criteria that encourage person–brand fit.

Although brand management is not our main focus here, selecting employees who are consistent with the brand and aesthetic of the organization may help employers to market themselves and provide consistent service encounters (Hancock and Tyler, 2007; Witz et al., 2003). We take this notion further by proposing that some recruitment and selection practices will be more successful than others in achieving fit between employees and the brand, and that this will have implications for skill match and turnover.

In order to develop the idea of how recruitment and selection practices may facilitate person–brand fit and subsequently reduce skills deficits, we chose to contrast two hotels of comparable size and labour market, but different reported levels of recruitment and retention problems; that is, one hotel suffered from high levels of turnover and skills deficits while the other reported considerably fewer problems with these issues. Our specific interest was in their distinct service brands, the recruitment and selection strategies they used to align employees to this brand and whether this could be associated with their contrasting positions. The study, thus, had four objectives: (1) to examine managers' perceptions of soft skills deficits in each of the case study hotels; (2) to identify the service brands of each establishment; (3) to explore the relationship between the recruitment and selection of employees and the brands of each establishment; and (4) to determine whether any relationship found in (3) can be used to explain establishments' experiences of soft skills deficits.

METHODOLOGY

Futureskills Scotland's Scottish Employers Skills Survey (ESS) series shows that the hotel and restaurants subsector is the worst affected by soft skills deficits (Hurrell, 2009). For this reason, the present study focused on two (anonymized) hotel establishments chosen from respondents to the 2004 Scottish Employer's Skills Survey; one (Fontainebleau) had reported soft skills deficits while the other (Oxygen) had not. This within-industry comparison allowed determination of whether the types of HR practices in place affected soft skills deficits. We focused only on establishments employing 100 or more staff and who were parts of multisite operations as these are more likely to have formalized HR practices (Cully et al., 1999). Fontainebleau employed approximately 130 staff, and Oxygen 220 staff. Both hotels were drawn from the same labour market (Glasgow) in order to try to minimize potential variation in labour supply and both were part of prestigious international hotel chains catering for the mid-high end of the market. Oxygen was a five star hotel and Fontainebleau four star. Although both catered for the business and leisure markets, Oxygen tended to emphasize business and conference trade and Fontainebleau the leisure market and large events such as weddings and parties. Organizational brand practices and proprietary systems have also been anonymized within the research presented below.

The majority of staff in each hotel were employed in the Food and Beverage, Events (Meetings and Events in Oxygen, and Conference and Banqueting in Fontainebleau), Housekeeping, Front Office (reception) and Kitchen departments. In both hotels, the Food and Beverage and Events staff were the largest employee group, accounting for approximately 40 per cent of Fontainebleau's staff and 53 per cent of Oxygen's. The majority of employees in each hotel were part-time – approximately 62 per cent in Fontainebleau and 65 per cent in Oxygen, with such staff typically employed in Food and Beverage, Events and Front Office.

Employee and management interviews and employee focus groups were used. Five managers were interviewed in Fontainebleau and six in Oxygen. The Food and Beverage Managers, Front Office Managers, Head Chefs and HR representatives (The HR Coordinator in Fontainebleau and People Development Manager in Oxygen) were interviewed in both hotels. In addition, Oxygen's Head Housekeeper was also interviewed, with Fontainebleau's Head Housekeeper unable to give an interview. Oxygen's Deputy General Manager and a second HR Coordinator, who joined Fontainebleau during the study, were interviewed regarding the skills of other managers in the hotel. Interview questions addressed service requirements (and relatedly the brand); which skills were important in selecting employees; whether skills deficits existed; levels of turnover; and recruitment and selection processes. HR representatives were asked to consider all employees within each establishment, while line managers were asked only about employees they directly managed.

Seven interviews with customer-facing employees were conducted in Fontainebleau. Four individual interviews and a focus group of eight employees were conducted in Oxygen. The interview and focus group respondents included male and female, full- and part-time and UK and non-UK staff. Questions included their experiences of recruitment and selection and what they believed management were looking for in terms of customer service and brand representation.

RESEARCH FINDINGS

Skills Deficits and Turnover

Consistent with the 2004 Scottish Employer's Skills Survey, Fontainebleau managers reported more problems with soft skills deficits than their Oxygen counterparts. Fontainebleau's managers reported soft skills shortages during recruitment ('skills shortage vacancies') in night staff, customer-facing breakfast staff, reception staff, and chefs in customer handling and communication skills. Only the Food and Beverage Manager reported no problems with skills shortages of any kind. In terms of soft skills gaps (lack of proficiency in current staff), the Front Office Manager reported these in four of the seven reception staff, especially in customer handling. The Head Chef reported that two of his eight chefs had soft skills gaps in oral communication, team working and customer handling. The Food and Beverage Manager believed that 25 per cent of his front-line staff in waiting and bar jobs had soft skills gaps in customer handling and team working, while two Food and Beverage unit managers had soft skills gaps in communication and leadership. Customer service and team-working skills gaps were also reported by the HR Coordinator in approximately 30 per cent of elementary staff (including Food and Beverage, Conference and Banqueting, Housekeeping and support positions in the kitchen). Even the hotel's senior management team was reported by both HR Coodinators to lack oral communication and leadership skills. Although some skills gaps were in new employees who had not completed training, many employees with skills gaps had been in the organization longer. Some managers did report technical skills gaps alongside soft skills gaps (for example strategic planning in managers and practical skills in chefs) but these were considerably less of a problem and outside the focus of this chapter.

Fewer Oxygen managers reported soft skills shortages but these were reported in the largest employee group, Food and Beverage, in contrast to Fontainebleau. The People Development Manager reported skill shortages for a maintenance position, while the Food and Beverage Manager reported some difficulties finding candidates with the requisite customer handling, self-presentation and communication skills. He believed these shortages were because Oxygen was very 'picky' during selection.

When examining soft skills gaps, however, Oxygen managers reported higher levels of overall staff proficiency. The Head Chef reported skills gaps in approximately 20 per cent of chefs and 40 per cent of kitchen stewards (porters), some of which were in oral communication, and the Deputy General Manager reported that 20 per cent of the 21 managers had skills gaps, some of which were in soft skills. In Oxygen there were more technical skills gaps reported than soft (in similar areas to Fontainebleau above) although these remained rare. There were thus some isolated soft skills gaps in Oxygen, but considerably fewer than in Fontainebleau.

Fontainebleau had an overall staff turnover rate of 75 per cent in the previous year compared to Oxygen's 42 per cent. Turnover was particularly high among part-time staff with the rate in Fontainebleau twice the average for the establishment as a whole. In Oxygen 90 per cent of replacement demand generated by turnover was for part-time positions.

The Service Brands

Oxygen: the 'style' hotel

Oxygen had a clear service philosophy; 'nae bother', which was covered extensively during induction and re-communicated through annual training events, as well as permeating the organization's culture. When discussing 'nae bother', respondents stated that Oxygen was a very 'informal', 'young', 'fresh' and 'stylish' hotel. Indeed the hotel itself had minimalist, chrome and leather décor with modern art throughout. The building was designed specifically for Oxygen and had won style and architecture awards. Oxygen maintained the 'nae bother' approach to customer service through genuine friendliness on the part of the employees rather than overtly prescribed brand standards. Employees were encouraged to be polite yet informal with guests, for example calling them by their first names wherever possible rather than using surnames or 'sirring' and 'maddaming' guests.

A further distinctive aspect of Oxygen's approach to customer service was the requirement for 'style' in terms of dress, appearance, speech and deportment, summarized by the Deputy General Manager as 'polish'. All respondents with the exception of the Head Housekeeper reported the importance of 'style' and self-presentation for Oxygen's employees. While the requirement was not for being good looking per se, focus group respondents stated that Oxygen employees needed to be 'students', 'funky', 'friendly' and 'individual'. Although employees had a designer uniform, they were allowed bodily and uniform adornments, 'crazy' hairstyles (Focus group respondent 6) and facial hair as long as these were viewed as 'stylish' and consistent with health and safety legislation and the Oxygen brand:

> Facial piercings we're very liberal on. We've had people with their eyebrows pierced… some people with their nose pierced, some people with strange parts of their ears… pierced… Girls, I don't care if they've got red, blue and green in their hair as long as it's not over the top. (Food and Beverage Manager, Oxygen)

This manager stated that he had only needed to speak to someone seriously about appearance once in four years. This employee had grown a dark goatee beard that clashed with his bleached blonde hair, making him look 'more like an idiot than anything' and thus inconsistent with Oxygen's brand. The employees reinforced the integrity of this fit between employees' appearance and Oxygen's brand:

> I am! [an essential part of the brand] [All start laughing] It's just you enjoy working here, because you know what the hotel is all about and what the image is so you can be confident about representing it. Staff complement the hotel [All indicate agreement]. (Oxygen focus group respondent 6)

> You have got that whole lively look of the building. It wouldn't look as good if you didn't have the staff there giving the same impression. (Oxygen focus group respondent 8)

Fontainebleau: tradition and formality

Fontainebleau's service encounter was dictated by exacting and prescribed brand standards stipulating the exact steps and stages that had to be engaged in for each service encounter. Management and employees characterized Fontainebleau's service as 'formal', 'traditional' and 'professional', in keeping with its long-established reputation as one of the world's leading hotel brands. The décor of Fontainebleau also appeared to reflect this tradition and formality; furniture and fittings in the hotel were highly opulent and grandiose, with classical art prints displayed throughout. Employees were expected to call guests by their title and surname or else 'sir' and 'madam'. The Food and Beverage Manager did note, however, that there was a requirement for a level of erudition when selecting employees for customer-facing positions as: 'you'd be looking for… whether that person's bright, articulate… Whether they've got a bit of… spark.'

Fontainebleau's appearance policy was more prescribed than Oxygen's and provides further evidence of its brand. Unlike Oxygen, there was no mention of style, only that employees were expected to be polite, clean and tidy. Employees' uniforms were purchased from an industry clothing supplier and no personalization was allowed. The Conference and Banqueting employees referred to these generic uniforms as hot, restrictive, uncomfortable and poorly designed. Strict guidelines also existed regarding hair length and style, an absence of facial hair and visible tattoos and the fact that only one pair of earrings and a wedding ring could be worn as jewellery.

Alignment of Recruitment and Selection with the Brand

Recruitment and skills demand

The hotels used a similar range of recruitment methods for front line positions – internal advertising throughout sister hotels; the Job Centre; a Scottish recruitment website; adverts in schools colleges and universities; informal drop-ins; newspaper adverts; referrals from current staff; agencies; and adverts in a trade publication. For more senior positions, specialized hospitality recruitment websites were also used, although many supervisory and managerial positions were filled internally.

Oxygen's approach, in addition to using conventional methods, aimed to attract candidates who fit their service brand. For example, university careers services were reported as the most extensively used method by the People Development Manager and Food and Beverage Manager as students were seen to epitomize Oxygen's style of service. Although Fontainebleau also used employee referrals, the original HR Coordinator, for example, believed this fostered a 'happy' environment and better teamwork, this practice was extensively relied upon in Oxygen and aligned to the brand. The Oxygen focus group respondents, for example, believed that the Meetings and Events department, in particular, was populated by 'friends of friends of friends!' who tended to be '(the) same (as us) and the right kind of person' (Focus group respondent 5). Even Oxygen's local recruitment literature emphasized the fit between employees and the hotel. One advert, for example, gave a picture of the inside of the hotel alongside words such as 'distinctive', 'unmistakable, and 'unique' before adding 'but enough about you' and then describing what Oxygen offered to employees. This advert thus highlighted the importance of a fit between new recruits and the hotel's brand. Indeed a campaign was also run at the same time, using similar wording, but targeted at guests. There was no evidence of Fontainebleau emphasizing style in this manner.

In both hotels it was soft skills that were the main focus at the point of selection, especially in terms of the ability to interact with and deal with others. Only 'back of house' functions, such as junior kitchen positions, placed less emphasis on soft skills and more on 'sound character', experience or technical skill (Head Chefs). For front-line staff, managers emphasized the importance of 'personality' and how this was used in the form of interpersonal skills. As stated by Fontainebleau's Front Office Manager: 'From a personality you can find out if they're bubbly, they're cheery... obviously if they're outgoing and whatever you know they're going to be able to deal with a guest, compared to someone that's really shy and withdrawn.'

Contrasts between the two hotels however emerged when managers were asked to elaborate on skills demand. Fontainebleau managers emphasized technical and practical skills, 'common sense' and/or work experience in addition to 'personality', especially for managers and senior kitchen positions. For entry-level staff, the HR Coordinator noted that applicants were often apathetic, appearing that they did not actually want the job, although this was not so much of a problem for part-time jobs that were typically filled by enthusiastic students. A bundle of characteristics indicating reliability and a work ethic were identified. The Food and Beverage Manager stated that in selection he asked himself: 'Does it look like this person could hold down a job or does this person have an active life? Is the CV well written? What were the reasons for the people having left their last job? Are they potential trouble makers?'

Fontainebleau's Head Chef also brought up the issue of reliability for entry-level staff but appeared to go beyond a work ethic, looking for something bordering on obedience. Acknowledging that many jobs were not especially stimulating, especially for Kitchen Porters, he often needed someone to 'turn up and do the job reliably'. Somewhat tongue in cheek, he commented that he was looking for 'eyes open, ears open, mouth shut' when selecting apprentices.

A final factor that managers in Fontainebleau considered when selecting front line staff was the degree to which the individual would fit with the current team on an interpersonal level. The original HR Coordinator, for example, stated that one of the most important things in the hotel was that management had done their best to foster 'a happy place to work' and so it was important that everyone 'got on'.

In Oxygen, the emphasis on particular soft skills when selecting front-line employees was much more evident, even in 'back of house' functions. The Food and Beverage Manager emphasized that the main purpose of the interview was the identification of soft skills. In agreement, the Front Office Manager added that he was also looking for 'confidence and resilience' for working on the front desk. Both the People Development Manager and Food and Beverage Manager noted the manner in which applicants greeted them in interviews:

> I just like them to kind of look me in the eye when they're speaking to me, maybe just a wee bit of a smile. And if they try and spark a conversation while you're speaking to them, you're like daddy-o... you're the one for me. (Food and Beverage Manager, Oxygen)

For managers, as in Fontainebleau, there were additional requirements for experience and technical skills, such as forward planning, forecasting and financial management; but soft skills and customer handling were viewed as essential for all senior managers.

Overall, Oxygen's management was looking for a particular manifestation of soft skills. They placed a strong emphasis on articulation, the appearance and 'style' of customer-facing employees and also a sense of 'warmth' and 'genuineness' that fit with the service product of the hotel: 'Self-presentation is particularly important to us here just because of the product we have in the hotel... It's very modern and it's sleek. It's very stylish and it's very attractive in the most part, depending on your taste obviously' (Food and Beverage Manager, Oxygen).

Selection methods

In operationalizing selection requirements, Fontainebleau's HR managers described a strategy that aimed to replace indiscriminate hiring with greater structure and formalization: 'Some of the managers would recruit... based on the fact that "OK that person's willing to do the job and not necessarily concerned with what skills they have"' (HR Coordinator 1, Fontainebleau).

Two interviews, one with HR and one with the prospective line manager, had been introduced for entry-level positions. For managerial positions, further interviews were required, as well as personality tests, assessment centres and occasionally presentations. The interviews themselves used competency-based questions with standard rating forms for each job. Conference and Banqueting employees summed up their experience of a competency-based interview: 'All the questions were geared around if you were placed in a work situation within like what could happen in a hotel, how you would react to it. Like a complaining customer or a dissatisfied guest or something' (Conference and Banqueting employee 1).

The HR interview in Fontainebleau reportedly picked up on any gaps from the line manager's interview and expanded upon information provided on the candidate's application form or CV. The establishment had recently invested considerable resources in training managers so interviews were standardized for each position. For more senior positions the second interview concerned more strategic matters such as profit maximization. For the most senior positions further interviews with the General Manager and/or Area Manager were informal and used as a 'quality check'.

The extent to which managers followed the recommended approach in Fontainebleau varied. For outlet managers (such as the bar and restaurant) both interviews were conducted. The Food and Beverage Manager, however, acknowledged that for front-line staff only the line manager interview was used. Although he reported that this did follow the competency-based format, his interest was more on candidates' willingness to do the job as highlighted when interrogating skills demand. Notably, this manager also reported skills gaps in around a quarter of his front-line employees. Employees in Food and Beverages departments, apart from one member of (Polish) waiting staff where this was to confirm she had the right documents, confirmed that they had received only one interview. The second interview for the Polish waitress was thus a legal check rather than an attempt to engage in more systematic selection. Only the Receptionist reported having more than one person present at her interview. Three employees described unstructured interviews (two waiting staff and one Conference and Banqueting casual): 'he [the restaurant manager] was quite willing to take me on as long as I was happy with what he was offering [in terms of hours and pay]' (Waiting staff 1). The second member of waiting staff believed that anyone would have been hired and that the interviewing manager was 'just looking for a pair of hands!'. Consistent with the referral approach, the Conference and Banqueting employee who had been recommended by his sister's friend noted the manager's comment, 'I have to give you an interview for the record'.

> My interview was more of a chat really, because the girl [who had referred him] was my sister's friend and she worked in banqueting… so she just said, 'Yes. He's a good worker' and stuff… and he's [the Conference and Banqueting Manager] like, 'you've basically got the job then.' (Conference and Banqueting employee 4)

It must be noted, however, that employees believed that the selection process had prepared them for organizational life and that few 'nasty surprises' were apparent after joining. Even where managers may not have acted selectively, employees believed that they were given appropriate and relevant information about the organization and their jobs.

Oxygen's policy was also that all candidates should have at least two interviews (with HR and the prospective line manager), although once again the employees did not confirm this. What emerged from Oxygen managers and employees, though, were additional methods geared towards a two-way exchange between department managers and the hotel on one side, and candidates on the other. Housekeeping and kitchen candidates were given a work trial, whilst anyone applying for front-office positions had to be seen by the Hotel's General Manager or Deputy General Manager to ensure that they would be suitable brand representatives. For management and some supervisory positions (depending on the line manager's discretion) psychometric tests or presentations were also used. A final stage in which all interviewees participated was a tour of the establishment, during which they were given the chance to ask their own questions and discuss Oxygen with the interviewer. Housekeeping trials were also accompanied by lunch and a further informal chat to assess candidates' views of the job.

Interviews in Oxygen were deliberately kept informal, although there were rating forms to be completed so that managers covered core areas. The Front Office Manager believed that hypothetical competency-based questions were not useful as 'anyone can lie at interview' and he preferred to use the time to get to know the applicant and assess their interpersonal skills.

According to Oxygen's People Development Manager, the interview was used to learn about the individual and gauge relevant work or social experiences. All managers confirmed this. The Front Office Manager and Food and Beverage Manager gave examples of interview topics: work and non-work activities and interests; asking applicants to tell the interviewer about themselves; qualifications; what they were doing at university and why they went to university (if applicable); why they wanted to work in the hotel; what they were planning to do over their holidays; and whether they wanted to go travelling.

The interview was viewed as a two-way process, intended to establish what candidates expected from the job and whether this 'married up with reality' (Front Office Manager; People Development Manager). This was also essential for the Head Housekeeper, who believed that the main purpose of the post-work-trial chat was to see how the applicant had enjoyed their experience and whether they had any concerns or questions. The Front Office Manager found the tour of the establishment very effective for assessing the reality of expectations that the applicant had about the job. Employees agreed that their interviews had been 'much less formal' than they had expected (Front Office and Meetings and Events employees). One interview described lasted 'about five minutes', but this employee had also already had two trial shifts, which she believed had been the main hiring method. Another employee typified Oxygen's approach to establishing a positive image during these early encounters with employees: 'My first contact with the hotel was a very positive impression. Actually I had another job as well which I'd got already and I never went back to it; my first impression about Oxygen was really, really positive and it was through the interview' (Front Office employee).

Class and Gender Implications

Given the above findings on selection, Oxygen managers appeared to be looking for a certain style of speech and deportment, which may be seen as reflecting 'middle class' socialization and the accumulation of cultural capital (Bourdieu, 1984). The Front Office Manager, for example, stated a problem with applicants who spoke 'very Glasgow', while the People Development Manager believed that, as many of the hotel's business guests were middle class, those from commensurate backgrounds found it easier to interact with them. Although managers emphasized that employees from any class background would be hired if they showed the correct manifestation of interpersonal skills for Oxygen's brand, the implied association of the brand with being middle class, in part to mirror customer requirements, was apparent:

> I know I sound like somebody from Hitler Youth, but yes I do [think social background matters]... Do you know, unless people are polished there is no hope for them? And yes we'll employ them in back of house areas, but then they're trapped, and they're not trapped because they're not capable, they're trapped because they're not articulate. (Deputy General Manager, Oxygen)

The focus group employees were also aware of this requirement for 'middle classness' and seemed to happily buy into it. This was revealed in the following discussion about the hiring of those from the most disadvantaged backgrounds, referred to colloquially in Glasgow as 'neds' (or non-educated delinquents) for front-office 'First Time Service':

> *Respondent 6*: It's [the service style] how well you speak and clarity. It's really important because that's how you come across to them guest.

> *Respondent 4*: You're not going to hire a ned for First Time Service!

> *Respondent 6*: [Laughing] I know, imagine!

> *Respondent 4*: [Putting on a strong Glasgow accent] Awrite big man, how's it going?! [Group laughs] First Time Tam[2] here! [Group laughter continues].

Respondent 7: First Time Tam! It would be bad!

Respondent 3: It would be awful!

Oxygen's intentional recruitment of students and, in the words of one focus group respondent, those who were 'beautifully educated', also reflects an indirect advantage for those from middle class backgrounds (see for example Heckman, 2000). Indeed, when discussing the requirement for a certain demographic, the People Development Manager made explicit reference to a Glasgow private school where students tended to be highly eloquent and 'super confident', and could thus interact with middle class customers.

In Fontainebleau, the association of social background and brand image was not apparent. Apart from one Conference and Banqueting respondent mentioning that Fontainebleau probably would not employ a 'ned off the street', none of the respondents mentioned the issue of social background. That is not to say, however, that eloquence was completely unimportant in Fontainebleau, as identified earlier by the Food and Beverage Manager's requirement for those who were bright, articulate and possessing 'spark'.

Gender was not explicitly associated with possession of soft skills in either of the hotels and was raised only with respect to certain aspects of grooming and health and safety in Oxygen – the Food and Beverage Manager's references to girls' hair colouring (see quote above) and how they could not wear open-toed shoes for safety reasons. The only indirect evidence that gender may have played a part in selection processes came in a guarded statement from Oxygen's Deputy General Manager. He reported that while he did not believe it mattered whether Oxygen's employees were 'stick insect blondes' if they had the appropriate soft skills, he had 'seen some evidence' that other managers may have focused on certain 'aesthetic aspects'. Although this one guarded statement may reveal little, it is worth noting that this was a senior manager's observation and some Oxygen managers may have interpreted the hotel's brand requirements or 'aesthetic' in gender-specific terms.

CONCLUSIONS

The more 'traditional' hotel, Fontainebleau, suffered more from employee soft skills deficits than the 'style' hotel Oxygen, despite operating in a similar industry context and labour market. Our aim was to link these different positions; firstly, to a distinct brand identity within each hotel, and secondly, to different approaches to staffing. Our evidence suggests that these hotels' contrasting approaches to recruitment and selection, with Oxygen adopting hiring practices that allowed it to achieve 'fit' with their brand image, at least partially explain this variation in soft skills deficits. Employees' identification with 'the brand' was shown to begin even before they entered the organization, cultivated by a two-way exchange relationship with the hotel during the hiring process. In what might be referred to as a social-strategic approach to recruitment and selection, named after two of Iles' (1999) distinct staffing paradigms, Oxygen achieved what is more widely referred to as person–organization fit, where the soft skills of those who were eventually hired were more likely to match both managers' expectations and applicants' own expectations of the job. These findings have implications most obviously for what is to be considered 'best practice' in the hospitality context, keeping in mind the need to find strategies for dealing with the industry's persistently high turnover and skills deficits. We must also, however, consider the negative implications of a person–brand fit approach to selection.

'Best practice' HRM in hotels is generally thought to be exemplified by more structured approaches which eliminate managerial inconsistency and ad hoc decision-making, and focus on aligning practice with employee competencies that can deliver high performance (Hoque, 2000). Fontainebleau's stated policy appears consistent with this 'best practice' approach with its espoused service standards and structured hiring practices. In reality, however, the implementation of the policy was inconsistent and did not always adhere to conventional notions of best practice. There was evidence, especially for Food and Beverage positions, that managers were not hiring selectively or strategically on the basis of skills and the candidate's fit with either the job or the organization. Line managers often departed from the stated, formal, competency-based policy, appearing to be more concerned with a person's willingness to do the job. They were even happy to accept the word of a current employee alone, on an applicant's suitability. Although informal recruitment such as employee referrals may facilitate person–organization fit, particularly in hospitality contexts (Lockyer and Scholarios, 2004) or as part of a strategic response to difficult labour market conditions (Klehe, 2004), in this hotel, there appeared to be no consistent attempt to use these methods to address strategic goals or skills gaps. An 'arms and legs' approach to hiring was thus apparent even in this large multinational organization, where greater standardization is to be expected.

In Oxygen, there was greater selectivity of front-line employees with managers more consistently focusing on interpersonal and self-presentation skills and the extent to which these skills were appropriate for the brand. Informality appeared here too – for instance, managers used interview 'chats' as a way of establishing the suitability of employees' skills. It must be noted that Oxygen managers also appeared to depart from the hotel's two-interview policy although they appeared to be behaving strategically and selectively. The use of managers to identify person–organization fit through the interview process has been highlighted before (see for example Brannan and Hawkins, 2006; Moscosco, 2000) but in Oxygen this concept was extended to consideration of fit with the overall hotel brand.

As well as managers' apparent consistency in selecting according to a strategic brand identity, a further distinctive feature of Oxygen's selection process was its acknowledgement of applicant experiences in the two-way relationship building. As part of the apparent 'informality', applicants themselves could establish whether they wanted to work for Oxygen and 'fit' its style requirements, for example through informal tours of the establishment. Practices that allow employee agency in selection decisions have been acknowledged before as part of attraction-based recruitment (Rynes, 1991; Saks, 2005). Through informal events and work trials, it appears that Oxygen's applicants were able to gather important information about the organization's symbolic attributes, such as its brand or 'personality', allowing a self-assessment of fit (Highhouse et al., 2007). This partially reflects work conducted in the call centre industry by Brannan and Hawkins (2006), where introduction of the organizational culture through informal selection events was seen as developing pre-entry affective commitment to the organization. Oxygen employees were highly aware of the brand, their fit with the brand and the role that they played in personifying this brand through their soft skills, indicating brand commitment and identification (Burmann and Zeplin, 2005). It is also possible that they perceived the organization as 'honest' in not attempting to project an unrealistic image of the work itself, and this enhanced applicants' feelings of being fairly treated (Anderson and Witvliet, 2008).

Fontainebleau's employees also appeared to believe that the organization had been honest to them during the selection process. Although Fontainebleau's selection process did not, therefore, appear to consider brand communication, it did at least seek to try and outline the general expectations of the job. These apparently transparent approaches are preferable to the use of 'impression management' techniques that may not always remain true to the organizational reality, potentially leading to dissonance and attrition among employees (Brannan and Hawkins, 2006).

There did, however, appear to be greater success at avoiding attrition in Oxygen despite Fontainebleau's transparency. Oxygen's employees appeared to have developed a positive image of the organization during the recruitment stage, and were attracted to what they saw of the work environment and style of the hotel, which they saw as compatible with their personal characteristics and values. Indeed, Oxygen's recruitment literature emphasized this fit between employees and the hotel's brand. This appeared to have contributed to employees' decisions to join the organization, and although it was not possible to evaluate this here, could explain the lower levels of turnover (Derous and de Witte, 2001; Schneider et al., 1995). Oxygen's selection process can be represented as 'institutionalized informality', with a combination of strategic direction and two-way informal communication acknowledging applicants' self-selection decisions as an essential and formalized part of the organization's HR policy.

There is, however, a caveat to any recommendation that deviates from the conventional notion of 'best practice' as standardization and objectivity. Selecting for 'fit' may lead to capricious decisions on the basis of 'similar to me' evaluations or unintentional exclusion of some applicant groups. Some of the evidence gathered from Oxygen suggests that the alignment of selection practices around a shared perception of brand characteristics may have pernicious implications for the selection of those from certain class backgrounds. Those operating in the hospitality industry and seeking to differentiate themselves by offering a certain 'style' in their service may be privileging those from the middle class (see Nickson et al., 2003; Nickson and Warhurst, 2006).

In terms of potential gender issues Hancock and Tyler (2007) discuss how employers may communicate their image and brand through the embodiment of employees in the 'aesthetic economy'. They particularly interrogate the manner in which recruitment literature is used to reinforce expected gender roles, appropriate organizational embodiment and performativity, as a form of pre-entry organizational control. There was little evidence of gendering in the type of person–brand fit being practised here, although one senior Oxygen respondent did suggest that some of his colleagues may have been selecting females for their looks. In the absence of further concrete evidence little can be said other than employers should certainly be careful not to employ branded selection practices that are discriminatory or reinforce harmful gender stereotypes. It could be speculatively argued, however, that Oxygen's recruitment literature communicated the appropriate cultural capital and therefore social background of applicants (Bourdieu, 1984) (whether intentionally or not), extending Hancock and Tyler's (2007) analysis into a different sphere. Clearly branded recruitment policies are not unproblematic and employers need to carefully consider the potentially harmful effects of these on particular social groups.

In conclusion, a greater emphasis on selecting employees who fit the brand may help hospitality employers and others in interactive services to reduce soft skills gaps. While this research was conducted on only two case studies and a relatively small sample of employees, the proposed relationship between selection practices, person–brand fit and soft skills gaps can be tested in other service settings. This chapter has demonstrated how emphasizing person–brand fit through informal yet selective and strategically integrated hiring practices, which allow applicants agency in selecting the organization, may be superior to standardized, competency-based selection procedures.

Although more research is needed on the direct link between HR practices, brand identification and employee outcomes, it may also be argued that this fit with the brand not only reduces skills gaps, but also increases employee satisfaction and commitment to the organization, thus reducing turnover. Strategies that encourage person–brand fit, therefore, may also be beneficial for employees. Such policies allow potential employees to establish for themselves whether they fit the brand, facilitating the self-selection attraction and decision process, although the potential for negative stereotyping of certain groups must be borne in mind.

NOTES

1. The authors would like to thank Victoria Mathers for her research assistance.
2. 'Tam' is a Glaswegian version of the name 'Tom' or 'Thomas' associated with those from less affluent or socially excluded backgrounds.

REFERENCES

Aaker, D. and Joachimsthaler, E. (2002) *Brand Leadership*, London: Simon and Schuster.

Anderson, N. (2001) 'Towards a theory of socialization impact: Selection as pre-entry socialization', *International Journal of Selection and Assessment*, 9 (1/2), 84–91.

Anderson, N. and Witvliet, C. (2008) 'Fairness reactions to personnel selection methods: An international comparison between the Netherlands, the United States, France, Spain, Portugal, and Singapore', *International Journal of Selection and Assessment*, 16 (1), 1–13.

Baum, T. (2002) 'Skills and training for the hospitality sector: a review of issues', *Journal of Vocational Education and Training*, 54 (3), 343–64.

Baum, T. and Odgers, P. (2001) 'Benchmarking Best Practice in Hotel Front Office: The Western European experience', *Journal of Quality Assurance in Hospitality and Tourism*, 2 (3/4), 93–109.

Bourdieu, P. (1984) *Distinction: A Social Critique of the Judgement of Taste*, London: Routledge.

Brannan, M. and Hawkins, B. (2006) 'London calling: selection as pre-emptive strategy for cultural control', *Employee Relations*, 29 (2), 178–91.

Burmann, C. and Zeplin, S. (2005) 'Building brand commitment: A behavioural approach to internal brand management', *Brand Management*, 12 (4), 279–300.

Cable, D. and Judge, T. (1996) 'Person organization fit, job decisions and organizational entry', *Organizational Behavior and Human Decision Processes*, 67 (3), 294–311.

Cable, D. and Turban, D.B. (2006) 'The value of organizational reputation in the recruitment context: a brand-equity perspective', *Journal of Applied Social Psychology*, 33 (11), 2244–66.

Chartered Institute of Personnel and Development (CIPD) (2007) *Employer Branding: The Latest Fad or the Future for HR?* London: CIPD.

Cully, M., Woodland, S. O'Reilly, A. and Dix, G. (1999) *Britain at Work; As Depicted by the 1998 Workplace Employee Relations Survey*, London: Routledge.

de Chernatony, L. and Segal-Horn, S. (2003) 'The Criteria for Successful Services Brands', *European Journal of Marketing*, 37 (7/8), 1095–118.

Derous, E. and de Witte, K. (2001) 'Looking at selection from a social process perspective: Towards a social process model on personnel selection', *European Journal of Work and Organizational Psychology*, 10 (3), 319–42.

Gapp, R. and Merrilees, B. (2006) 'Important Factors to Consider when Using Internal Branding as a Management Strategy: A Healthcare Case Study', *Journal of Brand Management*, 14 (1/2), 162–76.

Grugulis, I., Warhurst, C. and Keep, E. (2004) 'Whatever Happened to Skill' in C. Warhurst, I. Grugulis and E. Keep (eds), *The Skills That Matter*, Basingstoke: Palgrave Macmillan, pp. 1–18.

Hancock, P. and Tyler, M. (2007) Un/doing Gender and the Aesthetics of Organizational Performance', *Gender, Work and Organization*, 14 (6), 512–33.

Heckman, J.J. (2000) 'Policies to Foster Human Capital', *Research in Economics*, 54 (1), 3–56.

Herriot, P. (1989) 'Selection as a social process' in M. Smith and I. Robertson (eds), *Advances in Selection and Assessment*, Chichester: Wiley, pp. 171–8.

Highhouse, S., Thornbury, E.E. and Little, I.S. (2007) 'Social-identity functions of attraction to organizations', *Organizational Behavior and Human Decision Processes*, 103 (1), 134–46.

Hoque, K. (2000) *Human Resource Management in the Hotel Industry: Strategy, Innovation and Performance*, London: Routledge.

Hurrell, S.A. (2009) 'Soft Skills Deficits in Scotland: Their Patterns, Determinants and Employer Responses', Unpublished Doctoral thesis, Glasgow: University of Strathclyde.

Iles, P. (1999) *Managing Staff Selection and Assessment*, Milton Keynes: Open University Press.

Klehe, U. (2004) 'Choosing how to choose. Institutional pressures affecting the adoption of personnel selection procedures', *International Journal of Selection and Assessment*, 12 (4), 327–42.

Knox, S. and Freeman, C. (2006) 'Measuring and Managing Employer Branding Image in the Service Industry', *Journal of Marketing Management*, 22 (7/8), 695–716.

Korczynski, M. (2005) 'Skills in Service Work: An Overview', *Human Resource Management Journal*, 15 (2), 3–14.

Lockyer, C. and Scholarios, D. (2004) 'Selecting Hotel Staff: Why best practice does not always work', *International Journal of Contemporary Hospitality Management*, 16 (2), 125–35.

Lievens, F. and Highhouse, S. (2003) 'The Relation of Instrumental and Symbolic Attributes to a Company's Attractiveness as an Employer'. *Personnel Psychology*, 56 (1), 75–102.

Lievens, F., Van Hoye, G. and Anseel, F. (2007) 'Organizational Identity and Employer Image: Towards a Unifying Framework', *British Journal of Management*, 18 (S1), S45–S59.

Moscosco, S. (2000) 'Selection Interview: A Review of Validity Evidence, Adverse Impact and Applicant Reactions', *International Journal of Selection and Assessment*, 8 (4), 237–47.

Nickson, D., Warhurst, C., Cullen, A-M. and Watt, A. (2003) 'Bringing in the Excluded? Aesthetic labour, skills and training in the "new" economy', *Journal of Education and Work*, 16 (2), 185–203.

Nickson, D., Warhurst, C. and Dutton, E. (2005) 'The Importance of Attitude and Appearance in the Service Encounter in Retail and Hospitality', *Managing Service Quality*, 15 (2), 195–208.

Nickson, D. and Warhurst, C. (2006) 'Opening Pandora's Box: Aesthetic Labour and Hospitality', in C. Lashley, P. Lynch and A. Morrison (eds), *Hospitality: A Social Lens*, St Louis: Elsevier.

Ostroff, C. and Judge, T. (eds) (2007) *Perspectives on Organizational Fit*, New York: Psychology Press.

Payne, J. (1999) All Things to All People: Changing Perceptions of Skill Among Britain's Policymakers Since the 1950s and their Implications, SKOPE Research Paper no. 1, Oxford University: SKOPE.

Payne, J. (2006) What's Wrong With Emotional Labour, SKOPE Research Paper no. 65, Oxford University: SKOPE.

Rynes, S.L. (1991) 'Recruitment, job choice, and post-hire consequences', in M.D. Dunnette and L.M. Hough (eds), *Handbook of Industrial and Organizational Psychology*, Palo Alto: Consulting Psychologists Press, 2nd edn, pp. 399–444.

Saks, A.M. (2005) 'The impracticality of recruitment research', in A. Evers, O. Smit-Voskuyl and N. Anderson (eds), *Handbook of Personnel Selection*, Oxford: Blackwell, pp. 47–72.

Schneider, B. and Bowen, D. (1993) 'The Service Organization: Human Resources Management is Crucial', *Organizational Dynamics*, 21 (4), 39–52.

Schneider, B., Goldstein, H. and Smith, B. (1995) 'The ASA framework: An update'. *Personnel Psychology*, 48 (4), 747–73.

Schuler, H. (1993) 'Social validity of selection situations: A concept and some empirical results'. In H. Schuler, J. Farr and M. Smith (eds), *Personnel Selection and Assessment: Individual and Organizational Perspectives*, Hillsdale: Lawrence Erlbaum Associates, pp. 11–26.

Van Hoye, G. and Lievens, F. (2005) 'Recruitment-related information sources and organizational attractiveness: Can something be done about negative publicity?', *International Journal of Selection and Assessment*, 13 (3), 179–87.

Witz, A., Warhurst, C. and Nickson, D. (2003) 'The Labour of Aesthetics and the Aesthetics of Organization', *Organization*, 10 (1), 33–54.

8. The brand I call home? Employee–brand appropriation at IKEA

Veronika V. Tarnovskaya

INTRODUCTION

Employee and employer branding have been broadly discussed in the literature as a source of competitive advantage (Rosethorn, 2009; Davies, 2008;
Mosley, 2007; Barrow and Mosley, 2005; Miles and Mangold, 2004, 2005,
2007; Ind, 2003; Ambler and Barrow, 1996). Such literature addresses questions such as: What makes employees enthusiastic about their organizations?
What makes them satisfied and happy? How do employee work experiences
translate into organizational performance? Broadly speaking two perspectives
of branding have emerged which reflect different views of the roles of staff
in the organization. In one perspective, employee branding represents a view
of organizational staff as a vehicle to communicate and manifest the brand
to customers and other stakeholders. In this perspective, employee branding
is a strong positioning tool towards organization's stakeholders with an ultimate goal of creating more value for them. The other perspective of employer
branding views employees as salient internal stakeholders. This is reflected by
the objective of branding to make employees feel valued and give them the
sense of belonging by providing them with a good and credible place to work
(Ambler and Barrow, 1996). Hence, branding is mainly used as a recruitment
tool aimed at employees. There is, however, an implicit notion that satisfied
employees will translate into satisfied customers.

In spite of the differences in perceived employee roles, both perspectives
look at branding as something that is done to, or with the help of, employees,
demonstrating a strikingly normative approach. In addition, existing studies
tend to explore employee and employer branding on the metalevel of the organization. As a result, we lack a more nuanced understanding of branding on the
microlevel of individual employees interacting with the brand in the specific
work situations. Therefore, in this chapter I investigate how branding manifests
itself in employees' meaning construction of their work. Using the notions of
human agency and structure (Sewell, 1992; Giddens, 1979, 1991), this study
focuses on the specific ways in which employees interpret brand messages and

mobilize these meanings in their identity work. I argue that brand meanings are not only imposed on employees by managers in order to achieve marketing goals, but also re-appropriated by them in order to frame their own goals. Thus, employees are viewed as active constructors of brand meaning who appropriate the brand through their specific experiences of the organization. The study seeks to develop a more comprehensive view of employee branding as appropriation work by active employees, sometimes in sync with the managerial intentions, sometimes totally out of sync. It also contributes to the integration of ideas surrounding employee and employer branding, which are still seen in the literature as two separate processes.

THEORIES OF EMPLOYEE AND EMPLOYER BRANDING

The concept of employee branding combines the traditional view of branding with the internal marketing concept (Miles and Mangold, 2004, 2005, 2007; Mitchell, 2000; Gronroos, 1981). It is defined as 'the process by which employees internalize the desired brand image and are motivated to project the image to customers and other organisational constituents' (Miles and Mangold, 2004: 68). These authors speak of employee branding as a strong positioning tool towards customers and other stakeholders. Miles and Mangold (2005) identified that the critical elements of the employee branding process include: the organization's mission and values, desired brand image, the variety of communication modes, employee's psyche (knowledge of brand image and psychological contract), employee brand image and consequences for customers and employees. Drawing on evidence from other literature (e.g. Mitchell, 2002), they have emphasized the role of consistent communication of brand messages to employees. Clear communication via all sources is needed to build and maintain the employees' knowledge of the desired brand image while the psychological contract is used to build trust and motivation with staff. Following Rousseau (1989), the psychological contract, defined as 'a perceptual agreement formed in the employees' minds about the terms and conditions of working relationship', is argued to be central to the employee branding process since the degree to which organizations uphold it influences employees' trust in their employer and their motivation to serve customers and cooperate with their co-workers (Miles and Mangold, 2005: 538).

There exists a plethora of studies on the content, typology and role of psychological contracts for understanding of employer–employee relationships (e.g. Cuyper et al., 2008). It is argued, for example, that explicit and implicit promises exchanged between the employee and employer constitute the basis of the contract. Moreover, promises play a critical role in employees' perceptions of contract breach and corresponding behaviours. De Jong et al. (2009) argue that both promises and their fulfilment matter, thus balanced contracts are most beneficial for high job satisfaction and loyalty. Other authors argue that what matters more are delivered inducements (benefits) as perceived by employees (Montes and Zweig, 2008). On the whole, the notion of the psychological contract is mainly discussed from the managerial perspective, without considering the employee's active role in the contract creation. This is seen, for example, from the methods applied in many studies when employee perceptions are probed via surveys with predetermined questions, leaving no room for employees' own insights into the contract (Montes and Zweig, 2009; Cuyper et al., 2008; Huibao et al., 2008; Miles and Mangold, 2007).

The reported consequences of a successful employee branding process are a strong brand image, increased employee satisfaction and reduced staff turn-over, as well as higher levels of customer satisfaction. Das (2003) adds to these outcomes employee engagement, defined as ways in which employees 'say', 'stay' and 'strive' for their organization, acting as brand ambassadors. The conceptualization of employee branding by Miles and Mangold (2004) has been used as a practical guide to 'growing the employee brand' (e.g. Miles and Mangold, 2007) with a special focus on organizational systems that ensure message consistency in communication of desired brand image to employ-ees. Their latter paper is a good example of an overall approach in studies on employee branding, which can be characterized as strictly normative since it prescribes the concrete measures to ensure that employees deliver the intended image to customers.

Employees seem to be of value themselves only when they faultlessly communicate the desired message to customers. In other words, they are valued as passive and anonymous communication means for the transmission of managerial ideas. This is seen in the common discourse in which employees 'deliver' and 'enhance' experience, 'reflect' and 'project' brand image while the task of managers is to 'shape' employees' brand perceptions as well as 'to create and instil the desired image in employee minds' (Miles and Mangold, 2004: 69).

The other perspective of employees in the literature is that of the key inter-nal stakeholders, which is reflected by the objective of employer branding to make people feel valued and give them the sense of belonging by providing them with a positive and credible workplace experience. A series of McKinsey surveys provide growing evidence that companies use employer branding to attract recruits, which leads to an increased competition for talent (Hieronimus et al., 2005). As a reflection of companies' interest, most studies in employer branding lie in the practitioner arena, which explains its increasingly function-alist approach (e.g. Rosethorn, 2009; Barrow and Mosley, 2005; Frook, 2001).

Barrow and Mosley (2005) describe the employer branding as a three-step process. First, a firm develops the employer brand value proposition that should provide a 'compelling, relevant and differentiating' reason for employees to choose the organization for their workplace. The value proposition needs to provide a true representation of what the company offers its employees as well as accommodate the existing beliefs of potential applicants about the company. Following the development of its value proposition, the firm should communicate it to its targeted potential employees and other related parties. Both external and internal communications need to be planned and carried out, and they are also presumed to be consistent with all other branding efforts of the firm. Thus, Barrow and Mosley (2005: 150) talked about the total brand mix including all external and internal practices aimed at employees (among them are HR practices, training, communications and working environment).

The academic discourse of employer branding draws extensively on product and corporate branding. Thus, Ambler and Barrow (1996) defined the employer brand in terms of functional, economic and psychological benefits provided by and identified with the employing company. Backhaus and Tikoo (2004) argue that the employer brand establishes the identity of the firm as an employer by encompassing the firm's value system, policies and behaviours towards new recruits. A few studies take an alternative perspective on employee branding, for example, by focusing on the closer concept of employer attractiveness (Davies, 2008; Berthon et al., 2005) or combining managerial brand promise with employee experiences in employer branding (Mosley, 2007). Thus, employer branding is mainly viewed in the literature as a tool for recruitment of new and engagement of existing staff (Mosley, 2007). Employer branding is also suggested to be a broader strategy aimed at other stakeholders, and not only employees (Sullivan, 2004). There is, however, a notion of different attitude towards employees, reflected by the discourse of 'human capital', 'people as a resource' and 'brand as promise to employees'.

To summarize, the two perspectives of employee and employer branding are inherently interlinked since both deal with the employer–employee relationships as the basis for branding. However, this is not sufficiently recognized in the literature, which still treats employee and employer branding as two separate phenomena. Nonetheless there are authors who use these concepts interchangeably (e.g. Davies, 2008). In doing so, however, they generate further confusion since we do not know which particular phenomenon is in focus.

There is also a deeper philosophical connection between the two branding perspectives, seen, for example, in the ways the existing studies 'treat' employees in both approaches. As argued above, employee and employer branding differ in their focus on staff as either a vehicle for communicating the brand image or human capital which is important per se. Nevertheless, these perspectives take a common approach to employees as an anonymous workforce that can be controlled through exposure to corporate influence.

As stressed in Seeck and Parzefall (2008), by viewing employee perceptions and behaviours as dependent variables influenced by employer actions, most studies fail to capture employees' roles in employer–employee relationships. More specifically, very little is known about the employees' perceptions of psychological contracts and the ways in which these contracts influence employee satisfaction.

In order to uncover employee perceptions, they have to be considered as an active party in the contract with the organization. By changing the focus from the metalevel of organization to the microlevel of an active individual, new insights can be added to our knowledge of both branding phenomena and their eventual integration. This is the approach taken in the following sections of the chapter.

EMPLOYEE–BRAND APPROPRIATION

The notion of appropriation has been broadly used in consumer marketing literature to describe the way in which consumers attempt to regain control over brands and branded spaces (e.g. Aubert-Gamet, 1996; Cova and Pace, 2006). It reflects the ability of individuals to act freely within the given environmental frame and use it for their own goals, expressed by the concept of human agency (Foucault, 1997) and structure (Sewell, 1992). In relation to surrounding structure, agents are 'capable of exerting some degree of control over social relations in which one is enmeshed, which in turn implies the ability to transform those social relations to some degree' (Sewell, 1992: 20). As far as structures are concerned, they 'are constituted by mutually sustaining cultural schemas and resources that empower and constrain social action and tend to be reproduced by that social action' (Sewell, 1992: 20).

Applying the concepts of human agency and structure to branding, we can view the employer brand as a structure – a set of cultural schemas (e.g. common practices and procedures, habits and norms) and resources (e.g. plants, stores, products), which taken together constitute the framework within which employees exercise their power and freedom to act. Consequently, employee branding is a process of employees' appropriation of the brand structure through their 'free' usage of the brand's cultural artefacts and their attendant meanings in their identity work. This conceptualization echoes Kay's (2006) notion of a corporate brand as a logical structure that channels stakeholder perceptions, however, stressing the active role of employees in this process. This conceptual frame is used below to analyse employees' individual stories, providing examples of the different ways they engage in brand appropriation practices as part of their own identity work.

METHOD

This chapter draws from a four-year project (2002–5) that examined both IKEA's branding on a corporate level, and its local market activities. The case study method was applied in order to explore the branding phenomenon over time and in depth (Yin, 1994; Eisenhardt, 1989). Among other issues under study, the specific focus was on IKEA's HR activities globally and in one of the company's new markets – Russia. The interviews on the corporate level were conducted with HR managers responsible for IKEA's global employee policy, while on the local level both HR managers and local staff were contacted. The goal of the first round of interviews was to clarify the strategies related to employer branding (e.g. vision, cultural values and HR activities) while the second round was aimed at generating insights into the employee branding process as reflected in their perceptions of vision, core values, the psychological contract and their overall job satisfaction. In total four HR managers were interviewed at the corporate level and one HR manager and four staff members at the local level. Interviews were conducted in the employees' native languages (Swedish and Russian) and later translated into English. Each interview lasted for approximately one and a half hours.

The empirical material in this chapter draws mainly from two interviews of Russian employees taken from the larger study, although secondary data and selected quotes from interviews with corporate managers were also used. These cases were selected not because they were considered representative but because they provided most complete accounts of employees' experiences of IKEA as a place of work. When interviewed, these employees were willing to tell the stories that illustrate how individuals interpret corporate messages and construct meanings of their work. They also provided different cases of brand appropriation. Using interviews as social events and empirical situations of interest, rather than places and mediums to collect information, is emphasized in the literature (Alvesson, 2003) as a relevant method for studying meaning construction, and specifically for microlevel analysis (e.g. Thomas and Davies, 2005). In my interviews, the configuration of interview setting – an informal encounter in native language – increased the mutual understanding between the respondent and the interviewer. Given the situational, localized and partial nature of knowledge generated from these interviews, the logic of replication and generalizability are not really applicable (Yin, 1994). However, in line with the realist perspective of idiographic research (Tsoukas, 1989), the findings of case studies are nonetheless valuable for clarifying the generative mechanisms that are contingently capable of producing the employee branding phenomenon.

BACKGROUND TO IKEA

IKEA was founded in 1943 by Ingvar Kamprad, who was seventeen at the time, at his family farm Elmtaryd in Agunnaryd village in Sweden. His initials and the first letters in the farm and village names together make up the famous IKEA name. Since that time the IKEA Group has grown into a strong concept retailer with 267 stores in 25 countries. The company employs around 123,000 co-workers and generates annual sales of more than €21.5 billion. Among IKEA's new markets are China, Russia and Japan. The first Russian store was opened in Moscow in 2000. In 2010 there were 11 stores in Russia. IKEA retail stores specialize in large format warehouse retailing with an emphasis on low prices. They sell self-assembly furniture, which helps to keep costs down and enables them to undercut a vast majority of competitors on price. The furniture is heavily influenced by the Swedish design principles of minimalism and simplicity.

THE IKEA CORPORATE BRAND AS CULTURAL SCHEMA

Sewell (1992) conceptualized structures as mutually sustaining cultural schemas and sets of resources that empower agents who enact schemas. According to Giddens (1976), schemas are generalizable procedures applied in the enactment or reproduction of social life. The examples of schemas are rules, norms and notions that are most conventionally applied in many different situations. A central notion for the IKEA organization is its overall vision 'to create a better life for the many people' and HR vision: 'to give down-to-earth straightforward people the possibility to grow both as individuals and in their professional roles, so that, together we are strongly committed to creating a better everyday life for ourselves and our customers' (IKEA Group facts and figures, 2009). The IKEA vision is firmly rooted in IKEA's unique corporate culture, so pervasive that it influences every aspect of the company's activities both internally and externally. As commented on by the HR manager 1:

> When we talk about the IKEA culture, it is a huge subject. This is how we do things around here. A lot of culture is reflected in how we interact with each other, how we talk to each other. It is not necessarily something that is tangible.

Due to its inherently virtual character, culture constitutes a major element of the IKEA schema, reproduced in multiple store locations. It is made more tangible via a special focus on core values that have their origin in IKEA's history in Småland, the region in Southern Sweden where the company was founded. Core values are essential norms of organizational life at IKEA that are communicated to staff via specific examples of behaviours. For instance, the value of 'togetherness and enthusiasm' is specified as 'joining of efforts in everyday work, to work as a team and involve each other; to respect each other; to interact in an open way'. Managers also use values as written guidelines for staff recruitment in all markets.

Values are not only explicitly translated into behaviours but also in a more implicit way embedded into informal HR contracts between IKEA and staff. As one HR manager commented: 'The HR idea is very much about what you can expect from IKEA and also what we can expect from you. And it is trying to paint the picture of what it will be like to work for IKEA' (HR Manager 2). The idea of a contract is best illustrated by the internal document 'Our Human Resource Idea', which presents a list of employees' rights and responsibilities at each stage of their career at IKEA. The HR contract is about 'giving and taking on equal terms' and it has a goal 'to engage co-workers who get involved in their work and perform over and above the norm'. The responsibilities are about the employees' compliance with core values used as reference points for common behaviours. The rights are broad development opportunities that IKEA guarantees to every co-worker who can move between functions and countries. The essential employees' right is 'the working environment where people and team spirit are central values'.

It is important to note that the contract with an employee is not finally decided at the time of recruitment but it is presented as 'a journey' between different 'stations' with new responsibilities and new challenges at each next station. For example, one manager started her career as a trainee and later became manager at the Service department, then worked with logistics and customer orders at the store, then became an HR manager at the store level, and later the Global HR manager for Distribution and Range. In this 'career journey', the contract is negotiated between the employee and HR manager responsible.

Besides being used as guidelines for the contracts with existing staff, values play a central role in communicating the employer brand to potential employees. A respondent stressed the corporate feel of IKEA's recruitment advertising, which is standardized to get 'the same look and feel regardless of the type of company and market' (HR manager 1). Although the implementation can vary from market to market, IKEA's values are always included in their recruitment communications.

Values are also communicated internally via the 'Open IKEA' website accessible to all staff and a corporate magazine, *Read Me*. Thus, values are used as cultural texts to actualize and reinforce IKEA culture. Another important communication means is the store itself with its open spaces, simple and functional organization and product displays; there is a focus on low price and a general staff team spirit. Besides the store, the product range is a major material resource for staff in their enactment of the cultural schema.

Corporate managers play a central role in interpreting and translating the brand meaning and values; to this end they often lead brand-building activities at the local level. In Russia the essence of the employer brand was expressed as 'the right company for growing people'. The role of managers as the 'ambassadors of culture and values' (this term is widely used by IKEA corporate managers) is crucial in new markets. Thus, a group of experienced IKEA staff was sent to Russia in the late 1990s to 'build up' the local organization. That included recruiting of local staff, getting permissions for the first store, supervising the building process and literally assembling the departments of the store together with the newly employed staff. Thus managers can be viewed as both actors (enacting the employer brand) and non-material resources (constituents of the brand). The major elements of the employer brand as a structure are summarized in Table 8.2.

EMPLOYEES' APPROPRIATION PRACTICES

Appropriation practices are concerned with the ability of employees to find space for self-expression within the corporate brand. In this sense the accounts below illustrate two different sets of appropriation practices. In the first example, 'brand as "my home"' Irina's practices might be associated with accommodation; she appears to find plenty of space within the brand for her identity work. In the second example, 'brand as "constant trial"', Vladislov finds little space for his identity work. He finds it hard to 'be himself' at work, and observes that while he subscribes to the ideals of the corporate brand, the practices are often at odds with his identity. For him, trying to embody and live out the brand is a constant trial.

Brand as 'My Home'

Irina, a thirty-something enthusiastic woman, met me after her normal working hours in a small conference room in the IKEA offices. She had just been appointed head of the children's department at IKEA's Dybenko store in St Petersburg. She started at IKEA, St Petersburg in July 2000, which was a radical decision given her family situation (her family run their own business in Moscow). The decision to join IKEA was taken rather spontaneously – she visited the IKEA store in Khimki, Moscow and 'liked it a lot'. Her husband encouraged her to apply and, when she was hired as a team leader, he followed her to St Petersburg. The idea of working in the children's IKEA department excited her considerably since she had just had her first child.

Irina's career at IKEA went rather smoothly: 'I was a co-worker then a deputy, and later I became a group leader. It went on as if in a planned way.'

What made this development personally rewarding was her active participation in the build-up of the store in St Petersburg, the work she carried out together with her team. This is how Irina described her experience of this time: 'The build-up period was of great help. We were equal and we went along in the same direction. We've got goals, probably they were different with different people but we also had the common goal.' The feeling of participation and ownership was not only motivating for her personally, but also helped her to identify with the company: 'Well, first, I built the store, built up my department. I created it with my own hands!'

It was during the build-up time that Irina's department team was formed. When Irina talked about her team, her eyes sparkled. She raised her voice, gesticulated enthusiastically and completely dominated the conversation, trying to re-create the special spirit of her team for me as an outsider: 'We have a wonderful team! When you come to work you feel like being at home.' Irina described her relationship with her team as very trusting ('I don't have to follow and control everybody'), as open ('We talk every day!') and friendly ('I clearly know which of my team can oversleep and who will never oversleep and will come 20 minutes in advance!'). Irina observed that when problems arose she would consult her team members and could always rely on them to work through the problem with her: 'I say: my dear friends, let's think what's wrong, what is happening!' When talking about the time in the future when she would eventually progress in her career and leave her team, Irina gasped: 'I will part in tears!'

When asked how she motivated her staff to work long hours, often involving a lot of physical work at the department, she explained that the 'elbow feeling' (the feeling of closeness and mutual support) they have created together provided a strong motivational factor, which could even outweigh the material side of the job. Among other motivational factors at work, she mentioned the free lunch that was so appreciated by one of her team members, different corporate events and competitions, rotation to other store positions and very good opportunities for professional development. Many of her staff members – students working part-time – placed their hopes in IKEA since they knew that they 'had very good prospects' at the company. As far as relationships with other departments and within the management team were concerned, Irina described them as warm and cooperative: 'Nobody tries to show up his department, to grab the biggest piece of the pie, we come and consult each other.' She even referred to the corporate managers as 'our dear Swedes'.

Speaking about her daily work at the department, Irina mentioned many of IKEA's core values, which she referred to as underpinning her own, as well as her team's, actions. Speaking about low price, she used a rather normative style: 'It is actually our strategy. Low price is at the heart of IKEA's concept. We are to open a department which will display the lowest priced products in each product category. This then gives everybody a starting point.' When she further explained how she applied this principle in her department, she became much more personal, speaking in the first person, and used a more relaxed discursive style. However, she justified her actions in having additional, more expensive, articles in her department by reasoning: 'But I can save on me and never on my child. I've got the same attitude to my department.'

Irina placed great emphasis on customer service issues, such as being attentive to customer needs: 'To my mind, it is necessary, to give a person a clear explanation, first of all. Here, again, one should be a psychologist to some extent, understand what amount of information the person can bear.' She also recounted how she is 'absolutely delighted' with the way one of her team members treats customers at the department: 'When customers come to our department and I see S. speaking with them my soul sings, because he speaks with them as if they were his personal friends.' During the discussion Irina also emphasized the importance of simplicity and clarity in communications with customers recounting a discussion with a staff member that she personally had worked hard on training: 'Could you find simpler sentences so that the customer might understand you clearly, and not leave being shocked?' Irina also provided personal examples of other core values: 'You never feel shy asking somebody, and you are never afraid to seem silly or ridiculous' (the brand value of: no fear of making mistakes); 'How can I work carelessly, throw away anything? I can fail very much' (taking responsibility); 'To be friendly, to be a good example to everybody is very close to my heart' (leadership by example).

Irina mostly used the pronoun 'we' when speaking about her job and the company. She tended to address her staff as 'my people', 'my team' and 'my department', as well as using the expression 'my child' when talking about her department. All this demonstrated a high degree of identification with the company. Indeed, Irina expressed her feeling of complete confidence in IKEA in her observation that 'the company takes good care of us'. This, in her opinion, was what differentiated IKEA from typical Russian employers. Irina felt proud to work at IKEA and talked about the 'special pleasure' she experiences when talking about her job to her acquaintances. When asked what IKEA meant to her in a few words, she observed concisely: 'It is my home' adding that 'here we are really a family'. When asked about her future plans, she was very ambitious: 'Let's assume I want to be the director of the store. Why not? I really want to!'

Brand as a 'Constant Trial'

Vladislav constitutes a direct contrast to Irina in his orientation to the brand. A PR and Environmental Manager at IKEA Dybenko store in St Petersburg, he started at IKEA in 2000 as an accountant, but by 2001 had already been promoted to PR manager. For some time before this appointment he observed that he had felt a strong need for a job which involved 'communication with people, something creative, and something more vivid'. In spite of his strong motivation, Vladislav felt that he might not be the perfect candidate for his current job since it was so different from what he had done before. He described himself as a person who likes challenges mentioning his drive to show everybody 'what I am capable of'.

His first project as a PR manager was to organize the 'laying of the first stone' ceremony for a new store in St Petersburg. He realized already then that: 'In this job a trial period would never come to an end. All your former achievements are no longer recognized if you cannot work in the present, if you get relaxed.' Based on the subsequent conversation with Vladislav I have interpreted 'getting relaxed' as being complacent and lacking the motivation to change things. Vladislav's statement undoubtedly is in tension with IKEA's 'constant desire for renewal'.

Having succeeded in his initial projects, Vladislav was soon given responsibility for coordinating environmental projects in St Petersburg. He was required to combine this role with his other responsibilities as PR manager. He clearly felt the weight of this responsibility, commenting that: 'If something goes wrong, then my head will roll!' Although being very excited about the second part of his job, he found himself in the situation where he had to work almost entirely alone relying on temporary teams. Being a PR manager required him to communicate with many people, both his own co-workers and external partners, which Vladislav always found very stimulating. He observed that he did his best to 'always give a positive example to others, always be optimistic' since he understood that this was what his colleagues needed from him. However, it seems that this was not at all easy for him to do given his 'high degree of isolation'. He had to do many things at the same time, without being able to 'concentrate on a task', which in his eyes 'violated the main principle formulated by the founder of IKEA'. As Vladislav commented: 'My job often requires solitude and silence!' That was almost impossible in a room with thirty to forty people who also had to share computers from time to time. Commenting on his working conditions, Vladislav explained: 'It is very hard for those, who are not used to such things. It is very noisy. However, human beings are adaptable and can get used to anything.'

He also spoke with a certain degree of envy about his colleagues at the Trading Office who had a bigger and quieter room and explained that in his office the over-concentration of personnel had a purpose: 'So that people could see each other more often and communicate more. That unites people.' A second wish that Valdislav expressed was to have his own team: 'This would be fantastic. If there were such a team, I would do the impossible. It is very hard when you are alone!' Summarizing his experience of the job so far, he said proudly: 'In order to keep this position I had to go through really tough tests. I was thrown into the water. Will he come to the surface or will he drown? I came to the surface.'

Talking about his managers at the central office in Moscow, he suggested that 'they probably wanted to try and experiment' with his position. At the same time, he described his relationship with his immediate boss, a Russian manager, in very vivid terms: 'I sincerely admire this person.' In spite of his boss's general accessibility, they did not communicate much on a daily basis. Indeed, they only met 'when absolutely necessary'. Even in these latter cases Vladislav usually wrote to his boss, who responded by 'just looking and commenting'.

In his account, Vladislav almost always used the 'we' pronoun, talking both of the company and of himself in the job. This demonstrated his high level of identification with the company, as he admitted: 'I like the company a lot and I've not worked here for more than four years without a reason.' Vladislav also identified himself quite closely with IKEA's cultural mission in Russia: 'We want to be the guides of this culture, a positive feature for us is the partnership between the Swedes and Russians. At the end of the day, this partnership creates the brand image, and this is my job.' He also identifies with IKEA's ecological stance: 'We consume a lot of trees, this is an issue we need to address.'

In his daily work, he admired the openness at IKEA, especially on the management side. He observed that managers were willing to listen and were diplomatic. 'If your idea is good, you get carte blanche and this is fantastic!' This was in stark contrast with his experience of Russian managers, characterized by 'arrogance and swaggering', when 'he is everything and you are nothing'. On the other hand, when talking about his specific projects such as a Midsummer event in St Petersburg in June 2004, he echoed the 'them and us' culture in observing that he felt he had to prove himself to management: 'And then I'll show them what I am capable of!' He also used the term 'them' when talking about his future plans at IKEA. This feeling of uncertainty was mixed in his account with a strong desire to show how confident he felt about his job and his abilities. He expressed these conflicting feelings in this extract:

> No, I'm more than confident in my abilities. It is possible to resolve issues and be creative in everything I do. If I don't know something myself, I'll find sources and people, who can assist me. No, I'm very confident in myself, however, I don't know what will happen in the future. I may change the direction of my work.

Vladislav was very cautious about admitting his feelings of uncertainty. It was also clear that he was also trying to conceal signs of tiredness and physical exhaustion; at times in our interview he would lose the track of our conversation and ask me: 'So where were we?' He also observed that what was missing from his job was 'the satisfaction at the end of the day', which he associated with 'having a voice' and 'being appreciated everywhere'. He talked about the possibility of changing his job and moving to another company or just taking a break.[1] It was clear, however, that he had absorbed some of IKEA's principles and core values since in his future job he observed that he was looking for work that involved 'creativity, development, and responsible business management'.

DISCUSSION AND CONTRIBUTIONS

The purpose of this chapter has been to study how employee branding manifests itself in employees' brand appropriation practices. The findings reveal manifestations in employees' usage of core values as sources of motivation, their assessments of the fulfilment of brand promise and the fairness of the psychological contract.

Most strikingly, the brand was visible in the ways the respondents used core values as sources of motivation in their everyday work at IKEA store and/or office. Both respondents had a very good understanding of IKEA's core values but differed in their perceptions of these. Among the most motivating values were those that really worked in each respondent's individual situation. Table 8.1 provides a summary of respondents' perceived core values as sources of motivation. Irina has come up with nine of eleven core values, all of them being perceived as motivating. This respondent was energetic, happy and seemed really empowered by her job, as seen from her ambitious future plans. Vladislav, on the other hand, identified seven of eleven values but was really motivated by only four of them. He was only exposed to values of 'cost-consciousness' and 'constant desire for renewal', and he only observed 'togetherness and enthusiasm'. This respondent expressed the feelings of isolation, resentment, overall physical tiredness and unclear, even contradictory, future plans.

Other manifestations of employee branding included the ways in which the respondents assessed the fulfilment of brand promise (value proposition) and fairness of their psychological contracts with the organization. Irina's interpretation of IKEA's value proposition was the company that 'takes good care of us', which might suggest a fulfilment of the contract from the IKEA side. Regarding Irina's own role in this contract, she took an almost maternal stance towards her team, department and the company as a whole, characterized by both great care and great responsibility. Thus, her contract with IKEA seems to be not only fulfilled but also fair (mutual). On the other hand, Vladislav perceived IKEA's value proposition as an individual 'trial that never comes to an end'. This was not perceived as a fulfilled obligation since the major brand promise of togetherness was not realized. As to Vladislav's own role in

Table 8.1   The stated versus perceived values in the respondents' accounts

IKEA values	Perceived values: Irina	Perceived values: Vladislav
Togetherness and enthusiasm	Feeling good: confident, full of energy and inspired at work. Actively connecting personal life with the job. The company as an extended family.	Loneliness in an atmosphere of visible collectiveness. A constant trial period without any support from his managers. Constantly feeling the need to prove himself and demonstrate what he could contribute to the organization.
Accepting and delegating responsibility	A certain balance of accepting personal responsibility for her team and delegating tasks to other group members.	A focus on accepting responsibility, strong motivation to realize his ambitions.
Daring to be different	Not really accentuated in her account. Perceived more as company value.	Understood as daring to take risks. A way to show others what he was capable of.
No fear to make mistakes	Understood as admitting a lack of knowledge to her colleagues and asking for help when needed.	Feeling afraid to make mistakes; however, daring to take on new challenges.
Constant desire for renewal (developing oneself and others)	Both developing herself and motivating her people to develop professionally.	A desperation to hold onto the job and succeed in it. Having no time to develop others.
Constantly being on the way (growth and change)	Welcoming change both personally and professionally.	Feeling that he was not able to engage fully with the organization's growth and change mission but still wanting to move the company forward.
Cost-consciousness, achieving goals with small means	Distinguishing corporate goals (regarding keeping costs low) from her personal goals. In so doing, finding her own ways of how and when to cut costs.	Understanding the need to cut costs and therefore not complaining or asking for help when faced with increased workload.
Simplicity	Clarity in combination with simplicity in her relations with staff and customers.	
Closeness to reality	Understanding customer and staff perspectives, both of importance.	
Environmental responsibility		Demonstrating a strong sense of (environmental) mission.

the contract, internally he stressed his multiple attempts to prove that he was capable to stand up to the trial, while externally he aimed to reproduce the positive (responsible) image of the company as both employer and retailer. Hence, his psychological contract with IKEA seemed to have two conflicting sides: the unfulfilled internal and seemingly fulfilled external one.

Based on these findings, it can be suggested that core values as sources of motivation, and brand promise (value proposition) as a basis for the perceived psychological contract, are the key manifestations of employee branding in the individual employee experiences of a branded organization. They are also closely linked to employee job satisfaction and their eagerness to stay with the organization. These findings are in general agreement with the literature stressing the central role of the psychological contract for successful employee branding (Miles and Mangold, 2004; De Jong, 2009; Das, 2003) as well as the literature that links the fulfilment of the contract with a higher level of job satisfaction (Huibao et al., 2008). However, the present study adds new insights to our understanding of the psychological contract; more specifically, its link to employees' perceptions of core values and brand promise. Thus, motivating values and fulfilled promises appear to be the prerequisites of fair contracts. Besides, the contracts are shown to be evolving in the constant inter-action between employees and their superiors as well as between different employees, adding to the ideas of flexible and multiple contracts in the litera-ture (Seeck and Parzefall, 2008).

The findings provide support and additional insights to the earlier proposi-tions of employer brand as a structure and employee branding as an appropria-tion work within and upon the structure. The respondents' accounts represented two different appropriation practices: accommodation and resistance (see Table 8.2).

These practices were not only characterized by different perceptions of the psychological contracts by employees but also by different levels of their engagement with the organization. While Irina talked enthusiastically about her team and other colleagues, strived and wanted to stay at IKEA, Vladislav had mixed feelings about his bosses and even thought about leaving the company. His attempts to conceal his true feelings of isolation and exclu-sion via active participation in the organizational process (his attempts to feel included) reflects a series of tensions. It is also noteworthy that Irina actively redefined the conditions of her contract (for example, by refusing to make additional savings at her department) while Vladislav, rather than actively seeking change, only complained about the unfair conditions and spoke of the possibility of change, while at the same time considering terminating his contract. Thus, feelings of inclusion and empowerment undoubtedly involve the active re-creation of brand meaning by employees. The reverse also appears to be true, where passive acts of resistance may result in, and perpetuate,

Table 8.2   The empirical data on IKEA's employer brand and employee branding

Type of brand	Schemas	Resources	Brand essence
Employer brand as a structure	HR vision; values as behavioural norms, written contracts, career as a journey	Store, product range, values as cultural texts Managers as value ambassadors	'Working environment where people and team spirit are the central values'
Employee branding as appropriation work: inclusion by Irina	Vision as a reason for doing things Values as reasons for acting and sources of motivation. Nine of eleven values motivating Contract as fair: 'The company that takes good care of us' Exciting career, high ambitions	Store as a home Department as a child Team as a family Corporate managers as 'my dear Swedes'	Brand as 'my home'
Employee branding as appropriation work: exclusion by Vladislav	Vision as an inspiration Values as reasons for acting and challenges to overcome. Four of eleven values motivating. Deprived of the value of togetherness Contract as unfair: 'Work as a trial that never comes to an end' Career as a challenge, high ambitions	Job as the water where one sinks or swims. Office as a crowded and noisy place Team as a dream An immediate boss as an admired person Other corporate managers as 'them'	Brand as 'a constant trial'

feelings of exclusion. However, the exact relationship between the two elements is not clear, whether feelings of inclusion result from an active motivation to change things and re-appropriate meanings, or whether indeed it is the other way around, that feelings of inclusion motivate employees to actively engage with the brand meanings.

The findings also reveal several elements to meaning making at work which include the brand cultural schemas (the brand core values, brand promises and the psychological contract), material context (the store and office) and relationships with superiors and colleagues. These elements are closely inter-related, as seen from the observed close link between employees' perceptions of brand values and their treatment of the material context and relationships (which might be termed 'brand resources'). For example, the highly motivated Irina views her team as a family and the store as a home while the demotivated Vladislav views the office as a crowded place and managers as strangers. Thus the creation and re-appropriation of brand meaning by employees is inextricably related to the brand context (internal and external), implying the inseparability of employee and employer branding processes. Indeed, they are both integral parts of a larger branding process, which I would prefer to call employee–brand appropriation to stress the importance of taking an active employee perspective of branding. Viewed from this standpoint, the meaning of the organizational brand is continuously appropriated and re-appropriated by both existing and potential employees. By connecting employee and employer branding at the level of individual employee practices, this study contributes to a more integrative view of branding to, and with the help of, employees.

The major contribution of this study lies in challenging the established view of employee branding as a predominantly external approach (image creation, positioning), in which the employees' roles are limited to those of passive actors communicating brand messages to customers (Miles and Mangold, 2004, 2005). This study has revealed links between employees' level of empowerment and sense of belonging in their organization, and their motivations to re-appropriate brand meanings. It might be argued that successful employee branding would eventually lead to a more robust external brand image and customer satisfaction but these outcomes should not be used as ultimate goals for employees. More empirical data on employees' individual work experiences at global branded organizations are needed to obtain a deeper understanding of the employee branding process.

NOTE

1.   Indeed Vladislav needed this break. One month after the interview he had to take sick leave.

REFERENCES

Alvesson, M. (2003) 'Beyond neo-positivists, romantics and localists: A reflexive approach to interviews in organizational research', *Academy of Management Review*, 28 (1), 13–33.

Ambler, T. and Barrow, S. (1996) 'The employer brand', *Journal of Brand Management*, 4, 185–205.

Aubert-Gamet, V. (1996) 'Twisting servicescapes: diversion of the physical environment in a re-appropriation process', *International Journal of Service Industry Management*, 8(1), 26–41.

Berthon, P., Ewing, M. and Han, L. (2005) 'Captivating company: dimensions in employer branding', *International Journal of Advertising*, 24 (2), 151–73.

Backhaus, K. and Tikoo, S. (2004) 'Conceptualizing and researching employer branding', *Career Development International*, 9 (5), 501–17.

Barrow, S. and Mosley, R. (eds) (2005) *The Employer Brand. Bringing the Best of Brand Management to People at Work*, Chichester: Wiley.

Cova, B. and Pace, S. (2006) 'Brand community of convenience products: new forms of customer empowerment – the case "my Nutella The Community"', *European Journal of Marketing*, 40 (9/10), 1087–106.

Das, S. (2003) 'Vacant and engaged', *Employee Benefits*, March, 24–8.

Davies, G. (2008) 'Employer branding and its influence on managers', *European Journal of Marketing*, 42 (5/6), 668–81.

De Cuyper, N., Rigotti, T., de Witte, H. and Mohr, G. (2008) 'Balancing psychological contracts: Validation of a typology', *The International Journal of Human Resource Management*, 19 (4), April, 543–61.

De Jong, J., Schalk, R. and de Cuyper, N. (2009) 'Balanced versus Unbalanced Psychological Contracts in Temporary and Permanent Employment: Associations with Employee Attitudes', *Management and Organization Review*, 5 (3), 329–51.

Eisenhardt, K. (1989) 'Building Theories from Case Study Research', *Academy of Management Review*, 14 (4): 532–50.

Giddens, A. (1979) *Central Problem in Social Theory: Action, Structure and Contradiction in Social Analysis*, Berkeley and Los Angeles: University of California Press.

Giddens, A. (1991) *Modernity and Self-identity: Self and Society in the Late Modern Age*, Cambridge: Polity Press.

Gronroos, C. (1981) 'Internal marketing – an integral part of marketing theory', in J. H. Donnelly and W. E. George (eds) *Marketing of Services*, Chicago, IL: American Marketing Association, pp. 236–8.

Foucault, M. (1997) in Rabinow, P. (ed.), Essential Works of Foucault 1954–1984, Volume 1: *Ethics: Subjectivity and Truth*, New York: New Press, pp. 303–19.

Frook, J.E. (2001) 'Burnish your brand from inside', *B to B*, 86, 1–2.

Hieronimus, F., Schaefer, K. and Schröder, J. (2005) 'Using Branding to Attract Talent', *The McKinsey Quarterly*, 28 September.

Huibao, C., Shuo, Z. and Qiang, D. (2008) 'The Empirical Research on the Relationship between Employee Psychological Contract and Job Satisfaction', 2008 International Conference on Information Management, Innovation Management and Industrial Engineering, pp. 265–8.

Ind, N. (2003) 'Inside Out: How employees build value', *Journal of Brand Management*, 10(6), 393–401.

Kay, M. (2006) 'Strong brands and corporate brands', *European Journal of Marketing*, 40(7/8), 742–60.

Mangold, G. and Miles, S. (2007) 'The employee brand: Is yours an all-star?', *Business Horizons*, 50, 423–33.

Miles, S. and Mangold, G. (2004) 'A conceptualization of the employee branding process', *Journal of Relationship Marketing*, 3 (2/3), 65–87.

Miles, S. and Mangold, G. (2005) 'Positioning Southwest Airlines through employee branding', *Business Horizons*, 48, 535–45.

Miles, S. and Mangold, G. (2007) 'Growing the Employee Brand at ASI: A Case Study', *Journal of Leadership and Organizational Studies*, 14, 77–85.

Mitchell, C. (2000) 'Selling the brand inside', *Harvard Business Review*, 80 (1), 99–105.

Montes, S.D. and Zweig, D. (2008) 'Do Promises Matter? An Exploration of the Role of Promises in Psychological Contract Breach', *Journal of Applied Psychology*, 94 (5), 1243–60.

Mosley, R. (2007) 'Customer experience, organisational culture and the employer brand', *Brand Management*, 15 (2), 123–34.

Rosethorn, H. (2009) *The Employer Brand, Keeping Faith in the Deal*, Gower Publishing Ltd., Surrey, England.

Seeck, H. and Parzefall, M.-R. (2008) 'Employee agency: challenges and opportunities for psychological contract theory', *Personnel Review*, 37(5), 473–89.

Sullivan, J. (2004) 'Eight elements of a successful employment brand', *ER Daily*, 23 February.

Sewell, W.H. Jr. (1992) 'A Theory of structure: duality, agency, and transformation', *American Journal of Sociology*, 98(1): 1–29.

Tarnovskaya, V. (2007) 'The mechanism of market driving with a corporate brand', PhD Thesis, Lund University Press.

Thomas, R. and Davies, A. (2005) 'Theorizing the Micro-Politics of Resistance: New Public Management and Managerial Identities in the UK Public Service', *Organization Studies*, 26, 683–706.

Tsoukas, H. (1989) 'The Validity of Idiographic Research Explanations', *The Academy of Management Review*, 14 (4), 551–61.

Yin, R. (1994) *Case Study Research. Design and Methods*, second edn, London: Sage.

9. Appropriating the brand: union organizing in front-line service work

Melanie Simms

INTRODUCTION

Branding is increasingly important in contemporary life; to consumers and to organizations. The notion that branding is conveyed or 'lived' through the employees of an organization, and especially those working in front-line services, is a well-established one and one that is receiving increasing attention in academic literature (Ind, 2004; Pettinger, 2004). Ind (2004) argues that the purpose and values of an organization should be developed and communicated to staff within that organization so that they can act in line with those service brand values to promote the organization and its values effectively and consistently, and that this is particularly important in front-line service work (FLSW) where the employees are very literally the 'face' of the brand. The importance of employees being 'on brand' is argued by authors such as Barlow and Stewart (2004) to be central not just to customer service delivery but also organizational success. Important questions therefore emerge about how branding affects front-line service workers (FLSWs) and the ways workers respond.

Throughout the discussion in this chapter, the term 'service brand values' is used in the same way as used by De Chernatony et al. (2004) to indicate the argument within much marketing and services management literature that brands reflect a series of values (for more on the role of values in human behaviour see Rokeach (1973)) and that 'for a services brand the values are largely contained in the interaction between consumer and employee' (De Chernatony et al., 2004: 75). Service brand values are closely linked to, but not identical to, concepts such as organizational brand values, corporate identity and corporate image. The reality of the customer–employee interaction in front-line service work means that, in practice, many of these concepts may well be conflated within that interaction. But, technically, a single organization may encompass several or many service brands. Similarly, corporate image and/or identity may encompass more than the brand of the immediate service interaction. Further, existing literature tends to differentiate usefully between (1) brand 'identity', that is, values internally within the organization held by founders, managers and, crucially, staff; and (2) brand 'image', that is, values held externally and, crucially, by customers or service users (De Chernatony et al., 2004).

In the context of delivering a service (as opposed to a product) the role of the front-line service worker is crucial. Central to much of the more prescriptive branding literature looking at how organizations can improve the branded customer experience is the view that effective human resource management is the key to delivering an appropriate quality of customer service interaction to ensure that employees are 'on brand' throughout the customer service interaction (Barlow and Stewart, 2004; Miles and Mangold, 2004). Specifically, recruitment and training are identified as opportunities to select and then reinforce service brand values that (hopefully) should then facilitate the process by which front-line service workers communicate the brand to the customer in a consistent manner. Building on a wide range of organizational behaviour studies, and particularly those emerging from labour process theory and critical management studies (Thompson, 2009), it is reasonable to hypothesize that resistance is more likely when a managerial practice is experienced and/or understood as a control strategy. Branding may, in certain circumstances, be understood as just such a strategy. Customer service branding may involve an effort to assert managerial control over what front-line service workers wear, how they speak and the tone of engagement with the customer (Sturdy, 1998). Importantly, in some forms of FLSW, branding can go alongside routinization of work as forms of control. Perhaps the clearest example of this is some call centre work where workers are required to adhere to scripts in their customer service interactions in an effort to ensure consistency of response and service quality levels (Bain and Taylor, 1999; Kinnie et al., 2000). In routinizing these interactions, managers can be understood as attempting to secure a consistent application of service brand values and customer experience. In doing so, the work becomes de-skilled as workers lose discretion over how to deal with customers.

It is notable that a great deal of discussion about how organizations can secure branded customer service is highly optimistic in relation to how employees may experience this process. Jobs are mainly assumed to pre-exist any managerial decision-making regarding branding and the emphasis of much of the customer service branding literature (Barlow and Stewart, 2004; Miles and Mangold, 2004, 2005) is on how to then recruit the 'right' staff into these roles and then to train them to promote service brand values in a way that adds competitive advantage to the employer. This perspective risks obscuring the many complex interactions and inconsistencies that occur in organizations and in customer service interactions. It assumes that with the 'right' hiring, training and performance management an organization can ensure that an employee is consistently 'on brand'. In practice, we know from a wealth of studies that take a more critical perspective on managerial control of work that such outcomes are rarely so linear or predictable. Even under 'ordinary' circumstances of organizational life, employees resist and 'misbehave' (Ackroyd and Thompson, 1999; Collinson and Ackroyd, 2006) in ways that managers rarely expect or anticipate. In some cases dissatisfaction and resistance may become sufficiently organized and formalized to involve a trade union.

This chapter looks at how the service brand values of four organizations are used in precisely these kinds of circumstances: what happens to the service brand values when a trade union starts to organize the workforce? Of course, in nearly 85 per cent of private sector service workplaces, there is no formally recognized trade union with which the employer negotiates (Kersley et al., 2006). But as unions have attempted to renew themselves over the 1990s and 2000s, they have placed more emphasis on attempting to expand into service sector workplaces (Heery et al., 2000, 2003). In doing so they have had to engage with, and respond to, the particular issues confronting front-line service workers. One of these issues is the complexity of being the 'face' of the organization and its service brand values. Studies looking at front-line service work frequently identify the paradox that dealing with customers is both a source of considerable pleasure for these workers, but also of 'pain' when dealing with objectionable, dissatisfied or sometimes frankly unreasonable customers and clients (Harris and Reynolds, 2003). Increasing attention has been paid to the challenges faced by workers in dealing with customers (Reynolds and Harris, 2006) and the pressures that confront FLSWs within their day-to-day work. But comparatively little attention has been paid to how those pressures can create dissatisfaction and discontent in the workplace which may build into more formalized resistance in the form of a union organizing campaign.

CASE STUDY ORGANIZATIONS

The evidence for this chapter is drawn from four longitudinal (1998–2005), ethnographic case studies of successful union organizing campaigns where unions have targeted relatively low-skill front-line service workers in workplaces that had not previously been unionized. Four employers were targeted: Scope, Typetalk, Ethel Austin and Gala Casinos.

Scope is a large charity employing around 4000 staff and representing the interests of people with cerebral palsy. It is a well-known charity which re-branded itself from being the Spastics Society in 1994 because, through prolonged misuse, the term 'spastic' had become a term of abuse. In 2006, the charity was rated as having the 48th most valuable UK charity brand – notably lower than its ranking of 29th largest measured by income. The re-branding has largely been successful with a growth in donations and a rising profile, particularly among corporate donors who had previous steered clear of the organization because of its unfavourable previous brand and associations. Lomax and Mador (2006) explore the dynamics of this re-branding in substantial detail but here it is sufficient to highlight that the central value of the re-branded organization is equality. Primarily, this is conceptualized as equality between disabled and able-bodied people, but central to all of Scope's branding is the notion of equality: examples include their Time to Get Equal campaign, and their slogan 'For disabled people achieving equality'. Workers in Scope are engaged in three main areas of activity: head office work including campaigning, running charity shops that raise income for the organization, and support work for people with cerebral palsy and their families.

Typetalk is a smaller joint venture between British Telecom (BT) and the Royal National Institute for the Deaf (RNID), employing just over 400 staff. It is a telephone relay service that allows deaf and hearing-impaired telephone users to interact with hearing people. Text typed by the deaf user is spoken by a call centre operator and any spoken message in return is typed by the operator and sent to the deaf user's screen. Typetalk itself is a relatively unknown brand outside the target user groups, but both BT and the RNID are well-established and well-known. In 2003, BT introduced new core brand values: trustworthy, helpful, inspiring, straightforward, and heart. In 2005 (when much of the research took place) the Chief Executive's statement in the Annual Report argued that the brand 'stands for excellent networking[1] skills and a genuine commitment to finding innovative ways of delivering what our customers want'. The RNID by contrast uses the core notion of 'changing the world for deaf and hard of hearing people' to underline their commitment to campaigning, championing and winning improvements for those who are hearing impaired. The vast majority of Typetalk staff are engaged as call centre operators undertaking the transcription and speech services described above.

In contrast to the charitable brand values of Typetalk and Scope, Ethel Austin is a low-cost clothes retailer mainly based in the North of England and employing around 2800 staff. Although by 2008 it had hit significant financial difficulties and is currently undergoing a significant restructuring and brand re-launch, during the research period it was still a brand with strong links to its past. Unsurprisingly for a low-cost retailer, 'value' was a core brand value but always allied to notions of honesty and quality – particularly service quality. Equally important was the long tradition of paternalism and loyalty among both staff and customers. Treating staff and customers well in comparison to competitor low-cost retailers was central to efforts to build that loyalty. Ethel Austin staff are largely employed in the retail function working in and managing small high street stores.

The final research site is also a commercial organization: Gala Casinos. The casino business is one arm of a larger Gala Coral Group, and is in the middle of the casino market. Although Gala Casinos do target the low-stakes end of the market, it has a lower stake business in Gala Bingo and largely stays out of the high-roller top-end market of the casino sector. The core values of the company relate to hospitality and responsibility; providing a welcoming environment for customers while also complying with the extensive regulation in the gaming industry, and promoting gambling as a socially acceptable pastime. Specifically, the Chief Executive's statement in 2009 refers to being 'a high performing team, which is customer focused, behaves ethically, and achieves outstanding results' (Dominic Harrison, Chief Executive, Gala Coral Group website). Gala Casino staff are mainly involved either in front-of-house work (croupiers, bar staff, waiting staff, security etc.) or back-of-house work (some security functions, food and drink preparation etc.).

TENSIONS IN FRONT-LINE SERVICE WORK: CUSTOMERS, ROUTINIZATION, BRANDING AND CONTROL

The challenges of unionizing service sector workers are compounded by tensions that are, to some degree, inherent in the nature of front-line service work. Previous research has emphasized the importance of acknowledging that the involvement of the customer in the day-to-day work of front-line service workers is a source of both considerable pleasure and satisfaction, but also the root of much discontent (Eaton, 1996; Sturdy et al., 2001). While workers may well enjoy the sociability of such work, and the opportunity to engage with customers, reports of abuse, of the challenge of engaging in emotional labour, and of the often humiliating interactions that are sometimes encountered, are well-explored by previous researchers (Cobble, 1996; Reynolds and Harris, 2006).

Similarly, emerging from the literature on call centres, we see that there are frequently tensions in the ways that managers attempt to manage low-skill front-line service work (Taylor et al., 2002). The identification of 'mass customized bureaucracies' (Korczynski et al., 2000) is helpful here. In some low-skill front-line service work, managers attempt to routinize the customer interaction in an effort to exert control, but the demands of individual customers and of the imperative to provide a service require some degree of customization of interactions on the part of FLSWs. Similar tensions are visible in some areas of routinized hospitality work, retail and catering. It is not uncommon, for example, for restaurants or shops to script customer interactions. Whether or not FLSWs stick to these scripts is a different matter. But the fact of scripting can be seen as an effort to exert a degree of managerial control over the customer–worker interaction. Korczynski (2003) identifies that when these kinds of contradictions in mass customized bureaucracies emerge, employees often form informal 'communities of coping' which allow them space to complain and perhaps reconcile the contradictory managerial rationales. Challenging this control raises important issues for unions as it is a direct intervention into those efforts at managerial control. As we shall see, the empirical evidence raises complexities that are often not envisaged by managers or by workers.

So the nature of front-line service work, and the ways that managers attempt to exert control over the customer–worker interaction, present unions with specific issues that are not visible in, say, manufacturing work. But there is a further, extremely important, way in which managers attempt to exert some control over front-line service work: branding. Without understanding how managers seek to use notions of branding in the customer–worker interaction, we cannot properly understand the dynamics of those interactions.

The ways in which employees are expected to 'live' the brand and the tensions that this brings both to managers and to workers is increasingly attracting the attention of academics (Pettinger, 2004), but overall it is an under-explored area. Even in the most routinized front-line work, employees are regularly encouraged to see themselves as the 'face of the brand'. Work in call centres has drawn our attention to the ways in which employees are selected, trained and monitored to ensure compliance with particular service brand values (Batt, 2000; Korczynski, 2003; Taylor et al., 2002). Some authors have identified the ways in which different brands hosted within the same call centre often use different employees to front those brands in order to differentiate between different service brand values ('bubbly', 'professional' or 'informal' for example) (Batt, 2000; Kinnie et al., 2000). There is a strong managerial perception in these circumstances that particular employees are 'more suited' to particular service brand values and vice versa. Indeed, in some cases, routinization can itself be seen as an effort to promote particular service brand values to ensure consistency of the service experience. Thus, we might reasonably expect the ways in which employers and managers seek to promote particular service brand values to cause tensions for workers and for the customer–worker interaction.

It is the central argument of this chapter that all of these tensions are inherent in front-line service work and present trade unions with opportunities as well as challenges in their engagements with service workplaces. In order to reflect on this more conceptually, it is important to restate what unions are seeking to do when they recruit and organize in a workplace. In essence, they are seeking to identify common, collective interests among workers which are differentiable from the interests of managers (Kelly, 1997, 1998). The identification of these interests is a complex, socially constructed process. In other words, during the process of deciding which interests the union should represent (and in rejecting others), the union gives legitimacy to the chosen interests which, in turn, reinforces those interests as being legitimate expressions of the collective will (see Hyman, 1999; Simms, 2007b for further discussion).

Mobilization theory (Kelly, 1998) suggests that not only must those interests be seen to be opposed to a powerful group, but some form of 'blame' must be able to be apportioned. In other words, for example, if workers are resentful of a wage freeze, but attribute that to the difficult economic conditions in which the organization is operating, then it is unlikely that they will mobilize against management because they do not attribute the cause of their situation to managerial decisions. Finally, mobilization theory indicates that there is an – often implicit – cost–benefit analysis to be made about the respective 'costs' of mobilization (risk of losing a job, risk of the company going bankrupt, risk of managerial retaliation, etc.) and 'benefits' of mobilization (improvement of terms and conditions of work, better working environment, etc.).

At its core, a union is trying to mobilize a collective group (workers) around shared interests. Important conceptual and empirical questions emerge in the setting of FLSW. How does the involvement of customers affect the process of mobilizing against managers? Can customers and customers' interests be used to support the process of mobilization? How does the process of managing FLSW through routinization, branding, etc., present opportunities and challenges for unions to mobilize workers? This chapter uses empirical evidence to show that the ways in which managers seek to exert some degree of control over the customer–worker interaction (largely through routinization and branding) presents unions with opportunities to collectivize and mobilize workers. Indeed, in certain circumstances, unions and workers are able to appropriate service brand values (customer service, quality, etc.) to challenge managerial decisions.

In the case studies, we see some of the complexities involved when front-line service workers are sufficiently dissatisfied with their working conditions to unionize. This is important because it tells us a great deal both about how employees understand the nature of their branded (working) lives and about how resistance to managerial control can sometimes be developed using some of the values of the brands being lived. In the case studies presented here, FLSWs do sometimes understand the service brand values as being mechanisms of control and therefore presenting opportunities for collective resistance (organizing issues).

But something much more interesting also emerged from the empirical data: the potential for unions to use service brand values against management. It is already well established that many front-line service workers identify with the service users/consumers and are often very personally supportive of the organizational and brand values of their employers (see Miles and Mangold (2005) for a highly optimistic account or Hurd (1993) and Eaton (1996) for a more critical engagement with these ideas). What is remarkable in the case studies presented here is that unions are sometimes able to use the service brand values to construct narratives and arguments that challenge managers to organize work in ways that improve the customer service and allow FLSWs to deliver service brand values more effectively. In turn, this is important because it shows how unions are able to respond to the needs of service workers and engage not just with the day-to-day employment problems they may have, but to develop responses that address the fundamental nature of front-line service work. Heery (1993) acknowledges the possibility that trade unions can, under certain circumstances, help forge alliances between workers and customers to promote customer service. He uses the example of alliances between workers and customers to oppose privatization of the water industry in the 1980s and a similar dynamic can be seen in the Royal Mail today. If we understand the satisfaction that front-line service workers can, and often do, derive from customer service interactions, it is not implausible to argue that there may well be potential for unions to promote customer service as an important issue to their (potential) members. Given the centrality of FLSWs in 'delivering' service brand values, it seems likely that a perceived mismatch between the actions of managers and the brand values that workers are expected to uphold in their day-to-day lives may well give rise to the kinds of dissatisfaction and, perhaps, resistance that is a prerequisite for collective action.

Service brand values can appear in union organizing campaigns when unions are able to use the kinds of 'gaps' (mismatches, breaches) between espoused values and the ways in which work is actually organized to argue for improvements to the working lives of FLSWs. In other words, where employers are perceived as not fulfilling their own brand values, or are creating working conditions that make it difficult for FLSWs to deliver those brand values, unions are not only able to identify that as a source of dissatisfaction but use those arguments to persuade employers to make changes to work that help employees. Although this is a logical extension of the idea that there can be gaps and inconsistencies between what employers want (or say they want) workers to do and the conditions within which they are expected to deliver those outcomes, this is a dynamic that has not previously been discussed in relation to front-line service work. It shows that trade unions can not only be sensitive to the particular dynamics of FLSW, but they can also use these inherent tensions to improve working conditions not just for workers but also, potentially, for customers and managers.

METHODOLOGY AND METHODS

The focus of the analysis presented here is the ways in which unions can engage with service brand values as they attempt to collectivize the workforce.

This process was observed using the trade union organizing campaign as the unit of analysis. The primary research interest was to explore how trade unions respond to the challenges of collectivizing front-line service workers. I was keen to understand not just what unions do when they talk to and organize these workers, but wider issues about how these employees understand their daily working lives, what causes them difficulties, and how a union can (or cannot) address those concerns. I deliberately identified campaigns that were 'successful' in the eyes of the union (mainly defined by the fact that they were successful in achieving bargaining rights) because I wanted to know more about the conditions that allow unions to organize these workers successfully. These campaigns were then observed from the very early stages through to securing formal collective representation rights for workers. It is difficult to say definitively when a campaign 'starts' or 'ends' but critical moments are when the union decides to allocate resources to it and then to withdraw specialist organizing resources. Given the research focus of exploring the complex social meanings of these processes for key actors, the focus was on observation and interviews and was supplemented with analysis of documentary materials such as recruitment materials, websites of the union and employers, background data on the employer (company reports, etc.) and collective agreements.

As a researcher, I observed the process of union involvement from the early stages of planning meetings between workers and the union (mainly in the form of union officers and specialist paid organizers), through to the development of collective actions (including, but not limited to, action such as petitions, grievances, efforts to bring collective concerns to the attention of managers, leafleting, demonstrations, press events, and eventually negotiations between managers and the union), and culminating in formal agreement from managers that the union had the right to represent workers' interests. This observation was overt and non-participant. In other words, the union officers and the employees knew that I was a researcher and I was not directly engaged in the work of the union or of the workers.

Over the seven years of involvement in these campaigns, 92 participants were interviewed and 32 of them were interviewed more than once during that period – some as many as four times. Key participants included senior decision-makers within the union, paid union organizers, generalist officers and negotiators, workplace activists, and workers including both members and non-members. Unfortunately, I had few opportunities to interview managers because the campaigns were, for the majority of the research period, taking place in a context of significant managerial resistance to unionization. Nonetheless, there was opportunity to observe managers during meetings and discussions and, of course, workers and union officers were a rich source of data in relation to their own perceptions of managerial decisions including service brand values. The research was a small section of a much wider project run initially at Cardiff University[2] looking at trade union renewal from 1998 to the present day.

SERVICE BRAND VALUE AWARENESS BY EMPLOYEES

In customer service branding, the centrality of employees being aware of the organizational or service brand values is highlighted as an important step in ensuring that they consistently deliver a service experience that reflects and reinforces those values (Barlow and Stewart, 2004). In this research, service brand value awareness was not measured quantitatively, but it frequently emerged as a spontaneous issue raised by workers in meetings, interviews and discussions. In this context, service brand awareness is taken to mean the extent to which employees understand their front-line service roles as involving a degree of promotion of a particular set of customer service values and, if they did see their roles in this way, what those values were and how they related to the organization.

Notably, even employees who had worked in the organizations for relatively short amounts of time were keen to explain how they understood the service brand values. Often these were explicitly addressed in induction training, but even where they were not (e.g. Ethel Austin), much of the training about customer service underlined managerial expectations about what kinds of behaviours, attitudes and values were expected. Although the research approach made it difficult to interview managers directly, there was a strong belief among interviewees that they had been recruited because they exhibited particular characteristics (comment was frequently passed about the need to be 'friendly' or 'welcoming'), attitudes and behaviours.

Interestingly, the employees working in the two charitable organizations (Scope and Typetalk) were extremely articulate about the ways in which their own personal values were reflected in the values of the organization for which they worked. Thus, for example, one employee commented that 'I work here because I like it. But I also believe in it. I believe in fighting for better rights [for disabled people]... I wouldn't do it if I didn't believe in it' (Scope employee, interview). This kind of attitude was prevalent and emerged in many of the interviews with workers. Even relatively low-paid workers in Scope doing care work in residential homes or driving vans for collecting second-hand goods donated to the charity shops expressed a close association with the values of the organization. 'It's important that I'm doing something that's doing some good' (Scope driver, interview). 'It's hard work, but I know it makes a difference' (Scope care worker, meeting). Typetalk is essentially a call-centre-based service, so alternative employment for these workers might be in a commercial call centre. This was an important point of comparison to many of these workers: 'It's better than working for [insurance company]. Here, it's harder, you have to type quicker, but at least I know I'm doing something worthwhile' (Typetalk operator, interview).

By contrast, the employees in the commercial organizations often spoke more dismissively of the values of their employers. One Ethel Austin employee laughed, 'We're just a cheap knicker shop really!' (Ethel Austin worker, interview). Nonetheless, they identified the value of loyalty and frequently expressed pride in the paternalism of the senior management team. 'Old Mr Austin used to come around and give us all chocolates at Christmas until he retired. I know it's silly, but that kind of thing is important' (Ethel Austin clerical worker, interview). When prompted, employees in both Ethel Austin and in the casinos recognized that quality of service was important to them, to their employers and to the customers. 'Oh yes! It's important to be polite and all that. Even when they [customers] are buggers – complaining and everything' (Ethel Austin worker, interview). 'Managers come down hard on us if they think we've been arsy. Even if you've been provoked [by the customer]. It's important that our attitude's right' (Gala Casino bar staff, interview).

Arguably, service brand awareness is more important within the charity sector, which relies heavily on donations (both individual and corporate) for income. Having a 'bankable' and recognizable brand (i.e. brand equity) is often central to securing continued support and investment. Equally, there may well be an issue of self-selection whereby workers with particular values are more likely to actively seek out employment in the not-for-profit sector. But it is nonetheless notable that, when prompted, Ethel Austin employees did identify value and service quality as core values of the organization, and Gala Casino interviewees identified hospitality as a core part of the values of their employer. This is important because, as we shall see in a moment, there was a widespread perception that the employers were not always upholding these brand values in the management of staff.

BRANDING AND ROUTINIZATION AS INTERRELATED CONTROL STRATEGIES

What is clear from these case studies of low-skill, front-line service work is that both branding and routinization are central to managerial control strategies. Although none of the jobs in these environments is as tightly scripted as, say, in a routine commercial call centre operation or a fast food restaurant, it is evident that the ways in which jobs are designed and monitored routinizes the work to a considerable degree (Frenkel et al., 1999). In common with much FLSW, staff training in these organizations tends to focus on the ways in which service brand values can and should be promoted in front-line service interactions. Typically, workers reported that this involves suggested wording of particular service interactions, directions on the extent to which employees have (or do not have) discretion in dealing with customers, ways of dealing with difficult customers, etc. Clearly, training is only one mechanism through which to communicate the expectations and constraints of a job, but it is often one of the most visible, so demands attention. What this training does is to promote a standardization of customer service interaction across time and place so that there is a 'Gala experience', an 'Ethel Austin experience' or a 'Typetalk experience', even if this is not explicitly the language that managers would use to describe the service relationship. The work at Scope is inevitably harder to standardize as it is both more varied in its design and in the service user needs. In the facilities providing direct support to service users, front-line staff must respond to people with often very serious physical disabilities. Inevitably, the nature of those interactions is difficult to routinize. In the second-hand shops, the interactions are more often undertaken by volunteers, who are not the focus of this chapter. The point here is that in comparatively low-skill front-line service work, both routinization and branding can be important control strategies.

In other words, the routinization of the work through the explicit constraint of the extent to which FLSWs are allowed to exercise discretion in their service interactions is often justified by managers as being related to promotion of particular service brand values. An example of this can be seen in the ways that Typetalk operators are encouraged to start and end conversations. They are not technically scripted in the sense that operators can diverge from the guidelines if necessary and will not face any punishment if they do so, but they are actively encouraged to use particular phrases and wordings that appear friendly and open in order to promote a friendly and engaging experience for the service users. Certainly if they were perceived by managers as being surly, unfriendly or uncooperative, they would face discipline. This is actively presented as being part of the branded customer experience and can be understood as a form of workplace control through brand values. Similarly, Gala Casino hospitality staff are expected to promote a particular set of brand values as highlighted previously. In practice, the requirement to provide a hospitable environment limits staff options about how to behave in a situation where a customer is abusive. As we shall see in more detail in a moment, in the face of customer abuse, staff had little discretion to warn or eject problematic customers.

These examples show how brand values interact with service expectations and the ways in which jobs are organized. It is not the intention to suggest a simplistic relationship between these facets of front-line service work. Nor to suggest that they are always understood by managers as a way of controlling staff. The point here is that they can intersect as mutually reinforcing control strategies, particularly where managers are concerned to ensure the promotion of particular customer service experiences through standardizing interactions to some degree. This observation presents interesting possibilities to trade unions that are seeking to organize in these contexts.

VULNERABILITY OF BRAND VALUES DURING A UNION ORGANIZING CAMPAIGN

Without exception, an important issue in each of the four campaigns revolved around identifying discrepancies between the espoused service brand values and the ways organizations treated their staff. The extent to which this formed a core narrative of the campaign varies, but in all of the campaigns this phenomenon was visible. So, for example, in Scope the issue was initially identified by employees themselves. One key activist was at pains to point out that 'Scope is all about equality and fairness. All we want is some of that for us [employees]' (Scope activist, interview). The unions involved in the campaign often used the language and values of the charity to make the case for union membership and organization. Leaflets frequently and deliberately featured the words equality and fairness. One of the unions involved was, at the time, known as MSF[3] and the union regularly used the slogan Making Society Fairer to promote itself in the charity. MSF in fact stood for Manufacturing, Science and Finance union. This was a deliberate strategy on the part of the union organizers. In interviews and discussions they were keen to point out that this was an important way of engaging these workers. 'They [Scope employees] often do it because they want to help or improve society. We need to acknowledge that when we present them with the idea of the union' (MSF organizer, interview).

Indeed, this was precisely the strategy pursued by the union and it was highly successful. Negotiations and meetings with managers persistently pointed out how HR practices were often perceived as unfair by employees. Specific examples included selection for redundancy, or shift scheduling patterns in care homes. Initially managers reacted very negatively to the union pointing out inconsistencies in espoused values and HR practices and this was reflected in increasingly acrimonious relations between the union and management. But it played very well indeed with workers and was picked up by them as a campaigning slogan in leaflets and recruitment activities. Of particular interest here is that in a number of situations, this approach was used to highlight how service users were being let down. The example of shift scheduling in care homes illustrates this. Here the issue was about unilateral managerial decision-making in relation to shift scheduling, which sometimes created very irregular shift patterns for individual workers. This caused problems for some workers, especially those with care responsibilities outside work, which meant that in the worst case scenario they had to cancel or swap shifts with very little notice. In turn, this led to service users experiencing inconsistency in care provision or, at worst, staff being overstretched because of team member absence. The point is that the union worked hard to point out that the source of this problem was unilateralism in shift-scheduling processes. But the effect was not only that staff saw these processes as unfair, but that service quality may have suffered as well. This proved a persuasive argument and improved systems for consultation over shift-scheduling were agreed.

Similarly, in Typetalk, the union organizer was keen to emphasize that although this work shared many features of more conventional call centre work, the motivation for staying with the organization despite some challenging working conditions were often very different. 'These women could go and work in a bank. But they often want to be working here. So we need to understand that. Not be too confrontational' (CWU union organizer, interview). In this case, the union also played on the potential discrepancies between the espoused service brand values and the ways in which staff were being managed. Here, however, the approach was focused much more on directly engaging with management. At one point in the campaign, concern emerged about the content of the calls that operators were being asked to engage with; some were alleged to have sexually explicit content or be related to potentially unlawful activities. A profound tension emerged between those who believed that deaf telephone users have the right to use the telephone for any purpose that an equivalent hearing user would, and those (including the union) who argued that operators should be protected from having to engage with those calls. In this case, the brand values of BT (one of the joint venture partners) were extremely helpful in the union's mobilization efforts. With discussions with Typetalk management making little progress, the union threatened to go public with the story in the local newspaper. This was directly framed as a threat to bring BT into disrepute and to challenge its core values of trustworthiness and of being a reasonable employer. Unsurprisingly, even though BT were not directly involved in the day-to-day management of the service, this prompted sufficient concern to ensure that some progress was made on this issue.

These examples show how both charitable and commercial organizations can be vulnerable to poor publicity (either internally or externally) framed around their own service brand values. Of course, any union organizing campaign is about building collective interests among employees and such activity is, on one level, unsurprising. However, in the two commercial workplaces (Ethel Austin and Gala Casinos) the dynamic played out slightly differently.

In Ethel Austin the tensions in service brand values and HR practices were mainly seen in the ways that particular services, most specifically returns of faulty or unwanted goods, were dealt with in a very routinized way. Rules set by managers dictated what could and could not be returned and some workers felt that the lack of discretion in making this judgement meant that the quality of service was sometimes undermined. Unlike the campaigns in the two charitable organizations, this was a minor issue and never fully developed as a campaigning or mobilizing issue by the union but it was, nonetheless, observed. What is illustrated in this case is that the managerial decision to routinize a process was perceived by workers as undermining their ability to deliver customer service. They argued forcefully to be allowed greater discretion so as to be able to reward the loyalty of some customers. As one shopworker put it, 'I think it's unfair that I have to say no to returns [except under certain conditions]. Some of the customers are regulars, like. And I just don't think it's fair to them… It's not what we're about' (Ethel Austin worker, interview). Clearly it is impossible to know how far this argument could have been taken by the union and whether an alternative arrangement could have been reached. But it shows how employees can perceive discrepancies between the service brand values managers say they want them to deliver and the ways in which jobs are actually designed. Here, the routinization and removal of worker discretion from the job was seen as potentially undermining the quality of service undoubtedly associated with the brand and causing dissatisfaction to workers.

In the casinos, these tensions in managerial control over front-line service work were much more problematic and gave the union one of its central organizing issues. Specifically, the issue of customer abuse and what employees were or were not allowed to do if they were abused by customers was an issue of major concern. Customer emotions often run very high in a casino environment; it is an environment in which money is made and lost, alcohol is consumed, and the casino tries to create an atmosphere in which the customer feels they are king or queen in an effort to get them to spend more money both on hospitality and at the tables. In this context, it is relatively common that staff have to deal with difficult situations (threats, abuse, violence) as well as positive situations. Prior to the involvement of the union, the rule of thumb – at least as practised on the floor on a day-to-day basis – was that staff had very few rights to walk away from an abusive customer. Security staff would eventually remove a customer if he or she became too abusive, but staff were generally expected to deal with the situation unless or until there was a threat of violence.

This seemed largely to be driven by a desire to accommodate all of the requests of the customer; especially the higher-spending ones. It was explained in both interviews and observed meetings that this seemed to be a formal policy promoted by management, although the research never revealed written evidence on this point and it was contested by managers. One interviewee commented, 'I don't know why they [management] are saying now that we can walk away [from customers] if needs be. I've never heard them say that before til the union got involved' (Gala front-of-house worker, observation notes of union meeting). Here, the commitment to promoting a hospitable environment for customers came into direct conflict with the interests of workers. The union was able to campaign around this with some reasonable degree of success and agreed guidelines with managers about what staff could do if they were confronted with such behaviour. In short, these guidelines emphasized that workers did have the right to walk away from such a situation, and to request support from managers and security staff. Again, this is an example where the tensions and contradictions of the ways in which brand values are conveyed to staff can not only create unintended consequences for workers, but also be used as a lever to identify mobilizing issues.

CONCLUSION

In short, we see, in all of these cases, ways in which service brand values can be vulnerable during union organizing campaigns. These contradictions and tensions are, to some degree, inherent in the nature of relatively low-skill, routinized front-line service work. Addressing them is not simply a matter of ensuring more consistent transmission of service brand values through human resource practices, although that may change the precise nature of the issues identified by the unions. The inherent tensions and contradictions of this kind of FLSW ensure that there will always be inconsistencies in customer service delivery around which unions can organize. And using the service brand values as a way of framing desired improvements to working conditions can be a powerful narrative at the union's disposal.

Many studies of workplace sociology highlight the ways in which workers identify tensions and contradictions inherent within managerial strategies and, unsurprisingly, branding is no different. What matters here is that the financial value attached to the brand means that organizations may well feel vulnerable to an attack framed around their brand values. Union organizers are skilled at seeing the potential to reframe the service brand values of organizations. As the 'embodiment of the brand' (Pettinger, 2004), front-line service workers often report positive attitudes towards the service brand values they embody in their work. Although this is a potential challenge to unions because it could constrain their ability to construct ideological frameworks in which the interests of workers and managers may conflict (Kelly, 1997), in these cases the unions have shown that they can use these contradictions as a 'way in' to opening a dialogue with workers and with managers.

In this context, union organizers are highly skilled in identifying ways in which the service brand values can be used to promote workers' interests; echoing the US organizing campaign among Harvard University clerical workers where the union adopted the slogan 'It's not anti-Harvard to be pro-union' (Hurd, 1993). In these cases, managerial failure to organize work in such a way that allows workers to promote customer service quality can be used to develop narratives to support unionization. In this regard, union organizers are skilled in identifying the tensions inherent in FLSW and can even appropriate contradictions in brand values, using them to construct a logic that favours the development of collective interests among workers and, eventually, unionization.

The conceptual importance of this argument lies in the fact that the notion of 'communities of coping' relates specifically to the ways in which workers cope with the contradictions inherent in mass customized bureaucracies; particularly the contradictions between promoting service quality whilst simultaneously pursuing managerial control strategies such as routinization that may impede service quality (Korczynski, 2003). The case studies presented in this chapter show that unions can also be attentive to these contradictions and are able to frame some of them in ways that facilitate the development and expression of collective interests. These narratives are presented to both workers and managers with considerable effect. This approach allows workers to build complex and overlapping loyalties to their work, customers, union, and the brand, while simultaneously challenging managers. A typical example is the way in which unions use the problems confronting both workers and customers generated by over-standardized work to show managers that the service brand values are not being upheld in the work, thus legitimizing the role of the union and, ideally, negotiating improvements in work that allow greater focus on service quality. It is the contention of this chapter that the specific nature of relatively low-skill front-line service work presents these opportunities. By designing work in a relatively routinized manner, managers in these organizations become concerned with the ways in which brand values can be promoted by workers whose scope for discretion in relation to the customer service interaction is considerably constrained. One way of promoting a particular brand experience is to promote particular service brand values. But in doing so, it is more than possible that workers develop a genuine concern for the quality of service experienced by the consumer or service user which may well not be able to be satisfied within the constraints of routinized work. This can then create space for collectivization. When unions enter the workplace they may well be able to identify and to develop this nascent resistance into more collective and formalized forms.

What is also important here is that unions do this very deliberately. Union organizers are trained to do it (Simms, 2007a) and are skilled in developing and presenting these alternative narratives in such a way that facilitates, expresses and mobilizes ideological resources in favour of collectivization (Kelly, 1997). A further noteworthy point is that this argument presents an interesting empirical extension of Rosenthal's view (2004) that managerial control mechanisms can be appropriated by workers (and here, importantly, unions) to further their own control. This stands as a counterpoint to (but not rejection of) the argument of Boltanski and Chaipello (2006) about the ability of capitalism to appropriate the values of resistance movements. Here, unions have become adept at appropriating the values of, arguably, the most striking expression of capitalism, the brand, to further their efforts to gain some collective influence over work.

NOTES

1. Networking in this context refers to IT infrastructure, rather than interpersonal skills.
2. The team originally comprised Professor Ed Heery, Professor Rick Delbridge, Professor Paul Stewart, Dave Simpson, John Salmon and myself. The research team has subsequently moved in different directions and to different universities. I am grateful to all concerned for the continued support and engagement with the project.
3. It has subsequently merged to form the union Unite.

REFERENCES

Ackroyd, S. and Thompson, P. (1999) *Organizational Misbehaviour*, London: Sage.
Bain, P. and Taylor, P. (2002) 'Ringing the changes? Union recognition and organisation in call centres in the UK finance sector', *Industrial Relations Journal*, 33 (3), 246–61.
Barlow, J. and Stewart, P. (2004) *Branded Customer Service: The New Competitive Edge, San Francisco*: Berrett-Koehler.
Batt, R. (2000) 'Strategic segmentation in front-line services: matching customers, employees and human resource systems', *International Journal of Human Resource Management*, 11 (3), 540–61.
Boltanski, L. and Chiapello, E. (2006) *The New Spirit of Capitalism*, London: Verso.
Cobble, D.S. (1996) 'The prospects for unionism in a service society', in C.L. MacDonald and C Sirianni (eds) *Working in the Service Society*, Philadelphia: Temple University Press.
Collinson, D. and Ackroyd, S. (2006) 'Resistance, misbehaviour and dissent', in S. Ackroyd, R. Batt, P. Thompson and P. Tolbert (eds), *The Oxford Handbook of Work and Organization*, Oxford: Oxford University Press.
De Chernatony, L., Drury, S. and Segal-Horn, S. (2004) 'Identifying and sustaining services brands' values', *Journal of Marketing Communications*, 10 (2), 73–93.
Eaton, S. (1996) 'The customer is always interesting: Unionized Harvard clericals renegotiate work relationships', in C. MacDonald and C. Sirianni (eds) *Working in the Service Society*, Philadelphia: Temple University Press.
Frenkel, S., Korczynski, M., Shire, K. and Tam, M. (1999) On the Front Line: *Organization of Work in the Information Economy*, Ithaca, NY: Cornell University Press.
Harris, L. and Reynolds, K. (2003) 'The consequences of dysfunctional customer behavior', *Journal of Service Research*, 6 (2), 144–61.

Heery, E. (1993) 'Industrial relations and the customer', *Industrial Relations Journal*, 24 (4), 284–95.

Heery, E., Simms, M., Simpson, D., Delbridge, R. and Salmon, J. (2000) 'Organising unionism comes to the UK', *Employee Relations*, 22 (1), 38–57.

Heery, E., Simms, M., Delbridge, R., Salmon, J. and Simpson, D. (2003) 'Trade union recruitment policy in Britain', in G. Gall (ed.), *Union Organizing: Campaigning for Recognition*, London: Routledge.

Hurd, R. (1993) 'Organizing and representing clerical workers: the Harvard model', in D. S. Cobble (ed.), Women and Unions: Forging a Partnership, Ithaca, New York: Cornell University Press.

Hyman, R. (1999) 'Imagined solidarities: can trade unions resist globalisation?', in P. Leisink (ed.), *Globalization and Labour Relations*, Cheltenham, UK and Northampton, MA, USA: Edward Elgar.

Ind, N. (2004) *Living The Brand: How To Transform Every Member of Your Organization Into a Brand Champion*, London: Kogan Page.

Kelly, J. (1997) 'The future of trade unionism: injustice, identity and social attribution', *Employee Relations*, 19 (5), 400–14.

Kelly, J. (1998) *Rethinking Industrial Relations: Mobilization, Collectivism and Long Waves*, London: Routledge.

Kersley, B., Alpin, C., Forth, J., Bryson, A., Bewley, H., Dix, G. and Oxenbridge, S. (2006) *Inside the Workplace: Findings from the 2004 Workplace Employment Relations Survey*, London: Routledge.

Kinnie, N., Hutchinson, S. and Purcell, J. (2000) 'Fun and surveillance: the paradox of high commitment management in call centres', *International Journal of Human Resource Management*, 11 (5), 967–85.

Korczynski, M. (2003) 'Communities of coping: collective emotional labour in service work', *Organization*, 10 (1), 55–79.

Korczynski, M. (2003a) 'The contradictions of service work: the call centre as customer-oriented bureaucracy', in A. Sturdy, I. Grugulis and H. Willmott (eds), *Customer Service: Empowerment and Entrapment*, Basingstoke: Palgrave.

Korczynski, M., Shire, K., Frenkle, S. and Tam, M. (2000) 'Service Work in Consumer Capitalism: Customers, Control and Contradictions', *Work, Employment and Society*, 14 (4), 669–87.

Lomax, W. and Mador, M. (2006) 'Corporate re-branding: from normative models to knowledge management', *Journal of Brand Management*, 14 (1/2), 82–95.

Miles, S.J. and Mangold, G. (2004) 'A Conceptualization of the Employee Branding Process', *Journal of Relationship Marketing*, 3 (2), 65–87.

Miles, S.J. and Mangold, G. (2005) 'Positioning Southwest Airlines through Employee Branding', *Business Horizons*, 48, 535–45.

Pettinger, L. (2004) 'Brand culture and branded workers: service work and aesthetic labour in fashion retail', *Consumption, Markets and Culture*, 7 (2), 165–84.

Reynolds, K. and Harris, L. (2006) 'Deviant Customer Behaviour: An Exploration of Frontline Employee Tactics', *Journal of Marketing Theory and Practice*, 14 (2), 95–111.

Rokeach, M. (1973) *The Nature of Human Values*, New York: The Free Press.

Rosenthal, P. (2004) 'Management control as an employee resource: the case of frontline service workers', *Journal of Management Studies*, 41 (4), 601–22.

Simms, M. (2007a) 'Managed activism: two union organising campaigns in the not-for-profit sector', *Industrial Relations Journal*, 38 (2), 119–35.

Simms, M. (2007b) 'Interest formation in greenfield organising campaigns', *Industrial Relations Journal*, 38 (5), 434–54.

Sturdy, A. (1998) 'Customer care in a consumer society: smiling and sometimes meaning it?', *Organization*, 5 (1), 27–53.

Sturdy, A., Grugulis, I. and Willmott, H. (eds) (2001) *Customer Service: Empowerment and Entrapment*, Basingstoke: Palgrave.

Taylor, P., G. Mulvey, G., Hyman, J. and Bain, P. (2002) 'Work organization, control and the experience of work in call centres', *Work, Employment and Society*, 16 (1), 133–50.

Thompson, P. (2009) 'Labour Process Theory and Critical Management Studies' in M. Alvesson, T. Bridgman and H. Willmott (eds), *The Oxford Handbook of Critical Management Studies*, Oxford: Oxford University Press.

10. Employer branding and diversity: foes or friends?

Martin R. Edwards and Elisabeth K. Kelan

INTRODUCTION

In this chapter we explore whether employer branding and diversity are diametrically opposed to each other or whether they could support the same aims. We argue that employer branding aims at creating a coherent employment brand but in the process of achieving this it can introduce pressures that lead to a homogenization of the workforce. Employer branding is a relatively new idea that has received a flurry of interest in recent years (Martin, 2008; Edwards, 2005); interest which ranges from HR practitioner literature (CIPD, 2008; Martin and Beaumont, 2003) to literature more oriented towards the marketing field (Ind, 2006; Sartain and Schumann, 2006). Although employer branding can take a number of forms (see below), in general, programmes designed to strengthen an organization's employer brand will tend to present a uniform set of organizational values that represent both the characteristics of the organization's corporate brand and a set of beliefs that employees ostensibly share; often employees are actively encouraged to share these values. Employer branding aims at creating a coherent and recognizable brand which, it is argued here, can potentially lead to the introduction of pressures that encourage a homogenization of the workforce. Diversity, in contrast, aims to bring out and make use of the differences between employees.

This chapter discusses the tension that exists between employer branding and diversity. To begin with, the growing interest in employer branding is examined, along with a discussion of the differing positions on employer branding that the HR and marketing literature may have. We highlight the different understanding of employer branding based on whether these approaches stem from an HR perspective or a marketing perspective. We argue that an understanding of these differences can help to identify the tension that employer branding can bring to concerns linked to diversity in organizations. The potential for this tension to lead to greater problems for those interested in encouraging diversity in organizations is likely to increase as employer branding activities become a norm in the management of human resources. With new initiatives and new methods and approaches to management in organizations come new (often unintended) problems that need to be reflected upon with careful consideration. The aim here is to reflect upon the notion of employer branding through a critical lens, with a view to examining whether the homogenizing tension created with branding programmes is inevitable. We show by using approaches from corporate social responsibility (CSR) in general and stakeholder engagement in particular that diversity and employee branding do not have to be opposed and we discuss how an employer brand can be designed to take different views and interests into consideration.

EMPLOYER BRANDING

In order to explore how far employer branding and diversity have opposing agendas, it is important to first establish what employer branding is and why it is growing, which varieties it can take and the difference it makes to employer branding whether the driving force behind it is HR or marketing.

GROWTH OF EMPLOYER BRANDING

Although a focus on diversity in organizations is not new (Thomas and Ely, 1996; Kossek and Zonia, 1993; Roosevelt, 1990), the concerns we raise in this chapter relate to the specific issues arising for diversity in light of the growth of employer branding. There is little doubt that employer branding is a new feature of people management; one of the first references to it can be found in 1996 in a paper entitled 'The Employer Brand' written by Ambler and Barrow (1996). Ambler and Barrow's work is generally recognized as the first explicit reference to employer branding (Barrow and Mosley, 2005; Edwards, 2005). There has, however, been a growth of interest in employer branding since then and a number of arguments have been presented to explain the growth in interest. For example, Martin (2008) argues that it can be explained partly by 'progressively more heated and global talent wars' (p. 252), a point which can be supported by recent interest in organizations wishing to become 'employers of choice' and 'best companies to work for'. Martin also argues that the interest is partly due to the increasing interest in managing organizations' corporate reputation, which employer branding naturally complements. Linked to this is the growing interest in corporate social responsibility and the increasing expectations that organizations are facing from investors (Bartels and Peloza, 2008) and potential employees (Edwards, 2005) to demonstrate their socially responsible credentials. Additionally, Edwards (2005) suggested that the growth can also be explained due to the increased interest in the branding concept generally.

As Olins (2000) argues, brands are 'taking over the corporation' (p. 51) and employer branding is a natural extension to this, indeed branding authors are arguing that employees are 'becoming central to the process of brand building and their behaviour can either reinforce a brand's advertised values or, if inconsistent with the values, undermine the credibility of advertised message' (Harris and de Chernatony, 2001: 442). With the growing interest in branding messages being reinforced by employees, pressure is likely to grow on employees to act in accordance with a brand's advertised values. This restricts the individual ability to be and act differently, thus introducing a growing diversity tension.

From an HR perspective, there are also a number of reasons why there may have been a growth in HR practitioner interest. Edwards (2005) argued that the interest in employer branding is partly due to previously disempowered (and excluded) HR practitioners (Guest and King, 2004; Legge, 1978) wishing to move more into 'the strategic engine room' of the organization. A focus on employer branding and involvement in the management of a company's corporate reputation is seen to enable this. Such a position is supported by arguments presented by Welsing (2006) that many HR professionals suffer from a certain stagnation in their field and by Barrow and Mosley (2005), who argue that collaborating with marketing will boost HR as 'HR departments in many cases do not have all the competencies and resources that are required' (p. 42); furthermore that involvement in employer branding activities 'will attract a wider range of capable people than HR may have done in the past' (p. 101). The argument being presented is that focusing on employer branding could increase the potential sphere of influence that the HR function can reach. These arguments are supported by the statement made by the Chief Executive of the UK's Chartered Institute of Personnel and Development that the HR profession is going through a 'quiet revolution' and that 'it used to be Christmas parties and inductions now we talk about employer branding' (cited by Logan, 2008: 8). Despite these reasons for why the HR function might be interested in employer branding, HR professionals will have to respond to and manage the diversity tensions which accompany such a programme. The need to respond to this tension will be particularly relevant given that the HR function is often the body responsible for ensuring that diversity concerns are addressed.

VARIETIES OF EMPLOYER BRANDING

Despite the potential diversity concerns being raised here, employer branding is today considered to be an important part of an HR practitioner's toolkit. One would expect that employer branding programmes are likely to differ across organizations and because of this one would expect the degree to which the programmes raise diversity tensions will also vary. In trying to understand the possible variety expected in employer branding programmes, one can examine the definitions and explanations of the phenomenon in the literature. Exactly what employer branding entails is not necessarily clear, and definitions vary. Martin and Beaumont (2003) argue that it involves managing 'a company's image as seen through the eyes of its associates and potential hires' (p. 15). This definition focuses on the management of the organization's image as the main focus of employer branding. Backhaus and Tikoo's (2004) definition, however, argues that employer branding 'suggests differentiation of a firm's characteristics as an employer from those of its competitors, the employment brand highlights the unique aspects of the firm's employment offering' (p. 502). Employer branding therefore is considered to involve identifying the uniqueness of the employment experience enjoyed at a particular organization. This unique offering is referred to as the employment brand, which according to Dell and Ainspan (2001) 'establishes the identity of the firm, as an employer. It encompasses the firm's value systems, policies and behaviours toward the objectives of attracting, motivating and retaining the firm's current and potential employees' (p. 10). From these explanations, one can argue that at the very least, employer branding involves an explicit attempt to clarify the distinctive features of the shared employment experience at an organization. This employment experience will include 'functional, economic and psychological benefits provided by employment' (Ambler and Barrow, 1996: 187). This unique package will then be communicated to current employees as well as potential new recruits (in recruitment material).

Whether an employer branding campaign goes beyond communicating an organization's unique package of tangible and intangible benefits and whether diversity concerns follow is likely to depend on the scheme's aims and objectives and how these have been translated into practice. The literature that discusses employer branding identifies a number of possible objectives to carrying out employer branding (Edwards, 2005); these include: (a) attracting high quality talent; (b) retaining current employees while encouraging their identification with the organization and fundamentally, with more extensive programmes; and (c) attempting to encourage current employees to take on board and identify with aspects of the organization's corporate brand with a view to assist in the presentation of branded messages to customers. The particular aims and objectives associated with any employer branding activities will determine the scope of what the programme entails in each organization; most employer branding progammes are likely to have (at least) the first two aims and objectives mentioned here. However, organizations that aim to encourage current employees to help present a branded message through their 'on brand' behaviour are likely to carry out additional activities that try to encourage employees to internalize the organizations corporate or product brand values (employee branding). When organizations take this step, we argue here, diversity tensions will be inevitable.

In many cases organizational values referred to as part of an employer branding programme (usually a key part of the employment 'brand differentiation') would be explicitly linked to an organization's existing corporate identity and corporate brand. It is argued by some that values associated with existing brands should steer the construction of employer brand value propositions so as to ensure a consistency in the branded message (Ambler and Barrow, 1996). One would expect such an argument to become particularly relevant in service sector organizations with employer branding programmes that aim to encourage employees to internalize corporate brand values so as to strengthen customers' branded experiences. When employer branding programmes have this as an aim, it follows that there would be expectations about the degree to which employees 'live the brand' (Ind, 2004). Initiatives that aim to encourage employees to internalize corporate or product brand values would include activities often associated with employee branding (Miles and Mangold, 2004), which can be considered either a part of a wider employer branding programme or an initiative in itself. Related to employer branding, employee branding is considered to involve 'the process by which employees internalize the desired brand image and are motivated to project the image to customers and other organizational constituents' (Miles and Mangold, 2004: 68). If employer branding initiatives do not include some form of employee branding then the diversity tensions are reduced. The degree to which employer branding programmes attempt to do this will depend on their aims, as mentioned the range and the scope of activities included as part of employer branding programmes across organizations will undoubtedly vary. However, where organizations do include explicit attempts to encourage employees to internalize the organization's brand identity, diversity concerns are almost certain to follow.

Some authors argue that employer branding activities should definitely include a form of employee branding activity. Sartain and Schumann (2006), for example, argue that the 'employer brand must define on-brand behaviour' (p. 36) and Mosley (2007) argues that employer branding needs to 'maintain the overall integrity of the corporate brand through appropriate communication and behaviours' (p. 130). Where employee branding does become a part of an employer branding programme, this can involve a fairly sophisticated range of initiatives. Harquail (2006 and 2007a) helps clarify what employee branding would involve when included in employer branding programmes. Firstly, training, where 'all employees are taught the basics of branding' and are 'instructed on the attributes to be associated with their brand'. Secondly, employees are taught how to represent the brand in their behaviour and they are 'given opportunities to practice representing the brand' (2007a: 7).

Thirdly, 'internal corporate press' is used to persuade them and influence their behaviour... [to] encourage on-brand behaviour' (2006: 163). Employer branding programmes would tend to involve such activities if one of its objectives is to strengthen the organization's corporate or product brand. The degree to which this is an aim, however, may well be determined by whether the programme is being driven by the marketing function or the HR function. It is likely that where a programme is driven by the marketing function, expectations that employees should support the organization's corporate or product brand and subsequent diversity tensions may be greater than when employer branding programmes are driven by the HR function.

HR VERSUS MARKETING

The link between employee and employer branding indicates a growing relationship between the marketing field and that of the field of HR. Recent developments within marketing, in particular growth in the fields of 'strategic marketing','integrated marketing' and 'integrated communications', can also help explain a growth in interest in employer branding. Rindova (2007), for example, and Ind and Bjerke (2007) discuss a strategic integrated marketing approach which aims to take a holistic perspective, where marketing should not just focus on customers but consider the interests of all stakeholders. Employer branding can be considered an example of how these new perspectives are translated into other organizational activities. The increasing influence of the marketing discipline in HR activities is marked, the consultancies that help carry out employer branding are often communications or marketing specialists rather than HR consultants (e.g. Universum), and many employer branding activities will increasingly involve the marketing/communications departments who have brand management expertise.

Some authors (Martin, 2008; Martin et al., 2005) argue that employer branding as a phenomenon was first discussed within the marketing literature and only recently have HR and organizational behaviour academics begun to take it seriously as an important process. It is argued here that employer branding as a concept may have met with resistance from HR practitioners and academics because discourse associated with branding in the marketing discipline often conflicts with assumptions associated with discourse within the academic field of HR. When comparing writings of employer branding academics and practitioners that tend to have a marketing background versus those of an HR background, there are often subtle differences that seem to conflict.

Unlike edicts common in the HR academic and practitioner literature that employees are an organization's 'most important asset', implicit in the way branding literature from a marketing perspective refers to employees is that they are a means to an end. Some marketing authors, for example, refer to employees as 'the company's most tenuous and vulnerable asset' (Punjaisri and Wilson, 2007: 59) and instead of respecting diversity and individual differences they refer to employee individuality as a threat to an organization's corporate brand and that the organization's existing brand should be defended. Authors such as Free (1999) argue that 'all staff must understand and commit personally to the brand values' and Mosley (2007) sees 'the HR-led role of employer brand management as a reinforcing counterpart to the marketing led role of customer brand management' (p. 130) and argues that the aim is to 'maintain the overall integrity of the corporate brand through appropriate communication and behaviours' (p. 130). Ultimately it is suggested that in order to ensure a branded customer experience, employees' values, attitudes and subsequent behaviour need to be moulded to reinforce the corporate brand (Miles and Mangold, 2004) and furthermore diversity in employee values, characteristics and behaviours would not be good for the presentation of a consistent corporate brand identity. Fundamentally, however, if one starts with a premise that the aim of an employer branding activity is to increase product or corporate brand recognition and loyalty, this will conflict with certain assumptions made by HR authors and practitioners who may make fundamentally different assumptions as to the aims of employer branding activities.

Although ultimately, many HR experts and practitioners discuss how good people management practices should contribute to the bottom line, generally speaking the interests of the employees and their well-being is, and should be, a key concern (Peccei, 2004). Whether the differences in discourse mentioned above become a concern for the HR function will ultimately depend upon the underlying assumptions associated with an organization's ideological perspective concerning the role of the HR function. If an organization sees that the purpose of HR management is solely to help increase business performance then the marketing oriented employer branding perspective (which includes employee branding and internal marketing/internal branding) will not conflict with the interests of the HR function. If, however, the people management related ideological position of an organization is one that is fundamentally concerned about employee rights and emphasizes employee well-being as a priority then internal branding or employee branding activities would not resonate well.

THE POTENTIAL CONFLICT BETWEEN EMPLOYER BRANDING AND DIVERSITY

In the main, employer branding activities try to ensure that employees are 'on brand', particularly where the branding programmes are driven by the marketing function. We argue that being 'on brand' in this context means by definition that where employees' attitudes or behaviour differ from the organization's branded message, they are delegitimized. This poses a potential challenge for diversity management, which focuses on allowing and encouraging employees to bring their diversity into the workplace. In the following section, we will discuss this potential conflict between employer branding and diversity.

From the 1990s onwards the discourse of 'diversity' has replaced earlier discussions about equal opportunities in organizations (Gatrell and Swan, 2008; Roosevelt, 1990). While discourses of equal opportunities focused on arguments around social fairness, diversity discourses tend to be driven by 'the business case'. This means that diversity is seen as adding value to the organization and to give it competitive advantage (Gatrell and Swan, 2008; Thomas, 2004). Diversity often focuses on demographic groups and tries to ensure that diverse individuals can contribute to the work environment. This difference has exchange value in organizational transactions and thus has to be valued (Roberson, 2006). Most organizations today have a programme to encourage and foster diversity and many claim that diversity is in fact one of its core values.

In essence, organizational approaches to diversity try to bring out the individual differences between and among people. This is diametrically opposed to what employer branding aims at doing. A central aim of employer branding is to unify employees under a shared brand. Implied in the arguments mentioned is that differences within a brand have to be negated for it to be effective. The introduction of employer branding in an organization will bring to the fore a key assumption that employees do, and are expected to, share a similar set of values. Management programmes that take such a position will inherently act as a homogenizing force that conflicts with the idea of diversity; diversity is not valued but rather subsumed under a brand that might not reflect or allow for the display of individuals' identity. Ultimately, arguing that all staff should share a particular set of values and behave in accordance with a particular brand identity goes against the principles of accepting differences in employee values and beliefs, something which diversity programmes have as a core principle. This problem goes somewhat deeper when employer branding is driven by the marketing function and involves employee branding (as recommended by Ind (2004) and Mosley (2007)).

In itself, presenting a uniform view of the organization where a particular set of values and characteristics are assumed is not necessarily a problem in relation to equality and diversity as people will inevitably self-select organizations that they perceive some fit with (Kristoff, 1996). Furthermore, there is a considerable amount of literature which shows the positive impact of person–organization fit which illustrates why communicating the shared organizational values might be a sensible strategy (Kristof-Brown et al., 2005; Judge and Cable, 1997). Research has reliably shown a positive relationship between person–organization value fit and organizational commitment, job satisfaction, co-worker satisfaction and trust in managers as well as negative relationship between person–organization fit and intent to quit and indicators of strain (Kristof-Brown et al., 2005). However, employer branding practitioners will need to deal with the problem that communicating the values, characteristics and personality of the organization's employer brand implies that 'we are all alike'; this in itself will have an unintended consequence of sending a message that you only need apply if you share these values.

Where employer branding programmes involve communicating existing corporate values to current employees, it is likely that this sends the message that employees are expected to share and internalize the organization's values or personality characteristics if they wish to stay in the organization. Issues have been raised with such activities by Cornellison (2002), who argued that managerial attempts to set out uniform values present 'managerially induced' values 'rather than offering individuals free choice of values and identification' (p. 267). Cornellissen (2002) is critical of management attempts to present a uniform picture of the organization where staff will share values and where a homogeneity of values is assumed. Cornelissen (2002) draws on writings of Willmott (1993) and argues that when management presents a uniform view of an organization's shared values, this creates an illusion of homogeneity and agreement of an overarching set of values. According to Cornellissen this aims to give the impression of a unanimous sense of purpose and shared view of the world, which, importantly, may not exist. Although the validity and fairness of Cornelissen's critique is challenged by some authors (Gioia et al., 2002), it seems logical that presenting a uniform set of values will lead to a fundamental tension for HR as it does seem to go against a key principle of diversity management: the acceptance that people are different (Kandola and Fullerton, 1994).

DEALING WITH THE OPPOSITION OF DIVERSITY AND EMPLOYER BRANDING

Thus far, we have outlined what employer branding means and how it can conflict with diversity. There are some approaches that organizations can take to reduce the conflict between diversity and employer branding. In order to explore potential ways through which this can be done, we will draw on concepts and methods used in relation to socially responsible employer branding and stakeholder engagement. The key argument being presented here is that in the construction of or design of an organization's employer brand the interests of key stakeholder groups must be incorporated.

SOCIALLY RESPONSIBLE EMPLOYER BRANDING AND STAKEHOLDER ENGAGEMENT

As a raft of authors discuss, acting with social responsibility is becoming of greater importance as organizations are increasingly under pressure to demonstrate their socially responsible credentials (Hollander, 2004; Craig Smith, 2003; Burke and Logsdon, 1996). This pressure is being applied from numerous sources, including consumers as well as a range of stakeholders such as investors, employees and the community (McWilliams and Siegel, 2001). The argument presented here is that organizations, when designing employer brands, need to act in a socially responsible way by engaging and integrating the interests of key stakeholder groups (in this case the employee group is a central stakeholder).

As mentioned, presenting a uniform set of values is likely to raise some diversity concerns. Importantly, the process used by an organization when reaching a decision on what values and characteristics are presented as part of the employment brand offering will determine the degree to which tensions and problems may materialize. Ethical problems arise when an organization presents a shared set of employer brand values and characteristics linked to the organization's corporate brand which it then expects employees to internalize without question. Some authors recommend such an approach, however. Harris and de Chernatony (2001), for example, suggest that 'managers need to first define a brand's values and then ensure employees' values and behaviour are consistent with them' (p. 442). The downward imposition (on employees) of values and characteristics that such an approach involves, however, will mean that the organization will not be treating employees as an important stakeholder group whose interests and rights should be respected. It sends a message that employees are to be considered a commodity (rather than a stakeholder) and that their attitudes and behaviour can legitimately be shaped in order to ensure greater levels of customer loyalty. This concern has been raised earlier by Edwards (2005), who argued that imposing corporate brand values onto employees implies a stakeholder power dynamic that would clash with tenets associated with corporate social responsibility.

Considering how important having a socially responsible organization is deemed to be, it would seem rather problematic for organizations to impose a set of corporate brand values (for example) onto employees. In a study (Maignan and Ralston, 2002), 43 per cent of a sample of 400 high-profile companies either discussed corporate social responsibility or presented themselves as being socially responsible on their corporate websites; it is argued that the expectations for organizations to do so are currently 'ratcheting' (Bartels and Peloza, 2008). Specifically related to employer branding, there is evidence suggesting that the more organizations are perceived to act in a socially responsible way, then the more potential employees are likely to see them as an attractive employer (Turban and Greening, 1997).

Central to CSR is the consideration of the valid interests of all stakeholder groups, especially employees. In CSR a move from stakeholder management to stakeholder engagement has taken place (Blowfield and Murray, 2008). The former implies that stakeholders were simply seen as groups or organizations that could be managed whereas the latter seeks to engage in a dialogue with the different stakeholders to find a consensus. This approach seems very useful to include groups like employees into the process of defining brand values. This means involving employees in the process of employer brand building, especially when building the employer brand value proposition. This is a position explicitly argued by Ind and Bjerke (2007), who raise interesting questions of the governance of a brand and consider who actually owns an organization's employer brand. Edwards (2005) and Ind and Bjerke (2007) argued that employees can be considered important stakeholders of employer branding; their participation in the employer branding process is therefore a very important part of the process. One of the benefits of such an approach is that it reduces the likelihood of any dissonance between the espoused values of the organization, the values of the employee group and importantly the values which underpin the way in which the organization treats its employees. The inherent contradictions and tension that such a dissonance could raise would be extremely problematic as it would undermine the legitimacy and authenticity of any branding claims that are made.

Although it is likely that engaging the employee group as a stakeholder body in the design of the employer brand will lead to a more effective, authentic and accurate picture of the employer brand, a problem exists that a uniform (homogenous) picture of the organization is still likely to be presented in employer brand communication. This ultimately implies a lack of diversity among the employee group, when in fact the employee group is in reality likely to be a complex and diverse group.

DIVERSE GROUPS AS STAKEHOLDERS IN EMPLOYER BRANDING

It can be argued that a diverse group of employees should be seen as a complex stakeholder group that have to be given special attention when it comes to defining employer brand values. This suggestion may be considered problematic by those who argue that brand identities need to be consistently reinforced in all corporate communications. It is possible that allowing staff to help construct the employer value proposition and allowing the employer brand values to change over time may mean that these values differ from the corporate or product value proposition. In branding, authors argue how important it is that an organization's brand message is not contaminated by different messages. Cornelissen et al. (2007) argue that considerable literature has been written on the importance of an alignment or 'consonance' between the identity that managers project of the organization, employees' perceptions of the organization's identity and external perceptions of the corporate identity. Where there is a misalignment, then 'a range of suboptimal outcomes is anticipated – including employee disengagement, customer dissatisfaction and general organizational atrophy' (p. S7). However, there is also literature that argues marketing communication needs to take account of the range of stakeholders associated with an organization's activities and that communication campaigns need to consider and manage these complexities rather than send a single message to all.

An organization's image and identity are complex and there will be a number of stakeholders with potentially different perspectives on the organization's image (Brown et al., 2006). Interestingly, research indicates that different characteristics of an organization's image will be more or less attractive and salient to different stakeholder groups. For example, Chun and Davies (2006) measured perceptions of an organization's characteristics and satisfaction with the organization from the viewpoint of employees as well as customers. They found differences between the two groups in what characteristics predicted satisfaction; employees were more satisfied with the organization when they perceived higher levels of agreeableness while customers were more satisfied with the organization when higher levels of the characteristic 'enterprise' were perceived.

Recognizing that different stakeholders may have different perspectives on the organization's image and that they may have different interests suggests the need to manage complex messages associated with the organizational identity or brand. It is possible that this could result in different messages being communicated associated with any particular organization and that this may well lead to contamination of the core brand message. However, in order to answer some of the diversity challenges raised above, it is important that any communication programme associated with employer branding needs to recognize the complexities of the different groups associated with the organization.

Rindova (2008) discusses strategies where messages associated with an organization's identity are presented in a complex way to take into account the different interests of particular stakeholder groups. She argues that a range of diverse strategies can help organizations build 'multiplex identities, that is, identities with many facets that engage stakeholders in different ways'

(p. 169) and that subtly different messages can be targeted at different groups. The complexities of a variety of perceptions and interests of different stakeholder groups associated with an organization's identity, and attempts to communicate a coherent representation of the organization's image, has also been discussed by Gioia et al. (2000). They argue that although there may be particular values imputed and expressed by an organization that will help present a consistent organizational identity, interpretations of observers or participants may not be fixed or stable. Furthermore, particular statements of the kind you would find in an employee value proposition such as 'we value innovation' will mean different things to different individuals. These arguments and those of Rindova do give some idea of how to navigate around some tensions that arise with the employer branding programme. That is, make the core values relatively benign (not values that would tend to be associated with particular groups within society) with the potential to be open to interpretation and then manage subtly different messages around these that represent different stakeholders. Therefore, a potential way out of this employer branding diversity dilemma is for the organization to present some core corporate values that employees have been involved in agreeing; these values should, however, not be presented as all-encompassing and they should allow for slight variations in interpretation. Furthermore, it is important that around this core message, organizations are creative and present additional subtly different messages that may be more complex and reflect the different concerns and viewpoints of a diverse set of stakeholders.

This approach resonates well with the fact that many organizations talk today not only about diversity but about inclusion. The move from diversity to inclusion means that different sets of ideals come to the fore. Whereas diversity focuses on the individual demographic differences, inclusion aims at increasing participation of all employees and changing systems and structures that might hinder this participation (Roberson, 2006). Inclusion focuses more on integration rather than separation and entails a more consensus-based decision-making akin to stakeholder management. The aim would therefore be to build employer brands that are inclusive of the different groups of employees that do work in an organization and to value and respect their differences and to ensure that they feel engaged and can participate in decision-making. However, any processes aiming to achieve this have to be carefully managed and monitored in regard to the effects they have.

DISCUSSION AND CONCLUSION

This chapter has considered the relationship between employer branding and diversity and has explored how far the two concepts are opposed or could be brought together. The chapter started by discussing the growth of employer branding, the varieties of employer branding and the importance that the different backgrounds of HR and marketing bring to employer branding. We then discussed the conflicting potential between diversity and employer branding, highlighting how branding tries to homogenize values whereas diversity aims to bring out differences between individuals. By drawing on the concept of stakeholder engagement deriving from CSR, we argued that it is possible to construct brand messages that take diversity into consideration. This would allow organizations to create employer brands that fulfil the important predicament of being inclusive. Inclusive employer brands are potentially much more effective in ensuring employee engagement and participation.

The very least an employer brand has to do is to avoid any messages that can be read as fostering non-diversity. Although many companies include diversity as a value which the organization and its members ostensibly share, it is unclear whether declaring that one values diversity eradicates the tension between employee-related branding activities and diversity programmes. Stating diversity as a value is unlikely to be enough; organizations will need to do more than this in order to alleviate the homogenizing forces of a branding programme. By encouraging a dialogue with employees when designing branding programmes and regularly monitoring the accuracy of the associated value proposition it can at least be ensured that many different perspectives can be considered in employer branding. Of course, while listening to different voices might be an approach to create more diverse and more inclusive employer brands, it seems questionable how far all perspectives can be heard and be included in the final employer brand. This is particularly relevant when the values or beliefs of different staff groups are opposed to each other and when differing values cannot be reconciled.

It is evident that many of the challenges which result from the seemingly opposing concepts of employer branding and diversity cannot be easily resolved and one would expect the tensions to remain an important issue to consider for academics and practitioners. What it surprising, however, is that very few commentators have raised the incompatibility between declaring that diversity is a key value and the fact that employer branding is likely to lead to a homogenization of values and perspectives rather than diversity. Future research could explore how this dilemma is dealt with in organizations and how they reconcile the apparent opposition between employer branding and diversity. Further research in this area would need to be conducted. This chapter outlined some of the challenges and contradictions when it comes to employer branding and diversity and is to be understood as a starting point rather than an endpoint in the debates.

REFERENCES

Ambler, T. and Barrow, S. (1996) 'The employer brand', *The Journal of Brand Management*, 4, 185–206.

Backhaus, K. and Tikoo, S. (2004) 'Conceptualizing and Researching Employer Branding', *Career Development International*, 9 (4/5), 501–17.

Barrow, S. and Mosley, R. (2005) *The Employer Brand: Bringing the best of brand management to people at work*, Chichester: Wiley.

Bartels, S. and Peloza, J. (2008) 'Running Just to Stand Still? Managing CSR Reputation in an Era of Ratcheting Expectations', *Corporate Reputation Review*, 11 (1), 56–72.

Berthon, P., Ewing, M. and Hah, L.L. (2005) 'Captivating Company: Dimensions of Attractiveness in Employer Branding', *International Journal of Advertising*, 24 (2), 151–72.

Blowfield, M. and Murray, A. (2008) *Corporate Responsibility – A Critical Introduction*, Oxford: Oxford University Press.

Brown, T.J., Dacin, P.A., Pratt, M.G. and Whetten, D.A. (2006) 'Identity, Intended Image, Construed Image, and Reputation: An Interdisciplinary Framework and Suggested Terminology', *Journal of the Academy of Marketing Science*, 34, 99–106.

Burke, L. and Logsdon, J. (1996) 'How Corporate Social Responsibility Pays Off', *Long Range Planning*, 29 (4), 495–502.

Chun, R. and Davies, G. (2006) 'The Influence of Corporate Character on Customers and Employees: Exploring Similarities and Differences', *Journal of the Academy of Marketing Science*, 34 (2), 138–46.

Cornelissen, J.P. (2002) 'On the Organizational Identity Metaphor', *British Journal of Management*, 13 (3), 259–68.

Cornelissen, J.P., Haslam, S.A. and Balmer, M.T. (2007) 'Social identity, organizational identity and corporate identity: Towards an integrated understanding of processes, patternings and products', *British Journal of Management*, 18, S1–S16.

Craig Smith, N. (2003) 'Corporate social responsibility: whether or how?', *California Management Review*, 45 (4), 52–76.

Dell, D. and Ainspan, N. (2001) Engaging employees through your brand. Conference Board Report, No. R-1288-01-RR, April, Washington, DC: Conference Board.

Edwards, M.R. (2005) Employer and Employer Branding: HR or PR?, In S. Bach, *Human Resource Management: Personnel Management in Transition*, Oxford: Blackwell.

Faurholt Csaba, F. and Bengtsson, A. (2006) Rethinking identity in brand management. In J. E. Schroeder and M. Salzer-Mörling (eds), *Brand Culture*, 118–135. London: Routledge.

Free, C. (1999) 'The Internal Brand', *The Journal of Brand Management*, 6, 231–6.

Gatrell, C. and Swan, E. (2008) *Gender and Diversity in Management: A Concise Introduction*, London: Sage.

Gioia, D.A., Schultz, M. and Corley, K.G. (2000) 'Organizational Identity, Image, and Adaptive Instability', *Academy of Management Review*, 25, 63–81.

Gioia, D.A., Schultz, M. and Corley, K.G. (2002) 'On celebrating the organizational identity metaphor: a rejoinder to Cornelissen', *British Journal of Management*, 13 (3), 269.

Harquail, C.V. (2006) Employees as Animate Artifacts: Employee branding by 'wearing the brand', in A. Rafaeli and M. Pratt (eds) *Artifacts and Organizations: Beyond mere symbolism*, Lawrence Erlbaum: NJ.

Harquail, C.V. (2007a) Employee Branding: Enterprising selves in service of the Brand, available at http://authenticorganizations.com/wp-content/uploads/2008/03/employee-branding-online.pdf accessed July 2008.

Harquail, C.V. (2007b) Practice and Identity: Using brand symbol to construct organizational identity, in L. Lerpold, D. Ravasi, J. Van Rekom and G. Soenen, *Organizational Identity in Practice*, London: Routledge, pp. 135–50.

Harris, F. and de Chernatony, L. (2002) 'Corporate Branding and corporate brand performance', *European Journal of Marketing*, 35 (3/4), 441–56.

Hatch, M.J. and Schulz, M. (2004) *Organizational Identity: A Reader*, Oxford: Oxford University Press.

Hollander, J. (2004) 'What matters most: Corporate Values and Social Responsibility', *California Management Review*, 46 (4), 111–19.

Ind, N. (2003) 'Inside out: How employees build value', *Brand Management*, 10, 393–402.

Ind, N. and Bjerke, R. (2007) *Branding Governance: A participatory approach to the brand building process*, Chichester: Wiley.

Joachimsthaler, E. and Aaker, D.A. (1997) 'Building Brands Without Mass Media', *Harvard Business Review*, 75 (1), 39–50.

Judge, T.A. and Cable, D.M. (1997) 'Applicant personality, organizational culture, and organization attraction', *Personnel Psychology*, 50 (2), 359–94.

Kandola, B. and Fullerton, J. (1994) *Managing the Mosaic: Diversity in Action*, London: Chartered Institute of Personnel and Development.

Kossek, E.E. and Zonia, S. (1993) 'Assessing the diversity climate: a field study of reactions to employer efforts to promote diversity', *Journal of Organizational Behavior*, 14, 61–81.

Knox, S.D., Maklan, S. and Thompson, K.E. (2000) Building the unique organization value proposition, in Schultz, M., Hatch, M.J., Larsen, M.H. (eds), *The Expressive Organization*, Oxford: Oxford University Press, p. 216.

Logan, G. (2008) 'Jackie Orme tells directors HR's quiet revolution not over yet', *Personnel Today*, 14 October, p. 8.

Maignan, I. and Ralston, D.A. (2002) 'Corporate Social Responsibility in Europe and the U.S.: Insights from Businesses' Self-Presentations', *Journal of International Business Studies*, 33, 497–514.

Martin, G. (2008) Employer branding and reputation management, in Cooper, C. and Burke, R. (eds) *Peak Performing Organizations*, London: Routledge.

Martin, G. and Beaumont, P. (2003) Branding and People Management, CIPD Research Report.

Martin, G. and Hetrick, S. (2006) *Corporate Reputations, Branding and Managing People: A Strategic Approach to HR*, Oxford: Butterworth Heinemann.

Martin, G., Beaumont, P., Doig, R. and Pate, J. (2005) 'Branding: A new performance discourse for HR?', *European Management Journal*, 23, 76–88.

McWilliams, A. and Siegel, D. (2001) 'Corporate social responsibility: A theory of the firm perspective', *Academy of Management Review*, 26 (1), 117–27.

Miles, S.J. and Mangold, W.G. (2004) 'A Conceptualization of the Employee Branding Process', *Journal of Relationship Marketing*, 3 (2/3): 65–87.

Mosley, R. (2007) 'Customer experience, organizational culture and the employer brand', *Journal of Brand Management*, 15, 123–34.

Olins, W. (2000) How brands are taking over the corporation, in M. Schultz, M. Jo Hatch and M. H. Larsen (eds) *The Expressive Organization*, Oxford: Oxford University Press.

Punjaisri, K. and Wilson, A. (2007) 'The role of internal branding in the delivery of employee brand promise', *Journal of Brand Management*, 15, 57–70.

Peccei, R. (2004) Human resource management and the search for the happy productive workplace, Inaugural address, Erasmus Research Institute of Management (ERIM).

Rindova, V. (2007) Starbucks: Constructing a multiplex identity in the speciality coffee industry, in L. Lerpold, D. Ravasi, J. Van Rekom and G. Soenen (eds) *Organizational Identity in Practice*, Oxon: Routledge, pp. 157–73.

Roberson, Q.M. (2006) 'Disentangling the Meanings of Diversity and Inclusion in Organizations', *Group and Organization Management*, 31 (2), 212–36.

Roosevelt, T.J. (1990) 'From Affirmative Action to Affirming Diversity', *Harvard Business Review*, March–April, 107–17.

Sartain, L. and Schumann, M. (2006) *Brand From the Inside: Eight Essentials to Emotionally Connect Your Employees to Your Business*, San Francisco: Wiley.

Swystun, J. (2007) *The Brand Glossary: Interbrand*, Basingstoke: Palgrave Macmillan.

Thomas, D.A. (2004) Diversity as Strategy. Harvard Business Review, September, 98–108.

Thomas, D.A. and Ely, R.J. (1996) 'Making Differences Matter: A New Paradigm for Managing Diversity', *Harvard Business Review*, September–October, 1–13 (reprint).

Turban, D.B. and Greening, D.W. (1996): 'Corporate social performance and organizational attractiveness to prospective employees', *Academy of Management Journal*, 40, 658–72

Welsing, C. (2006) *HR Marketing: A New Perspective on Human Resource Management*, London: Pearson Education.

Willmott, H.C. (1993) 'Strength is ignorance; slavery is freedom: managing culture in modern organizations', *Journal of Management Studies*, 30 (4), 515–52.

11. Placing branding within organization theory

Matthew J. Brannan, Elizabeth Parsons and Vincenza Priola

The aim of this volume has been to contribute to the emerging discussion surrounding employee branding with a series of studies focusing upon the realities of 'living the brand' for workers at the point of production. The chapters in this volume provide a rich insight into the experience of employee branding in various organizational contexts and in keeping with our aim, the approach taken by our contributors has focused on the lived experience of branding and its wider resonance for sociological debates on work. In this final chapter we seek to explore some of the key emergent themes and issues and call for more empirical work to critically explore the scope and limitations of employee branding from a socioeconomic perspective. We also seek to place employee branding into a wider theoretical debate informed by a sociological understanding of the role of branding in contemporary organizations and society. While we think this contribution does much to explore the experience of branding, there is a notable absence, both here and elsewhere, of systematic survey level work that might be used to explore the extent and scope of branding and its impact as an employment strategy for the macroeconomy. In considering the impact of branding at a micro level, we have provided an initial attempt to establish the wider importance of brand value in contemporary capitalism and the first and final chapters consciously 'bookend' the case study material, accounting for the significance of branding for financialization (the first chapter) and to diversity management in organizations (the final chapter).

The chapters present a range of illuminating themes and ideas providing a significant contemporary commentary on the brand experience. A central theme that cuts across the contributions is the complexity of the branding experience for employees and for employers. The degree of flux, dynamism and contestation that lies at the heart of the employee brand performance stands in stark contrast to the very notion of brand, which, at its core, attempts to bundle a range of themes and emotions into one simple universally communicative concept. We take this insight to be significant and, from a practitioner perspective, this alone should give at least, some pause for thought to those who would seek to harness employee branding in the service of organizational objectives. Those that have grown accustomed to the elegant simplicity of notions of brand image in contemporary capitalism should be aware that the overwhelming experience of branded employment, on the evidence presented here, does not correspond to a series of slickly replicated identical performances demonstrating neat alignment between employee and organization; rather the experience of branding demonstrates fracture, paradox and staccato subversions which have the capacity to thwart rather than to secure organizational objectives and desires.

Albeit primarily empirically based, it is notable that a number of chapters in this volume have, in various ways, attempted to theorize the experience of employee branding and this is something that we wish to continue in this final section. Offering a theoretical insight is of value as an attempt to explore not only the ways in which employee branding processes actually work, but also how they fit in relation to wider mechanisms and dynamics of organizational and social life. In this way we might better understand the scope and limitations of the branding idea and how it relates to macrolevel economic and political issues. In this task we feel that the use of a variety of theoretical resources may help to shed light on the branding process, thus we recognize that we offer these insights as initial engagements with the concept from a more critical perspective. We are therefore pragmatic, rather than partisan, with our choice of theory and are guided by explanatory capacity rather than ideological commitment to existing theoretical alignments. Rather than offering the 'final word' on employee branding, we seek here to make tentative steps towards a theorization of the complexity that has been amply demonstrated in the empirical accounts and see our conclusion as 'opening up' rather than closing down much needed discussion in this area. This final chapter, therefore, represents an initial attempt to present some theoretical remarks and make sense of the brand complexity.

Much of the initial literature on employee branding (e.g. Miles and Mangold, 2004) argues that branding can and should go beyond internal marketing tactics (Rafiq and Ahmed, 2000) to involve organizational-wide strategies (as noted in the case of HRM processes discussed in a number of chapters). Such strategies are designed to motivate employees to internalize and perform the desired brand image in order to enhance customer satisfaction and organizational productivity. Although the rhetoric of employee branding might originate from within specific forms of functionalist management literature, a key concern in all the contributions to this volume is the critical engagement with the branding concept. Limiting the analysis of employee branding to internal marketing and functional HR issues omits crucial wider political and ethical debates that we see as significant.

Further, the development of internal marketing into forms of employee branding represents symbolically, materially and bodily a move on the part of capital to shift the terrain of control from the interiority of organizational space to the outside life-space of employees *and* potential employees. The impact of this, not only on one's work identity, but also on other identities outside of work, clearly needs far more consideration and connects vividly to what some authors (e.g. Willmott, 2010) call the 'unseen' side of the production process, where user-customers and user-employees actively participate equally in the building and erosion of brand equity.

On the surface employee branding might be seen as a largely benevolent practice, which, in attempting to improve organizational performance, works to humanize employment relations. The unitarist logic behind this thinking, that happy workers will ultimately engender happy customers, finds little support in the work presented here, either in the voice of the authors, or in the voices of the participants represented in the case studies. Thus, we feel that it might be more instructive to consider alternative conceptions and to move away from functional or practitioner-orientated literatures to explore some of the organizational-theoretic constructs intertwined with employee branding processes in order to better understand its dynamics and political implications. It is to this that we now turn in the following subsections.

EMPLOYEE BRANDING AND ORGANIZATIONAL CULTURE

Our theoretical starting point is to recognize that employee branding, as a relatively new concept, has a deep resonance with wider organizational constructs such as that of organizational culture, itself subject to intense practitioner adoption and academic critique and evaluation. Theoretically then, branding might be seen as yet another attempt to 'engineer' organizational culture in pursuit of a rather narrow set of corporate goals, thus fitting into a neo-liberal inspired attempt at the colonization of worker identity in pursuit of accumulation. The 'culture debate' has had a significant impact on organizational practice, and has been both reflective and directive and employee branding may simply be the latest iteration of this practice. The trajectory of employee branding, for example, shares similarities with the organizational culture literature, initial enthusiasm and adoption by leading people-focused organizations collapsing into growing scepticism, cynicism, and critical inquiry by management and organizational studies scholars and researchers. Culture, like branding, suggests the notion that organizations can and do design the interiority of the employment relationship through careful recruitment and selection, employee development, communication and ownership of corporate values (Priola and

Hurrell, 2011; Ray, 1986) with given outcomes in mind. From within the so-called 'culture-as-control' perspective, employee branding can be seen as yet another way to manipulate the workforce in order to achieve organizational goals. As the chapters here demonstrate, branding, like organizational culture, certainly exerts influence on organizational members in that the beliefs and values they project work to shape employees' behaviour in specific ways; it is evident that some ways of being are 'legitimized' through the brand, while those that are not compatible with organizational brands are de-legitimized. This can be seen for example in the 'brand fit' recruitment practices discussed by Hurrell and Scholarios in this volume. It is also clear that, to various degrees, notions of brand are internalized and often misrecognized as something other than overt management strategies (see Ray, 1986). However, the assumption that such conceptions can be uniformly applied and relied upon remains contested and has its limits evidenced by examples in the work presented here. This is also supported by the wider, vigorous debate surrounding the possibility of cultural engineering, with many authors suggesting that organizational culture 'by design' is, in fact, an impossibility in any meaningful sense (see Muzio et al., 2007; Sinclair, 1991). Employees can and will deploy their own 'readings' of organizational attempts at branding. In the case studies presented here this is reflected in the wide ranging use of the term (re)appropriation to understand and unpack the employee branding process (see especially the chapter by Tarnovskaya).

Despite this, we think that the debate that surrounds employee branding, rather than being abandoned in the face of the post organizational culture debate, has, instead, much to learn from this discussion. In this sense it might be instructive to think about employee branding as a process of *becoming*, itself a performative act of production and consumption carried out in organizational and social flux. Thus, although the employee branding concept might be flawed intellectually and practically, its continued and growing use warrants further attention. Seen from this perspective, the notion that idealized conceptions of brands could ever be transferred unproblematically to employee performances is rendered fictive, yet wider interest among practitioners in attempting this, demands further explanation. Moving the debate away from the assumption that branding can ever be an unproblematic and unidirectional practice is, on the basis of the work presented here, both necessary and desirable. The central issue therefore becomes the need to apprehend the function, however incomplete, that employee branding plays and what impact its attempted implementation has on the experience and management of working life.

Employee branding clearly goes beyond processes of internalization of organizational values and behaviours (the aim of processes and interventions intended to create a strong corporate culture) in that it emphasizes identification but also the representation of the brand outside the workplace as part of the employee's lifestyle and identity. Yet as we have noted, this cannot and should not be read as an uncomplicated process. While we recognize that employee identities, both within and without work, will be influenced by employee branding activities, we also see its implementation as problematic in that it cannot result in a unified and unidirectional practice enacted by all organizational members in a similar manner. See for example the 'polysemic brand readings' in Smith and Buchanan-Oliver's chapter and the two almost diametrically opposed readings of the brand by IKEA employees in Tarnovskaya's chapter. As with many organizational interventions, processes of employee branding are developed within a specific organizational milieu, which will necessarily influence both design and implementation. Equally, processes of branding are always conditional, contingent and open to interpretation and negotiation (whether deliberate or unwitting) between various organizational actors. Employee interpretations of branding processes may lead to ambiguity but also to ruptures and resistance, as evidenced by some of the work included in this text.

It is perhaps employees' capacity for resistance, which many of the chapters here draw specific attention to, where employee branding may most easily be turned against its architects (see in particular the chapter by Russell). Workplace resistance, as a form of misbehaviour at its most basic level, has been defined as 'counter-productive activity' (Thompson and Ackroyd, 1995 and 1999) and it is clear that the brand offers employers (and customers) an important and effective resource to leverage their interests against those of the organization. Employee resistance is also intimately connected with employee identity and the 'appropriation of identity' (Thompson and Ackroyd, 1995 and 1999) remains a key dimension in which the conflict between capital and labour is played out. In an era where notions of 'identity performance' are so clearly articulated by organizations as central to their success, it is little wonder that savvy customers and employees can and do work to subvert this process in innovative and highly effective ways for a variety of ends.

At the heart of the control/resistance dialectic lies the concept of agency and this emerges in the empirical work presented in a number of chapters which highlight how branding (power) and resistance operate at multiple levels, resulting in dispersed and varied modalities of accommodation and struggle (as clearly illustrated in Cushen's chapter). The benefit of a collection of ethnographic work such as this resides in the fact that, while aiming to make sense of the complex social processes that structure employee branding in organizations, it also provides space for variety of voices and experiences that question the orthodox control–resistance duality. While the contributions in this volume do not attempt to reconcile debates on structure and agency in labour relations, on a theoretical level[1], they do provide evidence of multiplicity and inconsistency in the practices of labour relations, challenging not only functionalist and bourgeois analysis of workplace relations but also more traditional (orthodox) labour process theorizations. Therefore while we can be confident that branding is important and does have an impact on people at work, this must be tempered to acknowledge that the influence played by branding activities on employees' positioning in relation to their work is only ever in process and never unproblematic. Moreover, while rejecting the individualism and voluntarism of functionalist perspectives, the work presented here supports the view that as 'agents' (albeit in an asymmetrical relation), employees have the potential to embrace their organization's expressed brand values but also to resist them and re-articulate them for their own ends. This re-articulation might reside in the habitual, everyday individual responses to employee branding but equally it might be the result of deliberate organized attempts to re-articulate the brand for purposive ends. This is reflected in the chapter by Simms in this volume where trade union organizers deploy brand narratives in the service of union recruitment and organizing.

EMPLOYEES AS CULTURAL CARRIES

An alternative perspective that could be taken in theorizing the concept of employee branding might see employees as 'cultural carries' of the brand image (see cultural intermediaries in the literature, cf. Negus (2002), Nixon (2002)), required to deploy a wide arsenal of actions, meanings and symbols to demonstrate the consumption of organizational products. So, for example, the retail worker who wears the clothes that she sells embodies the image of an idealized customer giving customers a 'lived example' of the product in use (Pettinger, 2004). The emphasis on employees as cultural carries is often represented in the practitioner literature (e.g. Hemp, 2002; Walker, 2002) as key to achieving excellence, not only in customer service, but also in customer–employee relations. In assessing and theorizing this practitioner-oriented perspective, the work of Bourdieu (1984), and specifically the notion of 'cultural intermediates', is significant. Bourdieu applies the term to those groups of workers involved in the provision of symbolic services or products (see also Nixon and du Gay, 2002) and the concept is further explored by Negus (2002) and McRobbie (2002) who, in investigating the position and status of cultural intermediaries, focus on questions of cultural and social change within the service economy. Negus (2002) advocates the importance of understanding cultural intermediaries in today's economy, emphasizing the significance of these workers and their structural location 'in-between' production and consumption. Intermediaries are engaged in developing a point of connection between production and consumption, shaping use values and exchange values and managing how these values are connected to people's lives by forging a sense of identification and desire between the product or service and the consumer.

Ultimately, however, they are, of course, unable to bridge the distance between production and consumption and merely succeed in reproducing it, 'offering the illusion of the link rather than its material representation' (Negus, 2002: 509). Bourdieu uses the terminology for restricted categories of workers with a specific class connotation: 'the new petite bourgeoisie', made up of workers involved in sales, marketing, fashion, public relations, advertising and other areas of work concerned with presentation and representation. Negus, however, extends its use, moving away from the specific class position implied by Bourdieu and in this wider sense, the term and its conceptual apparatus is clearly of value in the discussion of the dynamics of employee branding. Seen from this perspective, and returning to our opening remarks, employees are invited to bring more of *themselves* into the workplace, not out of humane benevolence but because organizations consider those 'selves' to have specific value in the accumulation process, thus contributing to the generation of surplus for the organization. These selves are closely scrutinized for their 'brand fit' and in such cases the brand operates to govern subjective norms. Hurrell and Scholarios' chapter provides a fine-grained analysis of this governance in action. In their hotel case studies those that are invited in are described as having 'polish'. We should be left in no doubt that not everyone is welcome to bring their selves into the workplace; the act of invitation invokes the knowing discrimination of the host who compiles the 'guest list' and the unknowing embarrassment and shame of those refused entry. Indeed, in this vein, Edwards and Kelan complete the volume by demonstrating concern at the likely incompatibility of employer branding and its anti-inclusive foundations and diversity management.

The application of the concept of (cultural) intermediaries to employee branding turns upon an understanding of the process(es) of branding as a transmission mechanism, wherein intermediaries effectively communicate ideas about the organization and its product to a wide audience including potential employees and customers through emotions, aspirations and bodily dispositions. A number of chapters in this text provide good examples of this in practice and this is further illustrated by the number of employees who are required to 'Tweet' or 'Blog' at work to reproduce the brand norms and values in a public arena (see for example Land and Taylor's Ethico employees in this volume). Employees as intermediaries thus contribute to value creation (in terms of both brand value and equity) of the product or service with their unwaged labour in the same way as user-consumers participate brand value co-creation through their public and communal use of the brand (Willmott, 2010). Employee branding thus augments the traditional circuit of capital accumulation; employees are summoned to buy into symbolic representations of organizational values, as a precursor to the *production* of organizational capital, through performance for a commercial audience. 'Living the brand' consequently becomes a prerequisite for the *consumption* of capital reconfigured as *meaning*. Placing the employee, rather than the product, at the fulcrum of the production and consumption relation may, as Land and Taylor illustrate, have precarious organizational consequences.

EMPLOYEE BRAND AS ORGANIZATIONAL PUTTY

Existing studies of the experience of work, especially service work, from both an employer and customer perspective, have drawn attention to the contradictions and tensions that are characteristic of the forms. Most typically and prosaically these tend to be played out in the tension between fulfilling quality-based objectives, often expressed in terms of customer service, while at the same time fulfilling the quantitative goals of organizations usually formulated as numerical targets (Taylor and Bain, 1999). Symptomatic of a much deeper structural antagonism, the unattainable goal of balancing irreconcilable objectives is something with which many practitioners and employees will doubtless identify. From an organizational perspective, although attainment of both objectives is specified as a service or product offering, too strict adherence to these ideals, and the corresponding insistence on simultaneous achievement of both quality and quantity for example, can lead to moribund and catastrophic organizational outcomes. It is in this sense that some authors have argued that contemporary organizations, which appear to promise 'everything to all', require spaces of negotiation where meanings are malleable and ambiguous. Such spaces allow slippage between objectives without fear that failure will puncture the foundational logic, or the continued survival, of their space within the organization (Kelemen and Rumens, 2008). Seen from this perspective, the complexity and ambiguity of branding in practice may provide space for service and product promises to be pursued, but not met. In short, the employee brand in essence provides a narrative 'cover' for non-compliance and failure. A version of the style versus substance debate, employee branding seen from this perspective acts as a narrative that works to cushion the blow of non-performance. For example, organizational targets and pledges that are not met are made good by the conduct and style of employee performances in pursuit of those goals. The material reality that the promised goals are structurally unobtainable, a functional feature of the dominant logics of capital, may be lost on customers as they gaze anaesthetized by the spectacle of aesthetic display performed, more often than not, by those at the bottom of organizational hierarchies. Indeed, as Klein (2000: 22) observes, there is a sinister element of 'collective hallucination' engendered by such performances. The material reality of the situation is of course seldom lost on employees, who are never far from brutal reminders that performance alone is no longer quite good enough. Moreover, in an environment that desires youth and novelty, the cultural capital that secures their employment location is likely to be ebbing away by the day. As a number of chapters in this volume point out, perhaps the most malevolent aspect of employee branding lies in its promised solution to alienation while simultaneously leaving the underlying property relations untouched.

LOOKING FORWARD

In highlighting the key issues to emerge from the work presented in this volume, we have attempted to provide some theoretical directions that can be pursed to explore employee branding from a critical perspective. These ideas need further theoretical development and empirical investigation at a time when the idea of the brand has extended beyond the disarmingly simple notion of 'stamp of quality and authenticity' to represent a differentiation strategy for the corporation itself (Hatch and Schultz, 2003). As the values, vision and culture of organizations become the core of their unique selling proposition (Balmer, 2001), the role played by employees shifts dramatically from providers/sellers of labour to carries or intermediaries of such corporate values and visions. It is this crucial shift from product-brand to corporate-brand that has deeply enhanced the representational capital of the brand and the holders of that capital in wider social and economical spheres. The work presented here is a testimony of this shift as it is experienced and 'lived' within the workplace in a variety of organizations. Yet as evidenced by some of the work in this volume, employee branding, as a top-down process of influence and change, often generates resistance, particularly when the values represented by the brand do not 'resonate with the tacit meanings and values that organization members hold and use' (Hatch and Schultz, 2003: 1049). Moreover, we argue that even when there is alignment between brand culture, corporate image and employee identity, as publicly enacted by 'branded employees', processes and experiences of employee branding are far from straightforward and still remain contested within and between workers, and managers.

In closing we would like to reconnect our consideration of employee branding to contemporary experiences of work. What are the implications of these processes for the experience of work in the twenty-first century? Are experiences of branded working conditions more likely to produce anxiety or reassurance? Are they likely to promote numbness and despair or inspiration and fulfilment among workers? In answering these questions we return to our opening themes of control and consent.

One might argue that the brand embodies a *new form* of domination and control, one levied at the individual capacity for self-governance, one which calls forth the enterprising subject so central to neo-liberal forms of capitalist reproduction (Rose, 1992). Here the brand appeals to individual freedom to act while simultaneously capturing that action in the pursuit of capital accumulation. The brand has been posited as a new form of informational capital (Arvidsson, 2006) within capital accumulation. The circulation of this capital is facilitated by the advent of the knowledge economy where the ability to perform and reproduce certain modes of communication are essential, be these emotional, aesthetic or symbolic in form and content. Indeed it is the very weightlessness, virtuality and immateriality of the brand which allows it to travel so far, so fast and so often unseen. In many cases its effects most often pass silently and unrecognized through the workplace. Its ability to direct attention away from the material dimensions of hard and dirty work, while at the same time putting the individual to work in its service, might be seen as pernicious indeed. In addition, such lack of substance reflected in the immaterial and ephemeral dimensions of the brand may well not be enough to offer workers reassurance, inspiration and a sense of fulfilment but rather work to promote anxiety over never quite perfectly produced performances and communicative displays. If we lift the lid on the slick and shiny branded world, the same old social relations of production are revealed, where control over labour remains a stark divider between the haves and have nots. This element in the circuit of capital not only reveals the labour processes, previously hidden behind factory doors, but reminds us that the very act of such display has become central to the process of value creation itself. Correspondingly, such performances are often both tightly controlled and celebrative of a narrow set of class, race and gender norms in their promotion of specific communicative, bodily and aesthetic dispositions. Thus, while the brand offers a promise of the freedom to 'be yourself' in the workplace, this promise is never quite delivered, not least because at its heart, the brand requires the suppression of individuality to function fully.

Taking a less dystopic perspective, and turning to the theme of consent, the brand cannot travel and grow without the complicity and consent of employees, consumers and managers. Because the brand only exists in the minds of these constituencies and because it is predicated on a shared terrain of meaning we might argue that individuals are, to some degree, responsible for their own enchantment and thus entrapment, hold a key stake in the brand and offer potential for its transformation. The ways in which this shared terrain of meaning encompasses the context of work, as much as it does the context of consumption, inscribes the production of value in its dual functions, as symbolic value for employees and customers, and as value that can be translated into accumulation (as brand value) for the organization. In a time when the corporate brand is often what distinguishes one organization from another, it is not a surprise that what is being attempted through the various employment practices documented here is the accomplishment of a 'corporate identity' to uniformly represent the brand to the outside world and, in essence, to further build the brand's equity and to pursue accumulation by other means.

This volume offers an analysis of how organizations can and do mobilize employees to further build their brand equity while acknowledging how this is experienced by employees. The chapters provide a detailed and nuanced account which shows that the branding process is always complex, conflictual and contradictory to further remind us that the mutability of employee subjectivity is always, at heart, the shifting sands upon which branded empires are built.

NOTE

1. For a theoretical discussion of subjectivity and the labour process theory see O'Doherty and Willmott's 2001 article in *Sociology*, 35 (2), 457–76.

REFERENCES

Arvidsson, A. (2006) *Brands: Meaning and Value in Media Culture*, Routledge: Oxford.

Balmer, J.M.T. (2001) The three virtues and seven deadly sins of corporate brand management, *Journal of General Management*, 27(1), 1–17.

Bourdieu, P. (1984) *Distinction. A Social Critique of the Judgement of Taste*, London: Routledge.

Hatch, M.J. and Schultz, M. (2003) 'Bringing the corporation into corporate branding', *European Journal of Marketing*, 37 (7/8), 1041–64.

Hemp, P. (2002) 'My Week at the Ritz as a Room-service Waiter', *Harvard Business Review*, 80 (6), 50–59.

Kelemen, M. and Rumens, N. (2008) *An Introduction to Critical Management Research*, London: Sage.

Klein, N. (2000) *No Logo: Taking Aim at the Brand Bullies*, Knopf Canada: Toronto.

McRobbie, A. (2002) 'Clubs to companies: Notes on the decline of political culture in the speeded up creative worlds', *Cultural Studies*, 16 (4), 516–31.

Miles, S.J. and Mangold, W.G. (2004) 'A Conceptualization of the Employee Branding Process', *Journal of Relationship Marketing*, 3 (2/3), 65–87.

Muzio, D., Ackroyd, S. and Chanlat, J-F. (2007) Redirections in the Study of Expert Labour: Lawyers, Doctors and Business Consultants, in D. Muzio, S. Ackroyd and J-F. Chanlat, *Redirections in the Study of Expert Labour: Established Professions and new Expert Occupations*, Basingstoke: Palgrave Macmillan.

Negus, K. (2002) 'The work of cultural intermediaries and the enduring distance between production and consumption', *Cultural Studies*, 16 (4), 501–15.

Nixon, S. and du Gay, P. (2002) 'Who Needs Cultural Intermediaries?', *Cultural Studies*, 16 (4), 495–500.

Pettinger, L. (2004) 'Brand culture and branded workers: service work and aesthetic labour in fashion retail', *Consumption, Markets and Culture*, 7 (2), 165–84.

Priola, V. and Hurrell, S.A. (2011) Organizational Culture and Change Management. in M. Butler and E. Rose (eds), *Organisational Behaviour. An Introduction*, London: CIPD, 349–73.

Ray, C.A. (1986) 'Corporate Culture: The Last Frontier of Control?', *Journal of Management Studies*, 23 (3), 287–97.

Rafiq, M. and Ahmed, P.K. (2000) 'Advances in the internal marketing concept: definition, synthesis and extension', *Journal of Services Marketing*, 14 (6), 449–62.

Rose, N. (1992) Governing the enterprising self, in P. Heelas and P. Morris (eds), *The Values of the Enterprise Culture*, London: Routledge, 141–64.

Sinclair, A. (1991) 'After excellence: Models of organizational culture for the public sector', *Australian Journal of Public Administration*, 50 (3), 321–32.

Taylor, P. and Bain, P. (1999) '"An assembly-line in the head": Work and employee relations in the call centre', *Industrial Relations Journal*, 30 (2), 101–17.

Thompson, P. and Ackroyd, S. (1995) 'All is quite in the workplace front? A critique of recent trends in British industrial sociology', *Sociology*, 29, 610–33.

Thompson, P. and Ackroyd, S. (1999) *Organizational Misbehaviour*, Thousand Oaks, CA: Sage Publications.

Walker, M.P. (2002) 'Going for customer service gold', *T + D*, 56 (5), May, 62–9.

Willmott, H. (2010) 'Creating "value" beyond the point of production: branding, financialization and market capitalization', *Organization*, 17 (5), 517–42.

Index